ASK THE PASTOR

One Hundred Questions and Answers
Plus Twenty Bonus Questions and Answers
Volume I

Roscoe L. De Chalus M. Min.

First Edition

WESTBOW PRESS®
A DIVISION OF THOMAS NELSON & ZONDERVAN

WestBow Press books may be ordered through booksellers or by contacting:

WestBow Press
A Division of Thomas Nelson & Zondervan
1663 Liberty Drive
Bloomington, IN 47403
www.westbowpress.com
1 (866) 928-1240

ISBN: 978-1-9736-1268-1 (sc)
ISBN: 978-1-9736-1269-8 (hc)
ISBN: 978-1-9736-1267-4 (e)

Library of Congress Control Number: 2018900032

Print information available on the last page.

WestBow Press rev. date: 01/29/2018

Endorsements

Everybody has an opinion. And when it comes to biblical issues, diversity of opinion is the norm. So where do you find thoughtful, reasoned answers to your questions? From God's Word. Pastor Roscoe De Chalus searches the Bible to offer answers to people's questions. Real answers to real questions. You have to admire him for even trying when opinions vary so greatly, but *Ask The Pastor* handily tackles 120 tough questions people like you are asking. You'll be delightfully coached with the answers.

Dr. Woodrow Kroll, Woodrow Kroll Ministries

"Roscoe De Chalus is a man of God who has dedicated his life to helping people come to know the Lord Jesus Christ and understand His Word. The answers contained in this book demonstrate his passion for God and his gifting for explaining the Bible."

S. Michael Houdmann, President and CEO, Got Questions Ministries

As an individual who sees people in a variety of situations; such as crisis, support, encouragement, and education, I find that this book is helpful for people in each of these situations. It is written so that the layperson can use it to respond to questions, as well as the ministry person for education and support. This is a resourceful guide with practical responses.

Revita De Chalus, President of SHEMWomen, License Professional Counselor, Chaplin at Amita-Alexian Brothers Health System

Roscoe De Chalus delivers scholarly, yet practical and easy to understand responses to many of the difficult biblical questions of our time. His answers are thorough, extensively researched and fortified using the Bible as his proof source. Mr. De Chalus treats each question, as if he is answering it face to face in his living room. His depth presumes an ability to give the person exactly what they need. I applaud his courage, as he tackles controversial topics, with unwavering faith and candor, as he adheres to God's word.

Roscoe De Chalus does the research for you. He weaves the questions and answers together in a manner that makes them highly entertaining. The bonus questions are complimentary to the bonus information he provides when answering each question. Mr. De Chalus sends each reader through the Bible and numerous references to enhance their understanding of the questions. The profile of each person who asked the question is useful as it gives insight into the people posing the questions. Roscoe De Chalus approaches the information as a pastor who teaches his subjects in order to give them a better knowledge of the God we serve.

Orlando Ceaser, President & CEO, Watchwell Communications, Inc.

"What impressed me most was Roscoe's gentle, but truthful manner in responding to each question. Roscoe's use of scripture and in depth coverage of the questions was exceptional. Go for it brother! God bless you for your work for the Kingdom!

Gary Hrivnak, Former Defensive End of the Chicago Bears.

At this critical time in world history we need clear answers to life's most challenging questions. Roscoe tackles these questions with scholarly wisdom and tact. Ask a Pastor book of 120 questions is a must have for everyone's library.

Rev Huntley Brown
International Concert Pianist

Table of Contents

Question: 23 63

Why is most of Israel Jewish, and most of Greece Orthodox instead of Christian? I just say those because they were main areas in the bible, and books of the bible were written there, apostles were from there, they went to these places, and the two countries have huge biblical history; yet most of them aren't even in the religion, why is this?

Question: 24 67

Gen 22:18 declares the promise of God to Abraham that through his offspring all nations on earth will be blessed. Eph. 2:12 tells us that the gentiles are foreigners to the covenants of the promise. Paul is telling us that Gentiles are foreigners to the promise but Gen 22:18 says that they will receive the blessing. Please explain.

Question: 25 69

Why did God put the tree of knowledge of good and evil in the Garden of Eden?

Question: 26 71

The bible says there is a baptism of The Holy Spirit and a filling of the Holy Spirit. It distinctively states that they were filled with the Holy Spirit on Pentecost, Acts 2:4. Is it not reasonable to accept the breathing of Jesus as the initial baptism and the filling as receiving the power as Jesus said it would be in Acts 1:8? Were they baptized into Christ in John 20:22 as stated in Galatians 3:27?

Question: 27 73

What did Paul mean when he said in 1 Corinthians 9:27 that he buffets his body?

Question: 28 77

Your site says "Christians do not continually live immoral lifestyles, nor do they reject the faith and deny Christ. Such actions are proof that they were never redeemed." But what about me, who has a problem with an immoral lifestyle? I am/was addicted to cigarettes, and alcohol, and

Bonus Questions Table of Contents

Preface

Over the years I have always been a person who wanted to know biblical truths. I had bible questions, and religious questions that were increasing. Very little answers were forth coming as I did the day to day routines. I ended up enrolling in divinity school and studied many articles and videos on the web from credible ministries… I checked out what the false teachers were saying as well… I seem to be like a sponge absorbing all that was in my path and squeezing out any errors.

Unbeknownst to me, God had been preparing me to be one of His children who would be placed in a position to provide the answers, and make these answers available for others.

This book is one of the avenues being implemented to put questions and the answers in the hands of believers, churches, schools, and non believers.

This book is filled with questions I answered through Lord of Hope Ministries, and Got Questions Ministries. Many references to website articles were included to help the reader get a deeper understanding of the topics. This textbook was designed to be used at home, in churches, at schools, libraries etc…

This book is very important in that the reader will get answers and will end up being equipped to answer tough questions when they occur.

It is my heart's desire that this book will increase the reader's faith in the Lord. It is also my desire for this book to move those who do not believe into a faith relationship with the Lord. For some, critical questions have not been answered over the years. This book will get those questions answered, with the hopes that people will open their hearts up to accepting the Lord Jesus as their Savior.

The Glory shall be reserved for our awesome Lord!

Preface

Introduction

Ask a Pastor was put together because truth matters!

This book will help people get anchored in the truth that flows throughout the Christian bible. You can trust God's word.

Many answers exist for questions you may have thought of. May you become more confident in your belief in God and His word as a result of reading this book!

2 Timothy 3:16-17 English Standard Version (ESV)

16 All Scripture is breathed out by God and profitable for teaching, for
reproof, for correction, and for training in righteousness, 17 that the man
of God may be complete, equipped for every good work.

May you be able to do what it says in Psalms 119:30 (ESV).

Psalm 119:30 English Standard Version (ESV)

30 I have chosen the way of faithfulness; I set your rules before me.

May this book help your readiness in answering biblical questions…

1 Peter 3:15 English Standard Version (ESV)

15 but in your hearts honor Christ the Lord as holy, always being prepared to make a defense to anyone who asks you for a reason for the hope that is in you; yet do it with gentleness and respect,

Tell a friend about this book for it may be just what they need.

It will make a nice gift as well!

It is our desire at Lord of Hope Ministries to help everyone who comes to us asking for help with biblical questions find answers so that they can grow in the faith.

This book presents the many questions I received and answered through Lord of Hope Ministries and Got Questions Ministries. At the end of the book I included some bonus questions I thought someone might ask. All bible verses are taken from the ESV (English Standard version) KJV (King James Version) and NKJV (New King James Version), unless specifically noted. Please use this book as a reference book to answer questions that you or someone else maybe having. May this book enhance everyone's spiritual growth in Christ!

May God get the glory forevermore! The LORD is Worthy!

Question: 1

Profile: Male 18-30 Uganda East Africa

Dear pastor, I am so confused... How can someone distinguish the true miracle from God to that of the false prophets? In our place there is a false prophet who is doing a lot of miracles like we do. They also sing the same songs that we sing...

Answer:

There are false prophets out there and the best way to identify them is to know God's word.

Scripture says you will know them by their fruits:

Matthew 7:15-20 New King James Version (NKJV).

15 "Beware of false prophets, who come to you in sheep's clothing, but
inwardly they are ravenous wolves. 16 You will know them by their
fruits. Do men gather grapes from thorn bushes or figs from thistles? 17
Even so, every good tree bears good fruit, but a bad tree bears bad fruit.
18 A good tree cannot bear bad fruit, nor *can* a bad tree bear good fruit.
19 Every tree that does not bear good fruit is cut down and thrown into
the fire. 20 Therefore by their fruits you will know them.

Friend, study God's word thoroughly and all the days of your life... By knowing His word you will be able to identify false teaching when you hear it.

Read the book of Jude. It is another bible book that speaks about false teachers... Additional scripture warnings:

Matthew 12:33-37 New King James Version (NKJV) A Tree Known by Its Fruit:

33 "Either make the tree good and its fruit good, or else make the tree
bad and its fruit bad; for a tree is known by *its* fruit. 34 Brood of vipers!
How can you, being evil, speak good things? For out of the abundance
of the heart the mouth speaks. 35 A good man out of the good treasure
of his heart brings forth good things, and an evil man out of the evil
treasure brings forth evil things. 36 But I say to you that for every idle
word men may speak, they will give account of it in the day of judgment.
37 For by your words you will be justified, and by your words you will
be condemned."

Know this; our God is not fooled by the false teacher. The future is very bad for them…

Hope this helps… His Grace to you!

Question: 2

Profile: Male 18-30 Uganda East Africa

Dear pastor, is it true that some Bible readers say that in the Bible there is an error? Is it true or not?

Answer:

My friend, there are no errors in the bible. You can truly rest with confidence that there are no errors! When a skeptic says this, they are repeating stuff they heard or read from non believers who are dead wrong! Many of the skeptics have said negative things about the bible and its content, but then archeology has unearthen the facts that always support the bible! The skeptics are always proven wrong!

Please go to the website: http://www.gotquestions.org

There are many questions answered regarding biblical topics. For your convenience I have provided a copy of what is posted on gotquestions.org below...

I am also including the link http://www.gotquestions.org/Bible-errors.html in case you want to view it in a different language.

Question: "Does the Bible contain errors, contradictions, or discrepancies?"

Answer: If we read the Bible at face value, without a preconceived bias for finding errors, we will find it to be a coherent, consistent, and relatively easy-to-understand book. Yes, there are difficult passages. Yes, there are verses that appear to contradict each other. We must remember that the Bible was written by approximately 40 different authors over a period of around 1500 years. Each writer wrote with a different style, from a different perspective, to a different audience, for a different purpose. We should expect some minor differences. However, a difference is not a contradiction. It is only an error if there is absolutely no conceivable way the verses or passages can be reconciled. Even if an answer is not available right now, that does not mean an answer does not exist. Many have found a supposed error in the Bible in relation to history or geography only to find out that the Bible is correct once further archaeological evidence is discovered.

We often receive questions along the lines of "Explain how these verses do not contradict!" or "Look, here is an error in the Bible!" Admittedly, some of the things people bring up are difficult to answer. However, it is our contention that there are viable and intellectually plausible answers to every supposed Bible contradiction and error. There are books and websites available that list "all the errors in the Bible." Most people simply get their ammunition from these places; they do not find supposed errors on their own. There are also books and websites available that refute every one of these supposed errors. The saddest thing is that most people who attack the Bible are not truly interested in an answer. Many "Bible attackers" are even aware of these answers, but they continue to use the same old shallow attacks again and again.

So, what are we to do when someone approaches us with an alleged Bible error? 1) Prayerfully study the Scriptures and see if there is a simple solution. 2) Do some research using some of the Bible commentaries, "Bible defense" books, and biblical research websites. 3) Ask our pastors/church leaders to see if they can find a solution. 4) If there is still no clear answer after steps 1), 2), and 3) are followed, we trust God that His Word is truth and that there is a solution that just simply has not been realized yet (2 Timothy 2:15, 3:16-17).

May God's Grace envelop you!

Question: 3

Profile: Male 18-30 Uganda East Africa

There is a question about Christmas. Many people say that is the birthday of our Lord Jesus Christ. Even when we are at school they taught us the same that he was born on 25th of December. Some say it is just remembering His birth. I will be grateful for your help in understanding this. Is December 25 the birthday of our Lord Jesus Christ?

Answer: December 25, is not the birthday of Christ. It is just when everybody traditionally remembers it. It is not known the exact date. See the following article for more details.

"Was Jesus born on December 25?"

Speculation as to the time of Jesus' birth dates back to the 3rd century, when Hyppolytus (ca. 170-236) claimed that Jesus was born on December 25. The earliest mention of some sort of observance on that date is in the Philoclian Calendar, representing Roman practice, of the year 336. Later, John Chrysostom favored the same date of birth. Cyril of Jerusalem (348-386) had access to the original Roman birth census, which also documented that Jesus was born on the 25th of December. The date eventually became the officially recognized date for Christmas in part because it coincided with the pagan festivals celebrating Saturnalia and the winter solstice. The church thereby offered people a Christian alternative to the pagan festivities and eventually reinterpreted many of their symbols and actions in ways acceptable to Christian faith and practice.

December 25 has become more and more acceptable as the birth date of Jesus. However, some argue that the birth occurred in some other season, such as in the fall. Followers of this theory claim that the Judean winters were too cold for shepherds to be watching their flocks by night. History proves otherwise, however, and we have historical evidence that unblemished lambs for the Temple sacrifice were in fact kept in the fields near Bethlehem during the winter months.

The truth is we simply don't know the exact date of our Savior's birth. In fact, we don't even know for sure the year in which He was born. Scholars believe it was somewhere between 6 B.C. and 4 B.C. One thing is clear: if God felt it was important for us to know the exact date of the Savior's birth, He certainly would have told us in His Word. The Gospel of Luke gives very specific details about the event, even down to what the baby was wearing – "swaddling clothes"—and where he slept—"in a manger" (Luke 2:12). These details are important because they speak of His nature and character, meek and lowly. But the exact date of His birth has no significance whatsoever, which may be why God chose not to mention it.

The fact is that He was born, that He came into the world to atone for our sins, that He was resurrected to eternal life, and that He's alive today. This is what we should celebrate, as we are told in the Old Testament in such passages as Zechariah 2:10: "'Shout and be glad, O Daughter of Zion. For I am coming, and I will live among you,' declares the LORD." Further, the angel that announced the birth to the shepherds brought "good news of great joy that will be for all the people" (Luke 2:10). Surely here is the cause for celebration every day, not just once a year.

From: http://www.gotquestions.org/December-25.html

Question: 4

Profile: Male 18-30 Uganda East Africa

My dear pastor, there is still a question with me in the Bible. Why did Jesus use so many threes in His talking? Like: He is going to build the temple in three days, the cock will crow three times..., and in three days He will be risen from the dead, etc.

Answer: Not much is said in scripture regarding why Jesus at times reinforced his teaching using the number 3. It would be pure speculation on my part or anyone else to try using these numbers for some other meaning other than what is in the context of the scripture verses. . . The examples you cited can be explained this way: The temple and His rising from the dead were speaking of the same thing. The temple was His body… The cock crowing in three days was because that was when it was going to happen.

Coincidence that it was three times, we do not know….

Question: 5

Profile: Male 18-30 Uganda East Africa

Why did Elisha ask for double possession of anointing?

Question 5 Answer:

You are referring to 2 Kings 2:9 (English Standard Version (©2001)

When they had crossed, Elijah said to Elisha, "Ask what I shall do for you, before I am taken from you." And Elisha said, "Please let there be a double portion of your spirit on me."

God had promised Elisha through Elijah's words that he would have a double portion of Elijah's spirit, which meant that he would have twice as many miracles as Elijah.

Elisha double portion of anointing:

"You have asked a hard thing. Nevertheless, if you see me when I am taken from you, it shall be so for you; but if not, it shall not be so."

Shortly afterward as they walked and talked "suddenly a chariot of fire appeared with horses of fire, and separated the two of them; and Elijah went up by a whirlwind into heaven. And Elisha saw it, and he cried out, 'My father, my father, the chariot of Israel and its horsemen!' So he saw him no more. And he took hold of his own clothes and tore them into two pieces. He also took up the mantle of Elijah that had fallen from him, and went back and stood by the bank of the Jordan." 2 Kings 2:11-13.

After that Elisha received a tremendous anointing from the LORD God. The Spirit of God was evident in all of the things that he did and said. Exactly as Elijah had promised him Elisha performed twice as many miracles of healing and victories than Elijah had done. His life was filled with the power and anointing of God.

So let me clarify what was going on...

Elisha asked to be invested with Elijah's power as a prophet. Another important factor is that Elisha saw Elijah as his father.

So Elisha's request is an inheritance in the Spirit. He wanted a double share of that which was on Elijah as an inheritance, the same way a firstborn son would receive a double share of the natural inheritance.

According to Deuteronomy 21:15-17, if a man had two sons, instead of splitting the inheritance fifty-fifty, he had to divide it into three parts, giving two thirds to the firstborn (the "double portion") and one third to the second born son.

It is a share of inheritance. Instead of one share, he wanted double–the right of a firstborn.

Thank you for writing to Lord of Hope Ministries! May God grow your faith as you study His word the bible!

Question: 6

Profile: Male 18-30 Uganda East Africa

Who wrote the second Ten Commandments after Moses destroyed the first one?

Turn to Exodus 34:1 (ESV) for the answer…

Moses Makes New Tablets

1 The Lord said to Moses, "Cut for yourself two tablets of stone like the first, and I will write on the tablets the words that were on the first tablets, which you broke.

Question: 7

Why do people refer to God as He? Isn't that personification at its finest? And doesn't that void the entire conversation of God not being something but rather existing?

Profile: Male 18-30 North America

Answer: To answer this, I feel it is important not to over analyze the answer but to go to the basics. What does God's word say? To accept this answer, one must overcome the question of whether the bible is God's word. Christians believe the bible is God's word. Throughout scripture God is referred to as in masculine terms. If this was not so, God through biblical inspiration would have made sure His word was correct.

So what we have to support this view point is as follows:

Starting with the first book in the bible…

Genesis 1:5 King James Version (KJV)

5 And God called the light Day, and the darkness he called Night. And the evening and the morning were the first day.

Genesis 1:27 King James Version (KJV)

27 So God created man in his own image, in the image of God created he him; male and female created he them.

The Trinity describes God as Father, Son, and Holy Spirit.

So God the Father is being described as Father thus Masculine terms.

Scripture Reference to the Trinity:

16 Come ye near unto me, hear ye this; I have not spoken in secret from the beginning; from the time that it was, there am I: and now the Lord GOD, and his Spirit, hath sent me. 17 Thus saith the LORD, thy Redeemer, the Holy One of Israel; Isaiah 48:16-17

The New Testament doctrine of the Trinity is evident in such a verse as John 15:26, where the Lord Jesus said: "But when the Comforter is come whom I will send unto you from the Father, He shall testify of me."

Even the Holy Spirit is referred to in Masculine terms...

Jesus, God in the flesh came to us as a male.

Jesus, when he told us how to pray in Matthew 6:9 says to say: Our Father who Art in Heaven...

Masculine terms again...

Jesus is God.

Jesus used the same name given to Moses {Ref: Exodus 3:13-14 ESV} for God (I AM) to refer to his OWN eternal existence.

56 Your father Abraham rejoiced that he would see my day. He saw it and was glad." 57 So the Jews said to him, "You are not yet fifty years old, and have you seen Abraham?" 58 Jesus said to them, "Truly, truly, I say to you, before Abraham was, I am." 59 So they picked up stones to throw at him, but Jesus hid himself and went out of the temple. (John 8:56-59, ESV).

God is not something, but is a person, in fact "three who's in one, or from a biblical perspective, that there's **one** "What" and **three** "Who's". It's one God revealed in three Persons. Those three Persons are eternally distinct. So the Father never becomes the Son and the

Son never becomes the Holy Spirit. This one God has always existed. He is relational, loving, creative, all knowing, all powerful, gracious, just, and the list goes on forever. A thing or something cannot contain these attributes...

God is described as masculine because he told us so...

Question: 8

My friend goes to the church of the Brethren, and I like to know what they believe about God, Jesus, and the Holy Spirit, etc. Can you help me? Thanks So Much!

Profile: Female 31-45 North America

Answer: The Church of The Brethren espouses some of the basic beliefs of Christianity, such as the divinity of Christ. They believe in God as Creator and loving Sustainer. They confess the Lordship of Christ, and seek to be guided by the Holy Spirit in every aspect of life, thought, and mission.

The mode of baptism is a little different, is trine (three times) immersion in a forward direction in the Name of the Father, of the Son, and of the Holy Spirit. This is followed by laying on of hands for the impartation of the Holy Spirit. This is simply a difference in procedure, not something we should divide over...

I find a lot of good practices through works being implemented through the Church of the Brethren.

However there are some areas of concern:

1. Who is leading since the pastor's function is limited?

Priesthood of all Brethren Believers follows a non-hierarchical pattern of church life. Today, most congregations have paid pastors, but their function is still somewhat limited, with the laity still taking a very active role in ministerial work.

I could not find on their website a schedule for service times where organized pastoral teaching of scripture and worship of the Lord occurs.

When I called the telephone number posted on the website of a particular church located in Illinois the phone number was not operational. No other information given...

http://www.brethren.org/site/Dir?pg=vprof&sid=1011&mbr=1001828

http://www.brethren.org/

Doctrinal concerns: Some Church of The Brethren congregations accept or even encourage individual interpretation of the Bible and their faith.

This can become risky if one or a group interprets scripture in favor of ones sinful behavior.

The Church of the Brethren upholds the New Testament for all matters and do not indicate that they use the Old Testament for the same purposes...

Friend, we must remember what the bible says regarding the OT and NT: 2 Timothy 3:16 (King James Version)

All scripture is given by inspiration of God, and is profitable for doctrine, for reproof, for correction, for instruction in righteousness.

Question: 9

I sincerely strive to believe, yet I continue to have nagging doubts about the Bible, and Jesus being God, and rising from the dead, miracles, etc. How much belief is enough belief to be saved?

Profile: Male Over 60 North America

Answer: You are on the right path seeking answers for your skepticism. Know that answers exist for the issues you are expressing doubts. To build your faith you need to arrange time to study and meditate on the word of God. This will strengthen and support the reasons to believe. Here are some answers to some of your concerns.

1. The Bible is the Word of God.

The study of biblical inspiration can help answer this.

In short, God told Moses to write all of His words down and put them in a book because these words were a covenant between God and Israel.

These words of God included the Ten Commandments and all of the other laws given in the Torah (the Torah are the books from Genesis-Deuteronomy). So, not only were the Ten Commandments written in stone and kept in the Ark, but the same Ten Commandments along with all of the instruction concerning them (the other 603 laws) made up the Book of the Law which were placed in the side of the Ark (Deut.31:26) The first installment of the ten were not kept separate from the rest. Afterwards, God used over 40 Authors to construct the rest of His word.

Keep this is mind, many scholars studied the word of God and found it to be true. Archeological discoveries, historical evidence, documented prophesies and their fulfillment support the biblical accounts. The bible is a very unique, one of a kind book that has the power to change lives, and provide instruction for daily living. When you read it you can see the fingerprint of God throughout the recorded text.

2. Jesus is God

Study the following scriptures to support this:

Jesus is God Almighty (John 1:1-3, 14; John 10:33; Revelation 1:8, 19:13. The GODHEAD incarnate (Colossians 2:9; 1st Timothy 3:16).

Jesus never sinned, He was perfect (2nd Corinthians 5:21; Hebrews 4:15, 16). Jesus was born of a virgin (Isaiah 7:14).

3. Jesus was raised from the Dead

We have eyewitness accounts regarding the resurrection of Jesus.

In 1 Corinthians 15:3-6 (KJV), Paul established the following:

"For I delivered unto you first of all that which I also received, how that Christ died for our sins according to the scriptures; And that He was buried, and that He rose again the third day according to the scriptures: And that He was seen of Cephas, then of the twelve: After that, He was seen of above five hundred brethren at once; of whom the greater part remain unto this present, but some are fallen asleep."

Manuscript studies indicate that this was a very early creed of the Christian faith, written within a few years after the death of Jesus Christ. Therefore, it's dramatic that Paul ends the passage with "most of whom are still living." Paul was inviting people to check out the facts. He wouldn't have included a statement like that if he was trying to hide something like a conspiracy, hoax, myth or legend.

Resurrection of Jesus: More Eye-witness Accounts...

The resurrection of Jesus was also declared in numerous other accounts, including the appearance of Jesus to Mary Magdalene (John 20:10-18), to other women (Matthew 28:8-10), to Cleopas and his companion (Luke 24:13-32), to eleven disciples and others (Luke 24:33-49), to ten apostles and others (excluding Thomas) (John 20:19-23), to the apostles (including Thomas) (John 20:26-30), to seven apostles (John 21:1-14), to the disciples (Matthew 28:16-20), and to the apostles on the Mount of Olives (Luke 24:50-52 and Acts 1:4-9). The ultimate test of credibility for these eye-witnesses was that many of them faced martyrdom for their eye-witness testimony. This is dramatic! These witnesses knew the truth. What could they possibly gain by dying for a known lie? The evidence speaks for itself, these weren't just religious faithful dying for a religious belief, these were followers of Jesus Christ dying for a historical event – His resurrection that established Him as the Son of God.

4. Miracles

A miracle is an event attributed to divine intervention.

Miracles happened in the past and are happening occasionally today. One need only to speak to someone who survived an horrific accident or serious life threatening illness to hear some first hand accounts.

Bottom line, with God all things are possible. See Matthew 19:26.

5. How much belief is enough to be saved?

Matthew 17:19-20 tells us that a small amount of faith can do much:

19 Then came the disciples to Jesus apart, and said, Why could not we cast him out? 20 And Jesus said unto them, Because of your unbelief: for verily I say unto you, If ye have faith as a grain of mustard seed, ye shall say unto this mountain, Remove hence to yonder place; and it shall remove; and nothing shall be impossible unto you.

In Luke 18:17, Jesus says that anyone who does not receive the kingdom like a little child shall not enter into it.

Childlike faith trusts. Childlike faith knows no bounds. Childlike faith listens to what is said, and believes it.

In summary, you just need enough faith to trust God to save you.

This is more than a concept in your mind. If you are seeing results in your life that you can attribute to God's compassion for you then you can know that your faith is enough...

Question: 10

1. Could you tell me where I can find the scripture that says: "Come as you are" and 2. The scripture that says: "Whosoever will let him come?"

Profile: Female 46-60 North America

Answer: 1. there is no such scripture.

The thought is projected in a hymn "Just As I Am", and song "Come as you are" used before an altar call in certain protestant organizations.

The meaning is built off of some biblical text directing people to Christ. The following scriptures are a few examples:

Isaiah 55:1 (ESV) Come, everyone who thirsts, come to the waters; and he who has no money, come, buy and eat! Come, buy wine and milk without money and without price.

Matthew 11:28 (ESV) Come to me, all who labor and are heavy laden, and I will give you rest.

Isaiah 1:18 (KJV) 18 Come now, and let us reason together, saith the LORD: though your sins be as scarlet, they shall be as white as snow; though they be red like crimson, they shall be as wool.

Romans 5:8 (KJV) 8 But God commendeth his love toward us, in that, while we were yet sinners, Christ died for us.

Be sure to go to Christ, do what He says, and let God change you. Come as you are, but as you continue to seek God and follow what His word says, you will leave a different person.

2. The only scripture that is close to what you are looking for is in Revelation.

Revelation 22:17 (KJV)

17 And the Spirit and the bride say, Come. And let him that heareth say, Come. And let him that is athirst come. And whosoever will, let him take the water of life freely.

This is an invitation in the new heaven...

Question: 11

1) What is the meaning of the Presence of God? 2) What is the importance of the presence of God in our lives? 3) What is the difference between the presence of God and the Glory of God?

Profile: Female 46-60 Africa

Answer: While God is omnipresent, and His presence is always with us, we continue to long for an encounter with the Presence of God. When we talk about experiencing the presence of the Lord, we are talking about the realization of God's presence – of perceiving His presence and being conscious of Him. Practicing His presence through worship is one of the most valuable things we can do. God has promised that as we draw near to Him he will draw near to us.

James 4:8 (New King James Version)

8 Draw near to God and He will draw near to you. Cleanse your hands, you sinners; and purify your hearts, you double-minded.

God will draw near to us and we will experience His presence in ever increasing measures.

God is omnipresent, meaning that He is everywhere at all times. David said in Psalm 139:7, "Where could I go from Your Spirit? Or where could I flee from Your presence?" He concludes that there is no place that we can hide from God's presence. God is everywhere and sees everything. Because of this, we can know that we are never alone, and that He shall never leave us nor forsake us.

As well as being omnipresent, God also dwells in the believer. The indwelling presence of God is given to all who believe. "Do you not know that you are God's temple and that God's Spirit has His permanent dwelling in you?" – 1 Corinthians 3:16.

God reveals Himself to those that earnestly seek Him (Deuteronomy 4:29). If we want to walk in the presence of the Lord, then we need to be practicing the presence of God. One of the major ways we can do this is through worship.

2) What is the importance of the presence of God in our lives?

The Presence of God:

1. Brings rest (Ex. 33:14).
2. Sets us apart from the world (Ex. 33:15-16).
3. Brings the glory and honor of God, along with strength, and gladness into our lives (1 Chr. 16:7).
4. Our enemies, all the things that hinder or weigh us down, or would harm us, perish at His presence. (Ps. 9:3)
5. Spending time in His presence brings the fullness of joy and pleasure. (Ps. 16:11) and shows us the path of life.
6. Is a hiding place from the pride of man. Being in the presence of God is a sure fire way to remain humble. (Ps. 31:20)
7. Wickedness that might be plaguing us, or trying to defile our temple, will perish at His presence. (Ps. 68:2)
8. It is an awesome privilege to have. (Ps.95:2)
9. Hills melt like wax at His presence. Whatever difficulty in your circumstance or life that you think you can't overcome, He can. (Ps. 97:5)
10. There is no way to hide from His presence, so be reminded He said He'd never leave you, nor forsake you in Heb. 13:5. (Ps. 139:7)
11. His presence is the dwelling place of the upright. (Ps. 140:13) There is no better place to live than in His presence. Know that we can live in His presence, remember Paul said in Him we move and have our being. It's possible, according to the scripture to walk in the spirit, and dwell in His presence.

12. If you have a problem with your flesh, or idols that have been hard to let go, His presence can move those things right out of your temple and out of your way. (Is. 19:1)
13. If you are experiencing a seemingly insurmountable problem or mountain of obstacles; seeking and dwelling in His presence can be like mountains melting and flowing down like hot wax. (Is. 64:1)
14. His presence shakes men, makes the steep places fall, and knocks the walls to the ground of every stronghold. (Ezek. 38:20)
15. The times of refreshing come from the presence of the Lord. (Acts 3:19)
16. Christ, our High Priest, is in God's presence as our intercessor. (Heb. 9:24) He can present us faultless before His presence with exceeding great joy. (Jude 24)

Moses was convinced that without God's presence in his life, it was useless for him to attempt anything. When he spoke face to face with the Lord, he said, "...If thy presence go not with me, carry us up not hence" (Exodus 33:15). He was saying, "Lord, if your presence is not with me, then I'm not going anywhere. I won't take a single step unless I'm assured you're with me!"

Moses knew it was God's presence in Israel that set the people apart from all other nations. And the same is true of the church of Jesus Christ today. One important thing that sets us apart from nonbelievers is God's being "with us" - leading us, guiding us, working His will in and through us.

3) What is the difference between the presence of God and the Glory of God?

There is a difference between God's presence and His glory. In Exodus, we're given a glimpse of this difference: "Then a cloud covered the tent of the congregation, and the glory of the Lord filled the tabernacle" (Exodus 40:34).

The apostle Paul writes that all believers' bodies are the tabernacle of God: "Know ye not that ye are the temple of God, and that the Spirit of God dwelleth in you?" (1 Corinthians 3:16). Like the Israelites who lived under the cloud of God's presence, we're constantly under the covering of God's grace. Yet, what is the difference between beholding God's presence and beholding His glory? God did show Moses his glory. But it didn't appear in some luminous cloud or in an earthshaking demonstration of power. No, God expressed his glory in a simple revelation of his nature: "The Lord passed before him, and proclaimed, The Lord, the Lord God, merciful and gracious, longsuffering, and abundant in goodness and truth, keeping mercy for thousands, forgiving iniquity and transgression and sin..." (34:6-7). God's glory was a revelation of His goodness, mercy, love, power, and compassion!

We are to abide in His presence, so our eyes will begin to open to His glory. It is all revealed in Christ. He is the full revelation of God's love, grace, mercy, kindness.

"As you continually reflect on this revelation, it will cleanse and purify you - because you'll become more and more like Jesus. As you see how loving and merciful He is to you, you'll become more loving and merciful to others. And that will be God's glory revealed in you!" Seek God with all your heart, and desire His presence in your daily life. Then you will know and experience the incredible glory of God!

Question: 12

How should a Christian respond when treated unfairly or unjustly by another? For example: A coworker gets credit for your hard work or the promotion that you believe you earned. A friend gives something to another that was promised to you. Your neighbor regularly allows his pets to soil your yard. A waiter gives a table to someone that just arrived even though you've been waiting patiently for a long period of time. With patience in mind, should we ever tell the person that offended us how we feel or what we think about what they have done? Or should we do or say nothing and trust that it is God's will?

Profile: Male 31-45 North America

Answer:

As Christians we need to respond in a God honoring manner.

Proverbs 15:18 A hot-tempered man stirs up dissension, but a patient man calms a quarrel.

This does not mean that you are to sit on your hands and do nothing. There are times when you need to speak up...

Some matters are for God to handle exclusively. These are the things that we cannot influence change by our own hands.

When, in an unfair situation, we need to pray and ask for wisdom in responding and handling the matter. We need to release it to God and seek his will in handling the issue.

As believers, we should expect opposition from time to time. The more we move out for the Lord, the more attacks we may have to face from our adversary (The devil) through his various schemes (See 1 Pet 4:10-12 ESV). As Paul stated it in 2 Timothy 3:12 ESV [12] Indeed, all who desire to live a godly life in Christ Jesus will be persecuted,

Elisha handled in a calm fashion the situation where evil young people were calling him names. He saw their hardened and rebellious condition, unresponsive to correction. In the name of the Lord (i.e. by His authority) Elisha simply turned them over to the Lord and to their own devises, which had the effect of removing them from even the common protection of God. He probably said something like, "may God deal with you according to what you deserve," or "may you be cursed for your sins of rebellion."

The apostle Paul also on some occasions stood fast and acted in a biblical way leaving the results to the Lord. This is precisely what Paul did in connection with the strong criticism often leveled at him by some of the Corinthians (1 Cor. 4:1). As with Elisha and Paul, we need to move forward, always trusting God to make a way and remove the obstacles.

There are times when you need to speak up for yourself and address the infraction. The way you speak to the person will make all the difference. Speak the truth in a loving and non threatening manner can really make a difference. You can gain a friend and respect from the offending party if they repent.

English Standard Version (©2001)

Proverbs 15:1 A soft answer turns away wrath, but a harsh word stirs up anger.

Due to the sin nature of mankind this may not always work. The other party may just be a bully and will not listen. In this case, turn the issue over to the Lord and depending on the seriousness of the infraction, you may have to turn it over to the local police department…

When treated unfairly by a superior, we should submissively endure by entrusting ourselves to God, the righteous Judge.

God's way is for us to identify the nature of the relationship: Am I under the authority of the person who is treating me unfairly? That is the first question we must ask to determine how we should act in a given situation.

God has ordained various spheres of authority. He is the supreme authority over all, of course. But under God, there is the sphere of human government (1 Pet. 2:13-17; Rom. 13:1-7). Also, there is the sphere of the family, in which husbands have authority over wives (1Pet. 3:1-6; Eph. 5:22-24) and parents over children (Eph. 6:1-4). There is the sphere of the church, in which elders have authority over the flock (1 Pet. 5:1-5; Heb. 13:17). And there is the sphere of employment (either forced, as in slavery, or voluntary), in which employees must be subject to employers (1 Pet. 2:18; Eph. 6:5-9).

Once we've identified whether or not we are under the authority of the person who is mistreating us, we then must examine our own attitude and motives and ask: Do I have a proper attitude of submission, or am I selfishly fighting for my rights? If I'm truly in submission, and I'm not acting for selfish reasons, I would argue that there is a proper place for respectful communication that seeks to clarify falsehood and promote the truth. In other words, if our attitude and motives are in submission to God, we need not always silently endure unjust treatment as Christian doormats. There is a proper place for self-defense and for confronting the errors of those who have mistreated us, as long as we work through proper channels.

Jesus and the Apostle Paul who wrote under the inspiration of the Holy Spirit did not always stay silent in these situations. For example, in John 8, the Jews attacked Jesus' character and authority by saying that He was bearing false witness about Himself and that He was illegitimately born. Jesus did not silently endure this attack. Rather, He defended Himself as being sent from the Father and He attacked these critics by saying that they were of their father, the devil! That's hardly a passive, silent response! Nor was Jesus passive when He attacked the Pharisees for their hypocrisy (Matthew 23). The Apostle Paul wrote 2 Corinthians,

Galatians, and parts of other epistles to defend his character and ministry which were under attack. He put down his critics in a strong and, at times, sarcastic manner.

So the answer to your question is, yes, it is okay to speak to someone who has done you wrong. As believers we are not to be a doormat. You need to be prayed up and discuss the issues with the sole purpose of reconciling the issues. Know that there will be times when silence is golden.

Question: 13

I just read this verse and it kind of confused me.

Matthew 10:23 says at the end of the verse "Truly I tell you, you will not finish going through the towns of Israel before the Son of Man comes." Is this a prophesy for Christ's return? If so, hasn't the gospel been spread through all the towns of Israel? Is this a false prophesy? Thanks

Profile: Male Under 18 North America

Answer: Do not let it confuse you. No false prophesy exist with the Lord Jesus. His words are faithful and true. This is a prophesy of his return but not the second coming...

Matthew 10:23 English Standard Version (ESV)

23 When they persecute you in one town, flee to the next, for truly, I say to you, you will not have gone through all the towns of Israel before the Son of Man comes.

The notion that this text alluded to the Second Coming is negated by the fact that the passage clearly implies that Christ knew when the "coming" represented in verse 10:23 would transpire.

This is evidenced in that the Lord declared that the disciples would not be finished with evangelizing the cities of Israel before He "came." On the other hand, He did not know when the event of His final coming would occur (Mt. 24:36).

Matthew 24:36 English Standard Version (ESV)

No One Knows That Day and Hour

36 “But concerning that day and hour no one knows, not even the angels of heaven, nor the Son, but the Father only.

This coming, therefore, was not the Second Coming.

The fulfillment of Mt 10:23 occurred just as our Lord predicted it: within the perspective of the disciples - those to whom our Lord was speaking. Before the disciples finished proclaiming the gospel of the kingdom to the cities of Israel Jesus Christ as the Son of Man would make His triumphal entry into Jerusalem. Ultimately they rejected Him and crucified Him. After the crucifixion, He was raised from the dead and He returned to the disciples before his accession to heaven. This return is what He was referring to.

Question: 14

I desire to become a Pastor (apostolic), God's willing of course. Is it wrong to want to serve God as a Pastor? If not, from my baptism to becoming a Pastor, what minimum length of time does it take on average to become one?

Profile: Male 31-45 North America

Answer: You mentioned that you have a desire to become an apostolic Pastor. If this desire came upon you after baptism it maybe God's calling in your life.

There is nothing wrong with wanting to serve God as a Pastor.

Please know that to be a good pastor a lot of study and training is required. School or Seminary... There is a lot of responsibility in this role. The length of time to become a pastor can vary depending on you finishing the required training suggested by the church you are attending and becoming ordained...

You will need to spend time praying, determining, evaluating, and or developing some of the following:

- Character
- Philosophy of Ministry
- Skills
- Spiritual Gifts
- Education
- Doctrine
- Experience
- Personal Information
- Leadership Style

See how you measure up to what the scriptures say in the following list:

Pastor Qualifications in 1Timothy 3:1-7

- Above Reproach - An accusation of sin won't stick to him.
- Husband of One Wife - He must be faithful to his wife. He adores his wife and doesn't flirt with other women.
- Self-Control - He is the master of his behavior. His behavior doesn't control him.
- Lives Wisely - He makes good choices.
- Has a Good Reputation - People at church and in the community think highly of him. He is respected.
- Hospitable - His home is open to others.
- He Can Teach - He has gifted insight into the scripture and communicates well those insights to others.
- Not Addicted to Wine - He never gets drunk or over-indulges in alcohol.
- Not Violent - He resolves conflict peacefully.
- Gentle - His manner and words are not abrasive ...he has a good "bed side manner." This will be very helpful when visiting the sick.
- Loves Peace - Is someone who works toward peace in every relationship he encounters. Be approachable…
- Does Not Love Money - He is not consumed with his retirement fund or the price of gas.
- Manages His Home Well - His family and home are in order, not in chaos. His children are polite and respectful. His finances are in order.
- Not a New Christian - He has proven experience as a faithful follower of Jesus.

Other Pastor Qualifications in Titus 1:6-9

- His children must be believers who are not wild or rebellious.
- Not Arrogant - He must be humble, thinking of others first. He has a servant's heart.

- Not Quick-Tempered - His anger does not flare up at the least provocation.
- A Strong and Steadfast Belief - A conviction in the gospel that does not waver.

You must study to show yourself approved...

2 Timothy 2:15 New Living Translation (©2007)

Work hard so you can present yourself to God and receive his approval. Be a good worker, one who does not need to be ashamed and who correctly explains the word of truth.

You must study to be able to answer questions from the people you will shepherd.

You will need to learn how to preach etc... One way to begin is to seek a mentor. This should be a person who is already an Apostolic Pastor. Ask if they can mentor you.

Enroll in school…

Read the bible over and over memorizing various core texts...

Practice delivering sermons...

Evaluate your patience, endurance, faith, and confidence. These character qualities are just the type of pastor qualifications people are looking for.

Go out and disciple others...

Matthew 28: 19.20

19 Therefore go and make disciples of all nations, baptizing them in the name of the Father and of the Son and of the Holy Spirit, 20 and teaching them to obey everything I have commanded you. And surely I am with you always, to the very end of the age."

Above all else, pray...

Question: 15

I have a hard time getting excited over my nieces and nephews children getting baptized at 7-11 years old. I don't want to make any of the family mad, but wouldn't this be more like a christening?

Profile: Male 46-60 North America

Answer: There is a difference between a Christening and a Baptism.

Christening is defined as "Christian sacrament signifying cleansing and rebirth". The christening ceremony included giving the baby his/her "Christian name, sprinkling water on the head of the child, and welcoming him/her into the congregation. This is not required nor mentioned in scripture.

Note: if a baptism is included in the christening it is not biblical.

Infants are not capable of understanding sin or their need to be cleansed from it, so clearly this is not the time to do a baptism.

Baptisms are okay to perform when a child clearly understands his/her need for the Savior. So, 7-11 years, may be ok if they understand what they are doing.

Be happy for them... In the bible Jesus wanted children to come to him.

Luke 18:15-17

The Little Children and Jesus:

15 People were also bringing babies to Jesus for him to place his hands
on them. When the disciples saw this, they rebuked them.
16 But Jesus
called the children to him and said, "Let the little children come to me,
and do not hinder them, for the kingdom of God belongs to such as these.

17 Truly I tell you, anyone who will not receive the kingdom of God like a little child will never enter it."

There is no age limit put on who shall believe in Jesus. Just be capable of believing…

John 3:16 (ESV)

16 "For God so loved the world, that he gave his only Son, that whoever believes in him should not perish but have eternal life.

Question: 16

Why is God giving my uncle and sister-in-law new houses in great neighborhoods and I'm here in this bad neighborhood with no job and no money? I give myself to the bible daily and pray daily. They curse and cheat on their spouse, and talk bad about others, but they are rewarded...

Profile: Male 31-45 North America

Answer: Why are they prospering while sinning? God knows whether this is true. Trust Him...There is more then what you see going on. Their sins will catch up with them...

God is good all the time. He knows and sees all. He is never fooled by us.

Continue being faithful for God sees what you are doing. Persevere through...

Romans 5:3-5 (NKJV)

3 And not only that, but we also glory in tribulations, knowing that tribulation produces perseverance; 4 and perseverance, character; and character, hope. 5 Now hope does not disappoint, because the love of God has been poured out in our hearts by the Holy Spirit who was given to us.

God lets the sun rise on the good and the evil. Don't lose heart. In due season things will get better!

Galatians 6:9 (NKJV) And let us not grow weary while doing good, for in due season we shall reap if we do not lose heart.

Romans 12:12 (NKJV) rejoicing in hope, patient in tribulation, continuing steadfastly in prayer;

At times, you have to take action.

Not knowing your circumstance fully, or much about you, let me step out and suggest that you look for what areas in life you can improve.

Questions to ponder: Can you improve or change your job skills. Do you need more education? Seek free training if you cannot afford the going rate.

Sometimes you have to relocate to a different region to get a job. Are you willing to do this? Did you pray regarding this? Did God ask you to move?

Are you really living right? Do you have any unconfessed sins? Make sure you are honoring God. Don't let the fact that the perceived wicked or non believers are prospering. You do not know whether they have true peace in their hearts or whether trouble awaits them down the line.

Know this fact: the current earth is the best it is going to get for non-believers. When they die hell awaits. Heaven and a new earth await the believer. This is eternal life… Life on this earth is a short time in comparison.

Pray for your family. You might be the salt that is needed to save them.

Avoid listening to prosperity preachers. Not all people are called to be rich. In this life there will be trouble.

In conclusion:

Remember this, you are different and unique. You are responsible to God in the place where he has you! Love Him, obey Him, and serve Him. You are influential in that very sphere. How's your influence been this week? Ask the Lord to make you count for him this coming week. No matter what the situation is, no matter how your heart is crushed, no matter how despairing you feel, tell the Lord that you are willing to trust him to use all of these difficulties to bring blessing into your life.

One may never understand the reason or purpose behind bad circumstances. However, believers should take comfort in the fact that God is sovereign and has a purpose for what He is doing. Isa 55:8-9.

Bad things happen indiscriminately to both the wicked and the good. There is not necessarily a direct relationship between bad circumstances and sin or lack of faith. Sickness, death, and problems are not an accurate reflection of a person's spirituality. See Job 1:21.

Beware of "health and wealth" theology, which asserts that faithful believers will not experience illness, financial setbacks, or other difficulties. This is not the truth and is bad theology.

Problems, evil, and bad circumstances may be due to original sin, may be used by God to test a person, may be a means to display God's power and grace, may be a form of chastening, may be a result of sin, or may even come from Satan himself. (Luke 13:11-16; Job 1:12).

Many have succeeded from the position that you are in life. Ask for more people to pray for your specific needs. Consider fasting to enhance your connection to God. Whatever you fast from, replace it with deep prayer with our Great God. Hang in there, for you are not forgotten.

Question: 17

I have been reading, and listening to LWF ministry...

They are good in reaching out to people and spreading the Gospel... I have listened to a particular sermon about the coming back of our Lord Jesus...

Mentioned in there that if you are not raptured before the tribulation then you are destined for wrath... Something like this...

So, is it all those who will be left behind are only bad persons, and all will go to hell, and will not be saved? Thanks!

Profile: Female

Answer: If LWF is referring to "Love Worth Finding", this is a fine ministry that is very good in reaching out to people with the gospel...

Your question regarding the rapture can be answered this way.

If you are not raptured, it will be very difficult becoming saved during this time because Satan and the antichrist will have a very strong delusion going out to the remaining people fooling many. With that said, there will be those who will come to Christ after the rapture so not all left behind will go to hell.

Revelations 9:4 indicates that there will be those with the seal of God on their foreheads. And Matthew 24:22 speaks of for the sake of the elect the days will be cut short.

Revelation 9:3, 4 (ESV)

[3]Then from the smoke came locusts on the earth, and they were given power like the power of scorpions of the earth.

[4]They were told not to harm the grass of the earth or any green plant or any tree, but only those people who do not have the seal of God on their foreheads.

Matthew 24:22-25 (ESV)

And if those days had not been cut short, no human being would be saved. But for the sake of the elect those days will be cut short. [23] Then if anyone says to you, 'Look, here is the Christ!' or 'There he is!' do not believe it. [24]For false christ and false prophets will arise and perform great signs and wonders, so as to lead astray, if possible, even the elect. [25]See, I have told you beforehand.

There will be those who will come to Christ after the rapture so not all left behind will go to hell. It is far better to accept the gospel now while the church and the Holy Spirit are still present.

As for bad persons, remember all of us "fall short of the glory of God" and are filthy rags.

Romans 3:23 (English Standard Version)

[23] for (A) all have sinned and fall short of the glory of God,

Isaiah 64:6 (New International Version)

[6] All of us have become like one who is unclean, and all our righteous acts are like filthy rags; we all shrivel up like a leaf, and like the wind our sins sweep us away.

God cares and will provide a way for all who call on the name of the Lord to be saved.

John 3:16 (New International Version)

16 For God so loved the world that he gave his one and only Son, that whoever believes in him shall not perish but have eternal life.

In conclusion, new believers will be saved after the rapture but it will be most difficult for them...

Question: 18

What is the united church of god? http://www.ucg.org/

Profile: Male Under 18 North America

Answer: The United Church of God faithfully teaches the doctrines of the now deceased Herbert W. Armstrong, who was a very charismatic and controlling leader of the Worldwide Church of God (WCG), which was widely considered to be a cult.

Armstrong believed that he was an end-time apostle proclaiming the soon-coming 'Kingdom of God'. WCG discontinued Armstrong's teachings after his death, prompting members faithful to Armstrong doctrines to split and form their own organizations. The United Church of God is one of many of these offshoot organizations. These organizations vary from moderate to more extreme forms, the latter of which tend to have controlling leaders and exhibit clear characteristics of a cult. The more moderate groups, such as UCG, have departed from Armstrong's more eccentric teachings such as a ban on birthdays and makeup.

The United Church of God teaches a unique form of Christianity derived from the teachings of Herbert W. Armstrong, which is known by non-adherents as 'Armstrongism'. Armstrongism teaches that groups of the same beliefs are the 'only true church', and that all other religions are false or satanic counterfeits. 'Converted' members are seen as an exclusive and select group of people specially chosen by God to become 'first-fruits' - a future group of 'god-beings' and 'kings and priests' in the literal earthly 'Kingdom of God.' God has specially 'drawn' his 'elect' and revealed the hidden knowledge of his 'truth' only to them, whereas the rest of the world is blinded by Satan to this special knowledge. The 'sign' of God's 'chosen people' is literal Sabbath keeping and obedience to the Old Covenant (Mosaic) law, excluding temple and ritual laws. Significant demands are placed on members, such as two tithes and Holy Day observances. Members are not permitted to work from sunset to sunset on Holy-Days or the Sabbath (Saturday), even if they lose their employment as a result. Armstrongist groups, such as UCG, consider themselves as being different and apart from 'the world', i.e. non-believers. As an example, they will not celebrate Christmas in any form because Christmas is 'extra-biblical' and 'pagan' in origin.

Other key UCG beliefs that differ from traditional Christianity include the rejection of the Trinity, and their belief that Western white nations (predominantly England and the U.S.A.) are the direct lineal descendants of the northern tribes of Israel.

UCG rejecting the Trinity is a major issue. The following are scripture support for the Trinity:

Deuteronomy 6:4 ESV "Hear, O Israel! The LORD our God, the LORD is one!"

The case for the Triunity of God is even stronger in the New Testament. Here it can be unequivocally demonstrated the Father is God, the Son is God, and the Holy Spirit is God. Furthermore, the New Testament teaches us that these three names are not synonymous, but speak of three distinct and equal Persons.

(1) **The Father is called God** (John 6:27; 20:17; 1 Cor. 8:6; Gal. 1:1; Eph. 4:6; Phil. 2:11; 1 Pet. 1:2).

(2) Jesus Christ, the Son is declared to be God. His deity is proven by the divine names given to Him, by His works that only God could do (upholding all things, Col. 1:17; creation, Col. 1:16, John 1:3; and future judgment, John 5:27), by His divine attributes (eternality, John 17:5; omnipresence, Matt. 28:20; omnipotence, Heb. 1:3; omniscience, Matt. 9:4), and by explicit statements declaring His deity (John 1:1; 20:28; Titus 2:13; Heb. 1:8).

(3) The Holy Spirit is recognized as God. By comparing Peter's comments in Acts 5:3 and 4, we see that in lying to the Holy Spirit (vs. 3), Ananias was lying to God (vs. 4). He has the attributes which only God can possess like omniscience (1 Cor. 2:10) and omnipresence (1 Cor. 6:19), and He regenerates people to new life (John 3:5-6, 8; Tit. 3:5), which must of necessity be a work of God for only God has the power of life. Finally, His deity is evident by the divine names used for the Spirit as "the Spirit of our God," (1 Cor. 6:11), which should be understood as "the Spirit, who is our God."

If one carefully examines UCG's "free" literature (including their free 12-lesson Bible Study Course), they can clearly discern that it is filled with mind control methods of guilt, striving for perfection, fear and "only true church" dogma.

Attendance in UCG dropped from 20,000 to 12,000 as of 2004, and they continue to experience slow growth, even losing members in many areas. Most of their new members have been from those who have exited other "churches of God" (i. e., offshoots or splinter groups from Worldwide Church of God).

Former members of UCG, express that the group shows a lack of love and venerates Herbert W. Armstrong, have testified of spiritual abuse, suffering and exploitation, and having to go through a very difficult exiting process and recovery.

Before considering that the UCG might be a "good church" to join, and before giving away your time, your money and your life, thoroughly check out the history of this group (Worldwide Church of God), investigate the religious roots of Herbert W. Armstrong, along with his background, and educate yourself on mind control and exploitive groups in society.

If the leaders of the Worldwide Church of God (United Church of God) really want to obey the Word of God, they should consider disbanding their unscriptural organization and exhort their members to get saved by trusting in the finished atonement of Jesus Christ and to join sound bible teaching churches. By attempting to reform an unscriptural organization which has such a wretched and apostate history, the leaders of the USG are creating tremendous confusion.

This is not a recommended Church to be a part of. Doctrines held by the United Church of God are at odds with traditional and biblical Christianity.

Question: 19

How closely should I scrutinize my church's operating budget? Should the majority of tithes go to pay salaries and bills? What is the measuring stick for a church to be a good steward of the money they are given?

Profile: Male 31-45 North America

Answer: The way this question is answered depends on who is asking. If you are a Pastor or part of the leadership personnel of the church responsible for handling this, you are to make sure that every penny is leveraged for the kingdom of God. The tithes and offering is used to support all of the church operations. The percentage depends on the church size, and the budget set to meet the qualifications of its personal, and the funds needed for all internal and external operations. The leadership team of the church determines the ratio or percentage for the budget. A church with a high profile pastor should get paid comparable to other high profile pastors in similar situation. The same thing applies with other ministry positions. This amount will be affected by the budget depending on the fluctuations in the received tithes.

There are standards (A measuring stick) that are put in place for Churches to follow. The bible speaks not regarding a ratio or percentage for the budget but regarding accountability:

Accountability to God is vital, but people form their impressions of both people and organizations by looking at the outward appearances (See 1 Samuel 16:7 ESV). The basis for establishing a standard is stated clearly by the Apostle Paul in 2 Corinthians 8:20, 21 (ESV):

20 We take this course so that no one should blame us about this generous gift that is being administered by us,

21 for we aim at what is honorable not only in the Lord's sight but also in the sight of man.

The Standards, drawn from Scripture, are fundamental to operating with integrity.

Every church shall exercise the appropriate management and controls necessary to provide reasonable assurance that all of the church operations are carried out and resources are used in a responsible manner and in conformity with applicable laws and regulations, such conformity taking into account biblical mandates.

If you are one of the congregants you can only view the budget from the updates in the announcements or in the church bulletin/program. Also, if the church is open and discusses this with the core attendees. If the church has shown itself to be credible in the past trust them to do the right thing.

If you are a congregant having controlling tendencies that includes micro managing others, well, you have to let go and let's others do their job. If the church established a history of being authentic and trustworthy with the money trust them…

The size of the church plays a huge role in how the money is received and allocated.

A large church may have a very large cash flow that allows them to do greater things.

A small church may struggle to have enough money to meet the standard salary requirements and pay its bills.

Both need to have integrity in dealing with the budget.

Question: 20

What is a back slider? Are we considered to be a back slider each time we sin? What did God mean when He said he was married to a back slider? I know that the Bible says we have ALL sinned and come short of his glory; but each time we sin knowingly or unknowingly are we "considered" to be a "Backslider"?

Profile: Female 46-60 North America

Answer: A backslider is a saved person who falls into sin. A lost sinner cannot be a backslider. You have to go somewhere before you can slide back. But one who is truly born again, a child of God who falls into sin, is a backslider. It may be outrageous and gross sin known to everyone, or it may be merely coldness of heart, a luke-warmness of heart instead of the burning fire of love for God. But when a Christian loses any of his joy, or loses part of his sweet fellowship with God, or falls into sin, then he is a backslider. Remember that only Christians can backslide. So, yes, a Christian is considered a backslider each time they sin whether knowingly or unknowingly. A sin is a sin...

"The backslider in heart shall be filled with his own ways." - Prov. 14:14.

"Thine own wickedness shall correct thee, and thy backslidings shall reprove thee: know therefore and see that it is an evil thing and bitter, that thou hast forsaken the Lord thy God, and that my fear is not in thee, saith the Lord God of hosts." - Jer. 2:19.

Christians sin. Some of the saintliest of God's people have fallen into outrageous sin. And that has puzzled honest hearts and has been the sneer of the wicked down through the ages.

The word "backslider" or "backsliding" does not appear in the New Testament and is used in the Old Testament primarily of Israel. The Jews, though they were God's chosen people, continually turned their backs on Him and rebelled against His Word (Jeremiah 8:9). That is why they were forced to make sacrifices for sin over and over in order to restore their relationship with the God they had offended. The Christian, however, has availed himself of the perfect, once-and-for-all sacrifice of Christ and needs no further sacrifice for his sin. God himself has obtained our salvation for us (2 Corinthians 5:21) and because we are saved by Him, a true Christian cannot fall away so as not to return. Christians do sin (1 John 1:8), but the Christian life is not to be identified by a life of sin. Believers are a new creation (2 Corinthians 5:17). We have the Holy Spirit in us producing good fruit (Galatians 5:22-23). A Christian life should be a changed life. Christians are forgiven no matter how many times they sin, but at the same time Christians should live a progressively more holy life as they grow closer to Christ. We should have serious doubts about a person who claims to be a believer yet lives a life that says otherwise. Yes, a true Christian who falls back into sin is still saved, but at the same time a person who lives a life controlled by sin is not truly a Christian.

We have many examples of this in the Bible. What an honest book the Bible is to tell us of the failures and sins of God's people through the ages! God wanted us to know that the men of the greatest faith, saints who had truly been born again, were frail people such as we are and subject to the same temptations and surrendering sometimes to the same sins.

God tells how Noah got drunk and lay naked in his tent. He tells how Lot sought the fellowship of the wicked Sodomites, lost all his influence, got drunk etc... The Bible tells how Abraham deceived, calling Sarah his sister. Even saintly Moses lost his temper. When God commanded him to speak to the rock that Israel might be watered from it a second time, in a temper he beat upon it with his rod and so dishonored God that he lost his chance to enter the Promised Land.

David, a man after God's own heart, a man used to write the Psalms, that blessed book of devotions for the saints through all these centuries, committed adultery with Bathsheba and then had her husband Uriah slain to hide his sin. The Bible tells how Samson, a judge of Israel who had been filled with the Holy Ghost and was a Nazarite from his birth, kept company with harlots until God left him powerless, a slave of the Philistines with his eyes burned out.

The Bible tells how Peter denied Christ and cursed and swore; how all the disciples forsook Jesus and fled; how later Peter, fearing the Jewish Christians, played the coward again, and led even good Barnabas away with his dissimulations. The Bible tells how Joseph of Arimathea, a disciple of Jesus, was a coward, a secret disciple. Even Paul the apostle went up to Jerusalem against the plain leading of the Holy Spirit.

So the saints of the Bible fell into sin. They were backsliders.

These examples should humble us and teach us that even the mightiest of God's saints sometimes backslide, fall into sin, and so lose the sweet joy that every Christian ought to have.

A Christian who backslides is like a child who disobeys his parents. It does not affect His son-ship but it affects his fellowship, his joy, and the approval of the Father.

A person who rejects Christ and turns his back on the faith is demonstrating that he never belonged to Christ. Those who belong to Christ remain with Christ. Those who renounce their faith never had it to begin with. 2 Timothy 2:11-13, "Here is a trustworthy saying: If we died with him, we will also live with him; if we endure, we will also reign with him.

If we disown him, he will also disown us; if we are faithless, he will remain faithful, for he cannot disown himself."

Remember the text in Proverbs 14:14 says, "The backslider in heart shall be filled with his own ways." Backsliding is not necessarily getting drunk nor committing adultery, nor any outward course of sin seen by the public. Backsliding is in the heart!

It may be, dear Christian, that you have drifted somewhat but have never noticed it. You may be like Samson who "wist not that the Lord was departed from him" (Judges 16:20). We need to search our hearts and we need to watch and pray lest sin creep up on us.

If you are a backslider, then I have good news for you. The simplest and shortest part of this answer is how to get back to God. Simply turn to God in your heart, confess your sin and backsliding, and He will receive you with open arms and forgive you of all your sins, failures and mistakes.

In 1 John 1:9 is this sweet verse for Christians, "If we confess our sins, he is faithful and just to forgive us our sins, and to cleanse us from all unrighteousness." Isn't that simple? We simply confess our sins honestly, and then God is faithful and just to forgive us and cleanse us.

What did God mean when He said he was married to a back slider?

This is found in the book of Hosea. The book of Hosea is a picture story. Hosea's marriage to an adulterous woman was a picture of redemption - God rejecting adulterous Israel, sending her away to go after other men, and then redeeming her.

According to divine law, a divorced woman could not return to her husband. And yet, God's mercy overruled the law. God himself redeems his own beloved, though she rightfully is unredeemable. Mercy triumphs over judgment.

It is a tender story, one that causes us to weep because of the goodness of our Lord.

It is a picture of redemption – God snatching the sinner from the bondage of sin, and restoring a covenant relationship with her - even after a time of judgment.

".... I will speak tenderly to her....

In that day, declares the Lord, "you will call me "my husband... and they will say, You are my God. Hos. 2:16, 23

Question: 21

I have some personal questions. First, I am attending a church where I met the Lord. I have been growing in God in this church but I am planning on attending a university out of state. Moving out of state means leaving this church... Do you think it is wrong for me to do this? Second, this church, is a church where you grow in God and which preaches according to the bible. But you have to depend on them for every decision you make in your life; whom you marry, where you go to school, where you live etc... I like how this church teaches the bible and they make you grow in God, but I feel like I don't have that much freedom. Do I really have to depend on them on these things? Do you think I am wrong because I am not committing myself to the church? As I mentioned above, I am planning on moving out of state. This is something they will not like because they believe I will be leaving God's calling of becoming a college bible teacher. They will start telling me this is not God's direction for me, but I don't see anything wrong with this. What do you think? Besides the fact I am moving out of state, I also want to leave the church because I don't feel like I have that much freedom. Do you think this is the wrong reason to leave?

Profile: Female 18-30 North America

Answer: It is a good thing that you are asking this question. You are not doing anything wrong here. You should not feel obligated to put your life on hold to be controlled by this church. It sounds like you experienced some good things there, in addition to it being a place that has a tight grip micromanaging its people.

Without knowing the name of the church, I cannot really comment on whether they are truly a good biblically functioning church.

1 John 4:1 Test the Spirits

[1]Beloved, do not believe every spirit, but test the spirits to see whether they are from God, for many false prophets have gone out into the world.

You should pray and ask the Lord what you should do.

You are not wrong in the way you are feeling. There are probably others attending this church that feel the same way. Please know that in Christ there is liberty and Freedom… See 2 Corinthians 3:17 English Standard Version (ESV):

17 Now the Lord is the Spirit, and where the Spirit of the Lord is, there is freedom.

As long as you are still going to pursue growth in Christ by being fed the word of God, go out and pursue your education.

Keep the Lord always before you. See if you can find a bible teaching church near your school...

After you graduate, see if you can leverage your degree for the kingdom of God, or outside of your career, volunteer your time to leverage your gifts for the kingdom of God.

Question: 22

I need to know "should Christians be resistant to the government if something is incorrect?" Thank you!

Profile: Female 18-30 Asia

Answer: You asked a question that can have a profound effect on a person's life depending on what part of the world this resistance might be applied. Some persecution can result from direct refusal to follow a government's mandate. In some parts of the world this can be a life or death situation.

This decision does require prayer. Seek how to proceed from the Lord.

He may provide a way of escape… Perhaps you may have to leave to avoid the danger or the troubles that may result.

The bible says that we are to obey God rather than man (Acts 5:29).

If the government ask for a Christian to reject being a follower of Jesus then this government would be in direct conflict with the word of God. The Christian needs to follow God's will, not man.

A person in this position will need to count the cost and know that in this life there will be trouble as Jesus informed us and march towards the cross with confidence that absence from the body is where all believers will be with the Lord in heaven.

A believer needs to obey authority as long as it does not conflict with scripture.

Another example of such government mandate is in some countries you must pay taxes.

Paying taxes is not against the scriptures. We are to give to Caesar what is Caesar's and what is God's to God. Matthew 22:15-21.

Many believers face decisions that are troubling. Know that you are not alone. God will never leave you nor forsake you.

Question: 23

Why is most of Israel Jewish, and most of Greece Orthodox instead of Christian? I just say those because they were main areas in the bible and books of the bible were written there, apostles were from there, they went to these places and the two countries have huge biblical history, yet most of them aren't even in the religion, why is this?

Answer: Some history… Christians are presently the smallest religious group and denomination of the Abrahamic religions in Israel. Most Christians living permanently in Israel are Arabs or have come from other countries to live and work mainly in churches or monasteries, which have long histories in the land.

According to both historical and traditional sources, Jesus lived in the Land of Israel, and died and was buried on the site of the Church of the Holy Sepulchre in Jerusalem, making the land a Holy Land in the view of Christianity. However, very few Christians now live in the area, compared to Muslims and Jews. This is because Islam displaced Christianity in almost all of the Middle East, and the rise of modern Zionism and the establishment of the State of Israel has seen millions of Jews migrated to Israel.

In recent years, the Christian population in Israel has increased significantly by the immigration of foreign workers from a number of countries, and the immigration of accompanying non-Jewish spouses in mixed marriages. Numerous churches have opened in Tel Aviv, in particular…

Greece was an earlier evangelized area that was conquered first by Rome, then later when Greece was conquered by Ottoman' Turks 1453 AD emphasized Orthodoxy, 1831 AD Bavaria controlled Greece, 1863

Denmark, and Orthodox was brought by Constantine in Constantinople 8th century.

It comes down to choice. They all chose not to follow Jesus even with the rich history in both countries...

The Jews rejected Jesus because He failed, in their eyes, to do what they expected their Messiah to do—destroy evil and all their enemies and establish an eternal kingdom with Israel as the preeminent nation in the world. The prophecies in Isaiah and Psalm 22 described a suffering Messiah who would be persecuted and killed, but they chose to focus instead on those prophecies that discussed His glorious victories, not His crucifixion. The commentaries in the Talmud, written before the onset of Christianity, clearly discuss the Messianic prophecies of Isaiah 53 and Psalm 22 and puzzle over how these would be fulfilled with the glorious setting up of the Kingdom of the Messiah. After the Church used these prophecies to prove the claims of Christ, the Jews took the position that the prophecies did not refer to the Messiah, but to Israel or some other person.

The Jews believed that the Messiah, the prophet which Moses spoke about, would come and deliver them from Roman bondage and set up a kingdom where they would be the rulers.

Two thousand years after He came to the nation of Israel as their Messiah, Jews still (for the most part) reject Jesus Christ. Many Jews today (some say at least half of all living Jews) identify themselves as Jewish but prefer to remain "secular." They identify with no particular Jewish movement and have no understanding or affiliation with any Jewish biblical roots. The concept of Messiah as expressed in the Hebrew Scriptures or Judaism's "13 Principles of Faith" is foreign to most Jews today.

But one concept is generally held as universal: Jews must have nothing to do with Jesus! Most Jews today perceive the last 2000 years of historical Jewish persecution to be at the hands of so-called "Christians." From the Crusades, to the Inquisition, to the pogroms in Europe, to Hitler's holocaust—Jews ultimately believe that they are being held responsible for the death of Jesus Christ and are being persecuted for that reason. They, therefore, reject Him today for this reason and for the other historical reasons mentioned above.

The good news is that many Jews are turning to Christ today. The God of Israel has always been faithful to keep a "remnant" of believing Jews to Himself. In the United States alone, some estimates say that there are over 100,000 Jewish believers in Jesus, and the numbers are growing all the time.

Question: 24

Genesis 22:18 declares the promise of God to Abraham that through his offspring all nations on earth will be blessed.

Ephesians 2:12 tells us that the gentiles are foreigners to the covenants of the promise. Paul is telling us that Gentiles are foreigners to the promise but Genesis 22:18 says that they will receive the blessing. Please explain.

Profile: Male 31-45 Europe

Answer: Genesis 22:18 and Ephesians are unified without conflict for Genesis is saying that through Abraham's offspring meaning the promised Christ all nations will be blessed.

Paul in Ephesians 2:12 is giving details regarding the Gentiles who are part of the nations Genesis was referring to. If you read on in Ephesians 2:13-22 it further clarifies that the promised Christ did come and made both the Gentiles and the Jews one in this by reconciling both to God in one body through the cross... Verse 19 ... so then you are no longer strangers and aliens but you (the Gentiles) are fellow citizens with the saints and members of the household of God.

Both the Jews and the Gentiles, all nations on earth are blessed by Jesus arrival just as the bible has said. The promise was applied to both...

Question: 25

Why did God put the tree of knowledge of good and evil in the Garden of Eden?

Answer: God put the tree of knowledge of good and evil in the Garden of Eden to give Adam and Eve a choice to obey Him or disobey Him. Adam and Eve were free to do anything they wanted, except eat from the tree of knowledge of good and evil. Genesis 2:16-17, "And the LORD God commanded the man, 'You are free to eat from any tree in the garden; but you must not eat from the tree of the knowledge of good and evil, for when you eat of it you will surely die.'" If God had not given Adam and Eve the choice, they would have essentially been robots, simply doing what they were programmed to do. God created Adam and Eve to be "free" beings, able to make decisions, able to choose between good and evil. In order for Adam and Eve to truly be free, they had to have a choice.

For more study please read the full article at the following url:

http://www.gotquestions.org/tree-knowledge-good-evil.html

Question: 26

The bible says there is a baptism of The Holy Spirit and a filling of the Holy Spirit. It distinctively states that they were filled with the Holy Spirit on Pentecost, Acts 2:4.

Is it not reasonable to accept the breathing of Jesus as the initial baptism and the filling as receiving the power as Jesus said it would be in Acts 1:8?

Were they baptized into Christ in John 20:22 as stated in Galatians 3:27?

Answer: This can be a very long and involved theological subject, but I'm going to try to give you a quick answer. Please spend time looking up the scripture verses referenced that help support the answer now given.

On the day of Pentecost, the believers of Jerusalem were both baptized of the Holy Spirit and filled with the Holy Spirit, but those are two separate actions. The baptism of the Holy Spirit is the work whereby He brings the believer into spiritual union with Jesus and with all other believers who are saved. It is the Lord Jesus who does this baptizing (Luke 3:16; John 1:33) using the Holy Spirit as His Agent (the instrumental case [or dative of means] is used in the Greek for the word "in" [Greek en] in Matthew 3:11; Luke 3:16; John 12:33; Acts 1:5; 11:16; I Corinthians 12:13). This, of course, was Spirit baptism and not water baptism.

Today, at the moment of our salvation, the Lord Jesus baptizes us with or in the Holy Spirit just like the initial believers at Pentecost. The difference is they were done as a group because this had never been done before. We are done individually when we trust Christ as Savior.

Throughout our lives the Holy Spirit fills us with Himself. This does not concern our receiving more of the Holy Spirit, for being a person He wholly resides in us. To be filled with the Holy Spirit is to be under His control, not in an absolute sense so that we are passive and our personal faculties cease to function, but in a relative sense in which we cooperate with Him by doing our part and depending upon Him to do His work in us (Acts 2:4; 4:8, 31; 6:3, 5, 8-11; 11:24; 15:32). This should be a daily occurrence not an once-in-a-lifetime event. This is where we get our power to be like Christ and do His work.

The impartation of the Holy Spirit in John 20:22 was accomplished by Jesus breathing the Holy Spirit into his disciples: "He breathed into them and said, Receive the Holy Spirit" (a literal translation). In a sense this verse consummates the Gospel of John because the Spirit who had been promised in John 7:37-39; 14:16-20, 26; 15:26; and 16:7-15 is now at last given to the disciples. After the Lord commissioned the disciples, he breathed to them and said, literally, "Receive Holy Spirit". Jesus' breathing into them recapitulates God's breathing into Adam (see Genesis 2:7, LXX, where enephusesen is used) and thus denotes that Jesus' infusion inspired a new genesis, in which he regenerated the disciples (see 1 Peter 1:3). With this "in-breathing" came the actual impartation of the promised Holy Spirit. The apostles received the Spirit 'into' them on the evening of the resurrection and the Spirit came 'upon' them on the day of Pentecost. They were filled and endued with the same Spirit.

Hope this helps.

Question: 27

What did Paul mean when he said in 1 Corinthians 9:27 that he buffets his body?

Profile: Anonymous

Answer: After reading this in other translations it is clearer what Paul was saying. Check out the following translations:

ESV: But I discipline my body and keep it under control, lest after preaching to others I myself should be disqualified.

KJV: But I keep under my body, and bring it into subjection: lest that by any means, when I have preached to others, I myself should be a castaway.

Paul explains that he is always under the law to Christ and he is never free to do things that would be contrary to the new covenant. And in Galatians 5:13 he says, "For, brethren, ye have been called unto liberty; ONLY USE NOT LIBERTY FOR AN OCCASION TO THE FLESH, but by love serve one another."

Paul's liberty in his evangelism was not a freedom to serve the flesh in any way. Paul was always strict in regard to sin and he did not allow anything in his life that would bring the result of sin by spiritual carelessness. He would not become a glutton to reach other overeaters, and he would not become a drinker of alcohol to reach a drunk.

To get control over one's body may required a major battle when sin tries to lead.

Notice the translations express the opening sentences as Paul taking control:

But I discipline my body and keep it under control…

Instead I subdue my body and make it my slave…

No, I beat my body and make it my slave…

I really fight! I am my body's sternest master,

Those of us who are saved, have God's Holy Spirit, within our wicked bodies and mind: Therefore one part of living the Christian life, is bringing our body under control. This is the goal set before every Christian: To grow to the point that we are not following the will of the flesh, but the will of the Holy Spirit within us.

There are consequences, to not controlling ourselves, and yielding to our flesh: Paul took these consequences seriously.

Paul concludes this paragraph by expressing a sincere fear that he himself could fail to win the prize. Instead of running aimlessly or shadow-boxing (9:26), Paul makes this contrasting statement, "but I discipline my body and make it my slave, so that, after I have preached to others, I myself will not be disqualified." With the judgment seat of Christ in mind, Paul writes, "but I discipline my body and make it my slave." The word translated "discipline" literally means "to strike under the eye" or "to beat black and blue." Paul beat his body into submission by doing all that he could to ensure his success. He deliberately knocks himself into unconsciousness, so to speak, thus bringing his body into "slavery."

Most people, including many Christians, are slaves to their bodies. Their bodies tell their minds what to do. Their bodies decide when to eat, what to eat, how much to eat, when to sleep and get up, and so on. An athlete cannot allow that. He follows the training rules, not his body. He runs when he would rather be resting; he eats a balanced meal when he would rather have a chocolate sundae; he goes to bed when he would rather stay up; and he gets up early to train when he would rather stay in bed. An athlete leads his body, he does not follow it. It is his slave, not the other way around.

Many of us hate the word "discipline" as much as "self-control." Yet, Paul says both are necessary.

In closing, friend, may we all keep control of our bodies, and bring them into subjection to God's will.

Question: 28

Your site says "Christians do not continually live immoral lifestyles, nor do they reject the faith and deny Christ. Such actions are proof that they were never redeemed." But what about me, who has a problem with an immoral lifestyle? I am/was addicted to cigarettes, and alcohol, and cussing, but I still feel the Holy Spirit and read my Bible and pray - does that mean I am not saved if I live an immoral lifestyle, even when the Holy Spirit, I believe, resides in me, for it is very strong?

Profile: Female 18-30 North America

Answer: Thanks for writing us. Know that you matter to us and I hope my answer truly reflects this sensitivity.

In brief, the requirements to get saved are to come just as you are… Get saved… (John 3:16). Then let the Lord help you change the things that you could not prior…

Once saved does not mean that you won't sin again. There should be a noticeable difference in the sinning that use to occur. This happens over time as the Christian learns to walk by the Spirit and not by the flesh. It will be a battle all of your life because of our sinful nature inherited from Adam and Eve. The flesh wants to do one thing and Spirit wants to honor the Lord. Read Romans 7:14-25 ESV.

Note: You can be victorious over many sins through the power of Jesus.

Some questions for you. When you got saved, did you really mean the prayer from your heart making Jesus Lord and Savior of your Life? Did you mean that you want to turn from your sins? Repent? Etc… If so, as a believer growing in the faith there should be an increasing desire to do God's will. Are you growing? Do you attend church? Are you worshiping the Lord? Are you using your Spiritual gifts for the Kingdom building efforts? Do you spend time alone with the Lord? Do you confess your sins to God and ask for help to stop doing the things that do not please Him?

1 John 1:9 English Standard Version (ESV)

9 If we confess our sins, he is faithful and just to forgive us our sins and to cleanse us from all unrighteousness.

A person who is a Christian who is growing in the faith will not want to live an immoral life. This would grieve the Holy Spirit.

Ephesians 4:30. English Standard Version (ESV)

30 And do not grieve the Holy Spirit of God, by whom you were sealed for the day of redemption.

A person willfully living in a pattern of sin (Immoral lifestyle) would be bringing the Holy Spirit along into their sinful actions. In a believer the Spirit would be prompting the person to repent. So if you are saying the Spirit is very strong in you, what is the Spirit saying while you are living an immoral lifestyle? If you are not hearing anything, your sin has you far from God. Repentance is definitely needed.

Change the immoral way of living ASAP even if it cost you… Trust God to make a way. Honor God and He will honor you…

If you are truly saved, know that God does discipline His children who are rebelling against His word.

Cigarette smoking is an addiction and does not indicate whether you are saved or not.

Alcohol is also habit forming and can do more harm to you and others… If you are an alcoholic, please seek help… Decide right now, not another drink. Period!! You can be freed from these habits. A Christian needs to live their life glorifying God. Does getting drunk and cursing bring glory to God? No… Not now… Not ever…

Please pray and ask God to change you. God is faithful to His people. Ask God to bring you a mentor or accountability partner or friend that can walk with you through this stage in your life. Tell God that you want to Honor Him and you are sorry for not living right. Work hard every day trying not to curse. Replace the commonly used curse word with clean words that build up. Please memorize the following scripture and put it into practice:

Ephesians 4:29 English Standard Version (ESV)

29 Let no corrupting talk come out of your mouths, but only such as is good for building up, as fits the occasion, that it may give grace to those who hear.

Some years ago my wife Revita had a great idea she shared with our small group at that time.

She said when you want to curse, or call people names, replace the bad language with the word "Ephesians" This will remind you of this verse (Ephesians 4:29).

For example: If someone cuts you off in traffic [replacement word]: "Ephesians"

Give it a try…You can say if softly or with more strength…

Scripture says that we will know a believer by his/her fruits? What are your fruits telling others?

Please read more of the scriptural details to enforce God's teaching: Ephesians 4:17-32; 5:1-20.

If after reading this answer you are not really sure that you are saved, or you want to rededicate your life to Jesus, please say the following prayer and mean it from all of your being:

Salvation Prayer:

Dear Lord Jesus, I know that I am a sinner and need your forgiveness.

I believe that you died for my sins.

I want to turn from my sins. I now invite you to come into my heart and life.

I want to trust and follow you as Lord and Savior. In Jesus' name Amen.

Now walk towards the Lord Daily… Go to Church… Get involved in serving the Lord.

Hold on to Romans 8:1 in your heart:

Romans 8:1 English Standard Version (ESV)

Life in the Spirit

[1]There is therefore now no condemnation for those who are in Christ Jesus. [a]

Footnotes:

a. Romans 8:1 Some manuscripts add *who walk not according to the flesh (but according to the Spirit)*

Friend, I hope this helps you, influences your decision, and brings you into a deeper walk with God.

Question: 29

Hello, I was born 10-11-50. I am a recovering alcoholic. Sober since 1998. How can I either get saved or know I am saved?

Profile: Male, North America

Answer: First, I want to say congratulations on being sober since 1998! This is very good news!

Also, thank you for writing to GotQuestions.org. You asked the most important question all people need to ask.

There is life after this one and where you spend it depends on you appropriating the free gift of eternal life.

To get saved you have to accept Jesus as your Lord and Savior. Believe on the Lord Jesus Christ!

This is a step that you must mean from the bottom of your heart.

Come just as you are to God in prayer…

John 3:16 ESV

16"For God so loved the world, that he gave his only Son, that whoever believes in him should not perish but have eternal life.

Friend, you wanted to know "how do you know if you are saved?"

Scripture say we will know a believer by his fruits. What are your fruits telling others?

Please read more of the scriptural details to enforce Gods teaching: Ephesians 4:17-32; 5:1-20.

If after reading this answer you are not really sure that you are saved, or you want to rededicate your life to Jesus, please say the following prayer and mean it from all of your being:

Salvation Prayer:

Dear Lord Jesus, I know that I am a sinner and need your forgiveness.

I believe that you died for my sins.

I want to turn from my sins. I now invite you to come into my heart and life.

I want to trust and follow you as Lord and Savior. In Jesus name Amen.

If you meant this prayer you are saved!

Now live a life honoring the Lord daily… Go to Church… Get involved in serving the Lord.

Know that you will still battle sin all the way until you go to heaven. Keep reading and applying God's word, the bible, to your life and you will win many victories over the flesh.

By reading and applying scripture, you will be walking by the Spirit and not the flesh.

You will see a noticeable change as you grow in Christ… Others will see the fruits too!

When sin occurs, repent… Remember to confess your sins to God and He will be faithful to forgive you and help you.

1 John 1:9 English Standard Version (ESV)

9 If we confess our sins, he is faithful and just to forgive us our sins and to cleanse us from all unrighteousness.

Hold on to Romans 8:1:

Romans 8:1 English Standard Version (ESV)

Life in the Spirit

1There is therefore now no condemnation for those who are in Christ Jesus. [b]

Footnotes:

b. Romans 8:1 Some manuscripts add *who walk not according to the flesh (but according to the Spirit)*

Friend, I hope you have chosen Jesus today. If you prayed accepting Jesus as your Lord and Savior, eternal life awaits. Nothing can take you out of God's grip now. You are in God's family now. Let us know whether you prayed to receive Christ.

Question: 30

What part of the Trinity raised Jesus from the dead? Was it the Father because the Son was dead?

Profile: Male 46-60 North America

Answer: When it comes to the resurrection of our Lord, scripture gives us a pretty good amount of information that says who was involved in the resurrection of Jesus. Read the following verses and references:

- God the Father raised Jesus (Acts 2:24, 32; 3:15, 26; 4:10; 5:30; 10:40; 13:30, 33, 34, 37).
- God raised Him up again (Rom. 4:24; 6:4, 10:9 [through the glory of the Father]); 1 Cor. 6:14; Gal. 1:1; Col. 2:12);
- The Holy Spirit is somehow involved in the resurrection of Jesus:
  Romans 8:11 "But if the Spirit of Him who raised…"
  Romans 1:4 "who was declared the Son of God with power by the resurrection from the dead, according to the Spirit of holiness, Jesus Christ our Lord,…"
- The Son Himself lays down His life and takes it up again — John 10:17-18

Jesus, through His divine nature, even while His human body lay dead, displayed His power through resurrection. Jesus, speaking of His body said "Destroy this temple, and in three days I will raise it up." (John 2:19) Certainly, it was "God" who raised His body (Rom. 10:9, 1 Pet. 1:21), and Jesus is God. But Scripture also teaches that the Father raised Him (Gal. 1:1; Eph. 1:17,20). As mentioned above even the Holy Spirit is said to have raised Him (Romans 8:11). So, the act of raising Jesus from the dead was not the operation merely of one person within the Trinity, but was a cooperative act done by the God head. The fact that the Bible teaches that God raised Jesus from the dead, and that Jesus raised Himself is yet another testament to Christ's divinity.

The answer is that all of the Trinity was involved in Jesus resurrection. The Father, Son and Holy Spirit!

Question: 31

What does the Bible say about making deals with God?

Profile: Male 18-30 North America

Answer: The bible does not specifically say you should not make deals with God. It does say one should not take oaths and not tempt God. Read on as I unpack this…

Luke 4:12 English Standard Version (©2001)

And Jesus answered him, "It is said, 'You shall not put the Lord your God to the test."

Satan attempted to make a deal with Jesus (One of the persons in the God Head) in Luke 4:1-12. Jesus addressed each of Satan's points. In this, He did not say I don't make deals. Jesus did correct Satan each time and resisted him.

Perhaps when humans try to make deals with God, He listens to what is being asked and resists these silly requests. If God was to hold us finite sinners to our word, the human race would be eliminated…

Another thing to consider, if a person has requested a particular deal, it is really important to note the motive of the person. If a kid asks God to save his sick parents' life and in return he will do a deed for God is different than someone saying if you let me win the lottery I will go to church every Sunday.

God is not out looking to make deals with people. He is sovereign. He can go on existing without us. He loves us, and puts up with mankind.

Scripture tells us that we cannot control certain things so we should not be making these types of promises. Your word is so important!

Read the true story about Jephthah's Errant Vow in Judges 11:29-40.

In short, Jephthah uttered a vow (deal) to the Lord. When Jephthah returned to his home in Mizpah, who should come out to meet him but his daughter, dancing to the sound of tambourines! She was an only child. Except for her he had neither son nor daughter. When he saw her, he tore his clothes and cried, "Oh! My daughter! You have made me miserable and wretched, because I have made a vow to the LORD that I cannot break."

In the New Testament we are taught by Jesus regarding oaths:

Matthew 5:36 English Standard Version (©2001)

Oaths

33 "Again you have heard that it was said to those of old, 'You shall not swear falsely, but shall perform to the Lord what you have sworn.' 34 But I say to you, Do not take an oath at all, either by heaven, for it is the throne of God, 35 or by the earth, for it is his footstool, or by Jerusalem, for it is the city of the great King. 36 And do not take an oath by your head, for you cannot make one hair white or black. 37 Let what you say be simply 'Yes' or 'No'; anything more than this comes from evil. {Foot Note: or the evil one}

Covenants are also mentioned in the bible and were strong bonded actions.

Laying fleeces out or making deals was done by Gideon who was lacking courage and faith. God worked with him in this… Judges 6:36-40.

A problem with following Gideon's example of fleece-setting is that it does not take into account that our situation and his are really not comparable. As Christians, we have the complete Word of God which we know is "God-breathed and is useful for teaching, rebuking, correcting and training in righteousness, so that the man of God may be thoroughly equipped for every good work" (2 Timothy 3:16-17). God has assured us that His Word is all we need to be "thoroughly equipped" for anything and everything life throws at us. We do not need experiential proof (signs, voices, miracles, deals) to verify what He has already told us in His Word.

If a decision is not specifically addressed in the Bible every Christian has the Holy Spirit, who is God Himself, residing in his heart to guide, direct, and encourage. Prior to Pentecost, believers had the Old Testament only and were directed externally by God's providential hand. Now we have His complete Bible and His indwelling presence in our hearts.

Trying to establish a deal can lead to trouble if the person's heart is not right.

Scriptures tells us to guard our tongues for out of the mouth can produce Trouble:

Proverbs 21:23 ESV

Whoever keeps his mouth and his tongue keeps himself out of trouble.

Psalm 34:13 ESV

Keep your tongue from evil and your lips from speaking deceit.

If you have made a deal request to God, keep in mind that God may not have accepted your deal. He knows your maturity level as a believer or non-believer and will try to work with you.

God is also very gracious and full of mercy. Many of us would have been destroyed years ago for not keeping our end of a particular deal offered to the Lord...

Instead of seeking deal making, we should be content to know God's will for us in every situation every day: "Let the word of Christ dwell in you richly" (Colossians 3:16).

Pray asking for God's help but leave the deal making out of it…

Question: 32

Please reply in detail: What does the Bible say about Prophet Lot, was he greedy, selfish, or otherwise?

Answer: First let me address the title you have given Lot. My friend, no where in the Holy Bible is Lot referred to or called a prophet... The bible does not call Lot a prophet.

Lot was a nephew of Abraham (Gen. 15:4-6). His occupation: Herdsman who owned many flocks and cattle.

Lot preferred the comforts and some of the customs of wicked Sodom. He paid a heavy price for his poor judgment; he lost his home and possessions, his sons–in-law, and even his wife (Gen 19:1-26). His daughters were also affected by living in this immoral environment as shown in Genesis 19:30-38... In these scripture verses, pay close attention to the fact that Lot did not know what his daughters were doing.

Lot is given a positive evaluation in 2 Peter 2:6-9. He is presented as a righteous man whose soul was tormented day after day as he witnessed his neighbor's lawless deeds. But there he is only called a righteous man, not a prophet.

You also ask if Lot was greedy, selfish or otherwise...

The fact that Lot made the wrong choice does not indicate that he was an ungodly, selfish, unusually materialistic wretch (greedy).

In Genesis 13 we find that the herdsmen of Abraham and Lot were quarreling about where their herds should graze, so Abraham, a man of peace and good will, gave Lot the choice of which way they should go. Then we read in Gen. 13:10, "And Lot lifted up his eyes, and beheld all the plains of Jordan, that it was well watered every where, before the Lord destroyed Sodom and Gomorrah, even as the garden of the Lord, like the land of Egypt, as thou comest unto Zoar."

Now consider what I am about to say: After reading this passage, people have spoken of Lot characterizing him as being selfish, a materialistic man who had little concern for others or his own spiritual welfare. There is little doubt that he wanted for himself the best he could get of material things.

Many of us would see this as making, perhaps, a wise land decision.

If someone offered you a choice of a fifty dollar bill or a dollar bill which would you choose? If you had been in Lot's shoes, what would you have done? It is easy for us to say, "He should have left the choice to Abraham," but Abraham already had the choice, and gave it to him.

Let's look at how Lot lived in this land:

As we see in Genesis chapter 19, even after he lived in Sodom he still showed courtesy, hospitality, shame at ungodliness, loyalty, gratitude and other good attributes. He was basically a righteous man. The outstanding lesson is: Regardless of how good or righteous one may be, the wrong choice can reap unexpected horrible consequences. The fact that Lot may have reasoned, "I know the city is wicked, but I do not have to participate in its wickedness" did not change the consequences.

There is nothing in the story that indicates that he did not think he could obey God and still pitch his tent toward Sodom. There is nothing in the story that shows that he was disobeying God by moving closer to Sodom.

We cannot argue with the statement that he was a righteous man, at least compared to those around him, for the Bible says so. But we can recognize that even a righteous man can have improper motives and certainly unwise choices.

Question: 33

Thanks for your reply, but if the Bible says Lot was a righteous man, who are we to say Lot is not. Brother, we should obey the Bible which is the final word. When the New Testament says him to be a righteous man we should not say any more. It is clear that Abraham given him a choice to choose the land. Lot did not disturb Abraham, but disturbed himself. We can say that Lot respected his uncle.

Angels came especially from Heaven to save these four people and the angels saved them, and waited for them until they reached the near city. Angels said that they cannot do anything with Sodom until they reach in the safe city.

This is a follow up question to question #32

Answer: Hello again. If I understand your commentary I think you are in need of information regarding understanding righteousness and God's grace.

As for being righteous, this does not imply that this person "Lot" never sinned. All have fallen short of the glory of God (Romans 3:23). We are all, including Lot, filthy rags (Isaiah 64:6), wretches (Romans 7:24), sinners needing a savior.

You asked: who are we? We are sinners in need of a savior. This savior is Jesus. He takes our sin away making us righteous in God's site.

God knows the heart. Lot is a perfect illustration of the backslider. He could be considered righteous because somehow he believed, in spite of his compromise and sin. But how he suffered...He lost everything he had and ended up living in a cave. The passage of 2 Peter 2:6 through 9 says that Lot was vexed in his soul by the sin and the wicked people around him. The word here is actually stronger than what we think of as "vexed," a word that appears in some Bible versions; it is a word that indicates Lot was *tormented* day after day when he saw what was going on around him.

Believers in a backslidden condition today may appear to enjoy their "freedom," but they often don't let on that, inside, they are, like Lot, most miserable unless and until they get out of the state they are in.

Based on what is revealed about Lot's life one might wonder if he was righteous. However, there is no doubt that God had declared him to be positionally righteous, even during his time in Sodom. "God rescued righteous Lot, oppressed by the sensual conduct of unprincipled men (for by what he saw and heard that righteous man, while living among them, felt his righteous soul tormented day after day with their lawless deeds)" (2 Peter 2:7-8). At some point Lot had believed in the coming Messiah, and that faith resulted in a righteous standing before God. It is likely that Lot's uncle, Abraham, had passed this truth down to him.

Grace is God blessing us despite the fact that we do not deserve it. Grace is extending kindness to the unworthy. God did this for Lot when He sent the angel to save Lot and He has done this for us when we receive goodness when we do not deserve it...

The Righteous

One becomes *righteous* at the point of a trusting-submitting faith in Jesus, which includes repentance. Basic characteristics of the righteous include the following:

(1) they don't have anything to repent of (Luke. 15:7);

(2) they are not doing evil (1 Peter 3:12);

(3) they do what is right (1 John 3:7).

It is also clear from multiple Scriptures that the righteous will live because of his *faith:*

Habakkuk 2:4, Rom 1:17, Gal 3:11, Heb 10:38.

You must believe in the Lord Jesus to be considered righteous.

Do you have a personal relationship with the Lord?

Do you want to have this and have eternal life?

Say the following prayer. Really mean it from your heart:

Dear Lord Jesus, I know that I am a sinner and need your forgiveness.

I believe that you died for my sins.

I want to turn from my sins. I now invite you to come into my heart and life.

I want to trust and follow you as Lord and Savior. In Jesus name Amen.

If you said the prayer, I want to confirm your decision to receive Christ:

You are saved.

You are a Child of God.

You have everlasting life.

If you prayed to have Jesus Christ be Lord of your life and the forgiver of your sins we would love to hear from you. Let us know…

Question: 34

What does justify mean in Luke 10:29?

Answer: The conviction of God's word strikes the hearts of many. We try to justify ourselves rather than simply throwing ourselves on the mercy of God and changing our hearts and lives.

In the scripture verse Luke 10:29, a lawyer had come to test Jesus. He did not have honest motives… He is not sincere. If so, Jesus' question, affirmation, and reply would have been enough.

To further define how the lawyer was trying to justify himself, I will try to do this in brief… In reading this passage we see the lawyer's self-righteousness.

Friend, some parables answer a question and deal with an attitude. The attitude being dealt with in this parable is self-righteousness. The text says the lawyer was "seeking to justify himself."

The lawyer was looking for a loophole, wanting to look righteous more than he wanted to be righteous.

This pattern of behavior reflects what many others are doing in this world. Let's realize that we cannot justify ourselves, but can find our righteousness only in God's grace given to us in Jesus Christ.

Question: 35

How can I know that there are not more than three persons in the God head, is there a way that I can know for sure that there are not more than three persons in the God head?

Profile: Male 18-30 North America

Answer: Thanks for sending in your question. My answer to your question really comes down to how well you trust the only book that God wrote for humans. The bible is the infallible word of the living Lord. The bible from cover to cover gives a unified message that includes who God is. 1 John 5:7 tells us the answer to your question.

1 John 5:7 For there are three that bear record in heaven, the Father, the Word, and the Holy Ghost: and these three are one. (KJV)

Through faith that this is from God's word you must believe that His word is truth. Once you accomplish this you will know by faith and gain confidence that it is true.

God never lied to us and is not capable of lying to us.

God revealed the Godhead description in His word, the bible, and protected His word for many generations so many can know something about Him and His purpose for us. Jesus only spoke of 3 persons in the Godhead (The Trinity).

John 13-17 is a good read on the Godhead.

For more excellent details regarding the God head (the trinity) please visit: http://www.gotquestions.org/trinity-bible.html

If you need information regarding trusting the bible please go to the following link:

http://www.gotquestions.org/Bible-God-Word.html

Consider this, when God created the world He did not reveal to us additional members in the God head assisting Him. The bible shows God the Father, Jesus and the Holy Spirit were the only ones involved.

To know for sure is strongly tied to your trust in what God has said.

Trust the bible and the rest will fall into place.

Question: 36

Does GotQuestions.org have any opinions about specific ministries and preachers, like Reinhard Bonnke?

Profile: Male 18-30 Europe

Answer: I will try to answer your question with gentleness and respect for the individuals in question.

Any Preacher, Evangelist, Minister, Christian church or presenter of scripture must do so in a consistent accurate manner. This is a huge responsibly for the ministry. We must always line up what the ministries and preachers are saying with what the bible is saying. The bible is our guide. Teaching must without fail be consistent with scripture. This will ensure us that ministries are conforming to doctrine etc...

2 Timothy 3:16 English Standard Version (ESV)

16 All Scripture is breathed out by God and profitable for teaching, for reproof, for correction, and for training in righteousness,

Questionable ministries need to be put to the litmus test. What does the bible say regarding their teaching and claims? Compare what's being said. Pray for wisdom... Move away from false teaching...

You asked about Reinhard Bonnke. For this, I checked what others are saying on the internet, and what the history posted on the internet is concluding. The internet articles suggest that Mr. Bonnke's teaching is not consistent with the bible.

You can read a lot of information on this subject at the following website: http://www.deceptioninthechurch.com/bonnke4.html

Deception in the church apologetics coordination team speaks clearly and specifically regarding Mr. Bonnke's unbiblical teaching and actions.

Another website speaks regarding Mr. Bonnke's miracle claims.

You can read what they reveal at the following website:

http://cephas-library.com/evangelists_bonnke.html

One more website to review regarding Reinhard Bonnke raising the dead:

http://www.letusreason.org/Popteac13.htm

My friend, all whose teachings are deviating from scripture should repent, get right with the Lord, and read the bible. They need to get retrained from schools honoring God and His biblical doctrine.

Bible Verses to ponder:

Matthew 7:16 ESV

You will recognize them by their fruits. Are grapes gathered from thorn bushes, or figs from thistles?

Colossians 2:8 ESV

See to it that no one takes you captive by philosophy and empty deceit, according to human tradition, according to the elemental spirits of the world, and not according to Christ.

2 John 1:10 ESV

If anyone comes to you and does not bring this teaching, do not receive him into your house or give him any greeting,

Revelation 2:2 ESV

“‘I know your works, your toil and your patient endurance, and how you cannot bear with those who are evil, but have tested those who call themselves apostles and are not, and found them to be false.

2 Peter 3:16 ESV

As he does in all his letters when he speaks in them of these matters. There are some things in them that are hard to understand, which the ignorant and unstable twist to their own destruction, as they do the other Scriptures.

2 Timothy 3:6-9 ESV

For among them are those who creep into households and capture weak women, burdened with sins and led astray by various passions, always learning and never able to arrive at a knowledge of the truth. Just as Jannes and Jambres opposed Moses, so these men also oppose the truth, men corrupted in mind and disqualified regarding the faith. But they will not get very far, for their folly will be plain to all, as was that of those two men.

2 Thessalonians 3:14-15 ESV

If anyone does not obey what we say in this letter, take note of that person, and have nothing to do with him, that he may be ashamed. Do not regard him as an enemy, but warn him as a brother.

There is more information on this subject in God’s word.

Here are additional URLS at bible.org that speaks of false teaching:

http://bible.org/seriespage/false-teachers-2-peter-21-3

http://bible.org/seriespage/instruction-concerning-false-teachers-church-titus-110-16

Pray for the ministries and Mr. Bonnke to be open to correcting the teaching that is not matching scripture.

Avoid all ministries that are not teaching scripture correctly!

Scripture speaks of false teachers. Study it… Let the information in the bible provide the answer to your question. For it is the final authority!

Question: 37

Tithing: I have 2 sisters that are living outside of obedience to God's will. (Please forgive me; I do not want to sound self righteous. I am growing through God's Word). As a result, they suffer the consequences financially. They both asked us for help, they did need it. My husband and I did help them, but we used our tithe. Is this wrong? When they thank me, I say give the thanks to God, and I tell them that as long as they are living out of disobedience to God, they will continue to face these struggles. I want to honor God. It is hard to see your family make bad choices repeatedly. My husband and I have disagreements about tithing. He says we do not have to just give to the church. We can put the money toward any just cause that serves God. The Bible instructs us to support our place of worship. I know I have to honor my husband in his decisions despite my objections. Please clarify what you can. Thank you.

Profile: Female 31-45 North America

Answer: Thanks for writing GotQuestions.org. This issue can be difficult if both husband and wife do not agree. You are wise in standing with your husband. This is not a subject to divide over…

Please be reminded that the bible is full of information to help us in our walk with the Lord. In scripture remember we are also call to help our family.

1 Timothy 5:8 ESV

But if anyone does not provide for his relatives, and especially for members of his household, he has denied the faith and is worse than an unbeliever.

In Matthew 15:5-6 Jesus condemns the Pharisees' practice of consecrating their possessions to God while their parents suffered need:

Matthew 15:5-6 English Standard Version (ESV)

5But you say, 'If anyone tells his father or his mother, "What you would have gained from me is given to God,"[a] 6he need not honor his father.' So for the sake of your tradition you have made void the word[b] of God.

Footnotes:

Matthew 15:5 Or *is an offering*

Matthew 15:6 Some manuscripts *law*

Notice how it is worded in the NLT:

Matthew 15:5-6 New Living Translation (NLT)

5 But you say it is all right for people to say to their parents, 'Sorry, I can't help you. For I have vowed to give to God what I would have given to you.' 6 In this way, you say they don't need to honor their parents.[a] And so you cancel the word of God for the sake of your own tradition.

Footnotes: Matthew 15:6 Greek *their father;* other manuscripts read *their father or their mother.*

Since tithing is not to be legalistic you are not doing something wrong in shifting the funds to help your family.

In light of this, if the tithe is the only resource available to help your sisters, give it to them. However, be sure you have sacrificed your portion before you decide to give what really belongs to God.

Providing help to your sisters can do wonders in opening up their hearts to following the Lord.

You also provided them with godly counsel on how to possibly correct their situation. Hopefully it won't fall on deaf ears… Always do this in love and pray that it will take root in their hearts.

Note: I have witnessed a couple of young men who made a request for funds, received a lecture prior to getting funds from a particular person. They no longer go to this individual… Note: The person was really trying to give them some wisdom. These young men now avoid this person when they need money so they don't have to be lectured…

I would suggest that you limit the time frame (if this is regular monthly support) especially if your assistance is allowing them to continue living a lifestyle that is contrary to God's will. You do not want to support ungodly activity. In this case investing your funds in the kingdom is the smarter choice.

If they turn to God and become regular church attendees they could then go to their church seeking help.

Your Husband is correct and you are correct. The bible simply tells us to give to the Lord. GotQuestions.org holds that a believer's primary giving should be to his/her local church with any "additional offerings" to other Christian causes. We do not believe, though, that a believer is legalistically required to give 10% or any other set amount.

The Bible instructs believers in Christ to give generously, to give cheerfully, and to give regularly.

Gotquestions.org does have articles regarding the Tithe that I want to suggest. The links are provided below.

http://www.gotquestions.org/tithing-Christian.html

http://www.gotquestions.org/tithes-church-ministry.html

http://www.gotquestions.org/marriage-disagreement-tithing.html

May God bless you for your heart is in the right place!

Question: 38

A person that comes to my church travels about 20KM in his own vehicle; I would like to re-reimburse him for his petrol. Do you think this is ok?

Answer: Count the cost my friend…

Luke 14:28 English Standard Version (©2001)

For which of you, desiring to build a tower, does not first sit down and count the cost, whether he has enough to complete it?

It's nice that you feel compelled to assist this person. First consider, are they asking for help? Are they experiencing a financial problem? Is this person a big volunteer in your church? Are they a member? Are there other church options for this person? Are there some closer church options to their home that will still feed them spiritually? Are you afraid to lose them to another church? Are you prepared to pay for other congregants who may want this option? Can they or will they consider moving closer to the church?

Driving to a church is a choice. 20 kilometer = 12.427 miles…

This distance is not uncommon for my wife and me…

Unless he or she is on staff and you have a car allowance for certain staff members I would avoid doing this. If you do give money, limit the time… Keep in mind; they might become dependent on receiving these funds. When you stop how will it be perceived?

If you still feel moved to issue money for gas perhaps issue a one-time gift, a gas gift card or cash…

Pray for the best outcome to occur for this individual…

Question: 39, 40

Sir, please give me reply for my questions.

In bible so many times it is mentioned the "God Of Israel".

39. What is this meaning? Suppose I am from India. How can I believe that he is my God because I am not belonging to Israel? Please give me the reply soon. I am so confused about it?

40. And another thing... If God created man in his own image (Gen 1:27) but the scientists says that human arise from a monkey, which is correct? Please give me reply as soon as possible

Profile: Male 18-30 Asia

Answer: Greetings in the name of Jesus! Thank you for submitting your question. Friend, you have asked very good questions. I hope my answers will help build your faith and confidence in our Great God! You will need your bible to read the passages referenced in both answers.

Exodus 19:4-6 is a monumental Old Testament text that reveals the mission of God. In this passage, God declares that the nation of Israel was to be a holy nation and a kingdom of priests. When God delivered the nation of Israel from Egypt it was for a specific purpose – to serve or worship Him (Ex 3:12: 8:1, 20; 9:1, 13; 10:3). The nation of Israel was to worship God by serving in a mediatorial role between Him and all the other nations. It was God's will that all the earth know Him through Israel and for all the earth to be "filled with the glory of the Lord." (Num 14:21) As mediators, they were to live in a holy manner so that they would be recognized by the Gentiles as God's special people. "They were to be a missionary nation." Following the previously revealed purpose for Abram's blessing (so that he would be a blessing) Israel was to continue in this purpose.

In order to enjoy the benefits of their majestic calling, Israel was required to obey the Lord. Through their obedience, God's plan to fill the earth with His glory would be accomplished. The key to their obedience was faith. They were to believe God, trusting in His ability to give them victory while providing for their every need. Furthermore, they were to live according to God's standards being separate in that respect from the Gentiles. Unfortunately, they failed to believe or obey. Loss of privilege as well as a history of despair and defeat ensued.

The missionary purpose for the nation of Israel is made very evident throughout the Old Testament. They were to be a "light unto the Gentiles" (Isa 49:6). Jerusalem was to be the world's capital city where inhabitants from all nations would worship and praise the Almighty (Ps 87). The psalmist proclaimed, "That thy way may be known upon the earth, thy saving health among all nations." (Ps 67:2) God's plan was that when the nations saw the blessing of God upon Israel, they would come to believe in the God of Israel and be saved. The sending of Jonah to Nineveh makes known the will of God for Israel's evangelization of the nations. When Solomon's temple was built, it was not exclusive to Israel. Rather, it was to be a house of prayer for the nations (1 Kings 8:41-43; Isa 56:6-7). Both Zechariah and Malachi envision the Gentiles and Israel living together in peace. The whole earth was to be engaged in the worship of the God of Israel (Zech 2:11; Mal 1:11).

The message of the Old Testament longs for the redemption and restoration of the entire earth through God's chosen people. The prophesied kingdom is eagerly awaited by the prophets (Isa 2: 61-66; Ez 36:22-23) where the entire earth will live in harmony under the rule of God.

If you are a follower of Jesus, then the God of Israel is your God too! You were adopted into God's family of believers.

Now to address your other question (#40): "God created man in his own image (Gen 1:27) but the scientists say that humans arise from a monkey which is correct?"

Answer to Question 40: God is always correct. The scientists you are quoting are wrong. Some things to consider: There has never been any transition in the species where another kind turned into another.

A dog is always a dog, a cat is always a cat, a monkey is always a monkey and horse is a horse and mankind has always been mankind...

There is variance in the look of animals for example the color, size and type but the main model of the animal does not shift to a totally different kind. An example of this is a wolf, a German shepherd and a Chihuahua; they are all in the dog family.

There has never been a missing link discovered to bridge the huge gap in their logic. If you have been to a museum, they show what they have lied about and said there is transition in the species. What they don't tell you is that before the Biblical Flood, people used to live a long time. When you live as long as some of these people, your bone structure continues to grow, changing your face.

Disease came into the picture after Adam and Eve sinned, resulting in illnesses affecting the people and in some cases arthritis... What are on display at the museums is a fabrication and a lie. Some of this creativity may be based on some other arthritic people or animal remains that were discovered... Evolutionist Scientist assume that it was from some form of transition from apes or monkeys... There is no proof... Just imagination...

Evolution is a belief system. A religion... It is taught as fact when it cannot be proven. This has resulted in lies being taught in textbooks, movies and especially in schools.

Man is always trying to remove God out of the equation and they have taken what is a belief system and put these lies in the textbooks as if they are facts.

A good book to buy is called "Bones of Contention" It will open your eyes regarding evolution and the fossils.

http://www.amazon.com/Bones-Contention-Creationist-Assessment-Fossils/dp/0801065232

GotQuestions has a lot of interesting articles regarding evolution. Please go to the following links to select what best meets your interest.

http://www.gotquestions.org/search.php?zoom_sort=0&zoom_query=evolution

http://www.gotquestions.org/questions_Creation.html

My Friend, in the beginning God created everything. The scientist you are mentioning believes in evolution. Evolution is a belief system that says everything came from nothing. Nothing exploded and now there's life. This is not logical... And then they want you to believe that we came from a monkey!

In recorded history, no monkey has ever giving birth to a human.

You can be confident that you were made in God's image, for God's word, the bible informs us of this.

Question: 41

How can I know if God has anointed me for something?

Profile: Male 31-45 Africa

Answer: Hello Sir, to know the will of God on your life is vital in how we serve Him. There are some things you can do to know if God has anointed you or called you to do something. Start with the following:

Pray for discernment. If God has a specific (or more general) task for you, he will lay it on your heart. Spend time in prayer asking about it, and if God has something special in mind, he may just be waiting for you to ask. Ask the Lord… Ask one question at a time and listen for promptings or a whisper from within for each question. Try to discern if the answer is from God.

Ask yourself what you're good at. You may be like Gideon or Moses and not feel up to what God wants out of you. Ask Godly people what they see in you.

Many churches do gifts assessments, and part of a good program is to have others in the class tell you what they think you're good at. Many people are surprised at what they're told!

You may have to train for the task given you. You may be gifted to teach but need training in Bible study or lesson preparation. Don't confuse lack of preparation with the absence of a gift. It's easy to fool yourself. There are people who feel they are called to teach, but they have NO gift of teaching. God gifts those he calls. For a list of spiritual gifts see 1 Corinthians 12.

Seek outside advice to be sure you haven't turned a personal wish into a mission from God.

Gifted people generally enjoy using their gifts.

You may need help from others (Moses needed Aaron). Don't be afraid to recruit others to help you. God doesn't necessarily call you to do it alone. Jesus sent his missionaries out two by two. God gave Gideon a small army. Paul traveled with a group of missionaries.

Pray a lot. If you feel God has something in mind for you, then you aren't through praying. Rather, like Jesus, it's time to get serious about your prayer life.

Expect to have a hard time at times. Paul got beaten, shipwrecked, rejected…

Pharaoh didn't listen to Moses. David was nearly killed by Saul and spent years in the wilderness before he took the throne. Be patient. Persevere.

Study hard to be sure what you're doing is true to God's word. God never calls you to violate his word.

At times you may feel a little driven–even obsessed–even when you can't figure out your next step or things are going badly. It could be the Spirit pushing. Let the Spirit push.

Since we live by the Spirit, let us keep in step with the Spirit. (Galatians. 5:25)

HOW TO KNOW GOD'S ANOINTING

(a) Surrender absolutely to the Lordship of Jesus Christ.
(b) Believe the Word of God in its entirety.
(c) If you have never received any form of water baptism, ensure that you are baptized in water, thus identifying with Jesus Christ in His death and His resurrection.
(d) Repent from all sin, especially unbelief, doubt, fear, things of the occult, unforgiveness, blockage of mind, wrong doctrine.

(e) Read again the Scriptures in 1 John 2:20 and 1 John 2:27 which confirm that we have an anointing from the Holy One.
(f) Get on your knees in a quiet location free from distractions and say a simple prayer similar to this:

"Dear Heavenly Father, I come to you in the name of your Son Jesus Christ. I praise You Lord and I worship you… Father, I thank you that you love me so much that you sent your Son, Jesus Christ, to die for me and pay the penalty for my sins. I believe that I am reconciled to you through the blood of Jesus Christ and that I have received your peace. I renounce all sin, everything of the occult, all unbelief, all fear, all doubt, wrong doctrine, stubbornness of mind etc... These I renounce in the precious name of Jesus Christ. I confess that Jesus Christ was raised from the dead." LORD, I ask you to please let me know the anointing which you have already given me by the Holy Spirit. Show me what you want me to do with my life. I want to serve you with all of my heart. I need to know your will for my life. What did you anoint me to do as your child? Your servant is listening…

(g) If you will do this with all your heart then you will sense the peace of God coming around you…

Continue to pray and listen… Remember to ask others to pray for you…

Now step up in faith and start the process of following God's leadings.

1 Corinthians 15:58 New King James Version (NKJV)

[58] Therefore, my beloved brethren, be steadfast, immovable, always abounding in the work of the Lord, knowing that your labor is not in vain in the Lord.

Once you know what God has called you to do go for it… God will be with you!

(e) Read again the Scriptures in 1 John 2:20 and 1 John 2:27 [illegible] confirm that we have an anointing from the Holy [illegible].
(f) Get on your knees in a quiet location free from distractions and say a simple prayer similar to this:

"Dear Heavenly Father, I come to you in the name of your Son Jesus Christ. I praise you Lord and I worship you. Father, I thank you that you love me so much that you gave your Son Jesus Christ to die for me and pay the penalty for my sins. I believe that I am not called to [illegible] through the Holy Spirit. I thank you that [illegible] your [illegible] [illegible] all [illegible] all [illegible] [illegible] [illegible]

[illegible]

[illegible]

[illegible]

[illegible]

These [illegible] beloved brethren [illegible] know that [illegible] in the Lord.

[illegible] God has called [illegible] God [illegible]

Question: 42

Is it wrong for a church to set a member down from church activities and ministries because of public sin?

Profile: Male 18-30 North America

Answer: No, it is not wrong for a church to set a member down from church activities and ministries because of public sin.

Church discipline can be defined as the confrontive and corrective measures taken by an individual, or church leaders, or the congregation regarding a matter of sin in the life of a believer. Discipline in the church is not punishment. It is discipline and this discipline is designed to train and restore.

The Purposes of Church Discipline:

(1) To bring glory to God and enhance the testimony of the flock.
(2) To restore, heal, and build up sinning believers (Matt. 18:15; 2 Thess. 3:14-15; Heb. 12:10-13; Gal. 6:1-2; Jam. 5:20).
(3) To produce a healthy faith, one sound in doctrine (Titus 1:13; 1 Tim. 1:19-20).
(4) To win a soul to Christ, if the sinning person is only a professing Christian (2 Tim. 2:24-26).
(5) To silence false teachers and their influence in the church (Titus 1:10-11).
(6) To set an example for the rest of the body and promote godly fear (1 Tim. 5:20).
(7) To protect the church against the destructive consequences that can occur when churches fail to carry out church discipline. A church that fails to exercise discipline experiences four losses:

The loss of Purity, the loss of power, the loss of progress, and the loss of purpose…

Church discipline rests upon the divine authority of Scripture and is vital to the purity, power, progress, and purpose of the church.

You really cannot have someone in a high profile role in the church doing wrong, and not setting an example for the rest of the congregants.

If the person is caught up in a pattern of sin and refuses to stop, it may show that they are not growing in the faith and is backsliding…

A failure to exercise discipline in the church evidences a lack of awareness of and concern for the holiness of God. Ref: 1 Pet. 1:16; Heb. 12:11; 1 Cor. 5:6-8.

Church discipline is to be patterned after and based on the divine commands of Scripture (1 Cor. 4:6). We have numerous passages of Scripture which both command and give us God's directives on the how, why, when, and where of church discipline. Failure to exercise this responsibility demonstrates a lack of obedience and belief in the authority of the Bible (1 Cor. 5:1-13; Matt. 18:17-18; Titus 3:10; 2 Thess. 3:6-15; 1 Tim. 5:20; Gal. 6:1).

The necessity of church discipline supports the testimony of the church in the world (1 Pet. 4:13-19). The world observes the behavior and life of the church. When the church acts no differently than the world, it loses its credibility and authenticity (1 Pet. 2:11-18; 3:8-16; 4:1-4).

Church discipline is vital to the purity of the local body and its protection from moral decay and impure doctrinal influences. Why? Because a little leaven leavens the entire lump (1 Cor. 5:6-7). This is the "rotten apple" problem or the "snowball" effect.

Question: 43

Why are bishops and deacons only mentioned in the intro in Philippians? What I mean is, that it is maybe strange that Paul and the others didn't include 'bishops and deacons' in the introduction to the other letters. And why were they included here? Was it only in this church that there were bishops and deacons?

Profile: Male 18-30 Asia

Answer: Greetings in the name of Jesus!

Actually these titles were referenced in other areas of scripture as well!

Paul was taking a more personable approach when he addressed the Philippians… Philippians is probably the most personal of all his church epistles. He does not mention his office as an apostle in his salutation, as he had done in all his other church epistles except those to Thessalonica. It is only in Philippians that he greets "the bishops and deacons" of the church (Philippians 1:1). The entire letter reflects close friendship and affection for the church, some ten years after its founding.

In biblical history it began with the seven Deacons. The historical beginning of Deacon Ministry is recorded in Acts (6:1-6). At that time the number of disciples was growing. Friction developed between the Greek & Hebrew followers because their widows were being neglected in the daily distribution of food. So the twelve apostles called together the community of disciples and said, "It is not right for us to neglect the word of God to serve at tables. Brothers, select from among you seven reputable men, filled with the Spirit and wisdom, whom we shall appoint to this task, whereas we shall devote ourselves to prayer and ministry of the word." The proposal was accepted by the whole community, so they chose Stephen, a man filled with faith and the Holy Spirit, also Philip, Prochorus, Nicanor, Timon, Parenas, and Nicholas of Antioch.

They presented these men to the Apostles who prayed and laid hands on them. The term that was used to describe Stephen and the others selected was the Greek word diacona, which is translated as servant or minister. This is the root of the word Deacon.

As you can see, the early Deacons had a key role in the life of the Church. In fact, the first martyr was Stephen. For more information see Acts 7:1-53 (Stephen's discourses), Acts 7:54-60 (Stephen's Martyrdom), and Acts 8:26-40 (Philip and the Ethiopian).

The word, "diakonos," which is transliterated in our English Bibles, "deacon" is simply the Greek word of "servant." The New Testament gives examples of both "appointed" servants elected by the church to specific tasks and of "unelected" servants who served the Lord in a general sense in a local church. The noun "diakonos" is used thirty times in the New Testament and in only five of those does it refer to a specifically appointed servant.

Some scriptures to study:

Philippians 1:1 "Paul and Timothy, the servants of Jesus Christ, to all the saints in Christ Jesus which are at Philippi, with the bishops and deacons (diakonos - noun)."

1 Timothy 3:8 "Likewise must the deacons (diakonos - noun) be grave, not double tongued, not given to much wine, not greedy of filthy lucre."

1 Timothy 3:10 "And let these also first be proved; then let them use the office of a deacon (diakoneo - a verb), being found blameless."

1 Timothy 3:12-13 "Let the deacons (diakonos - noun) be the husbands of one wife, ruling their children and their own houses well. For they that have used the office of a deacon (diakoneo - verb) well purchase to themselves a good degree, and great boldness in the faith which is in Christ Jesus."

The word is generally used simply to denote one who served the Lord or ministered as a servant. Another example:

Romans 16:1 "I commend unto you Phoebe our sister, which is a servant (diakonos - noun) of the church which is at Cenchrea."

The word translated "deacon" in 1 Timothy 3:13 is the verb "diakoneo" is found only in 1 Timothy 3:10, 13. The single word "diakoneo" is translated into the phrase, "use the office of a deacon. The word means servant and the context tells you if it is an elected position or simply one who served in the church. Phoebe was a faithful member and servant in her church. Phoebe worked faithfully in daily ministration of the local church, helping many people including Paul.

The earliest organization of the Church in Jerusalem was similar to that of Jewish synagogues, which were governed by a council of elders (Greek: πρεσβύτεροι *presbyteroi*). In Acts 11:30 and Acts 15:22, we see this collegiate system of government in Jerusalem, and, in Acts 14:23, the Apostle Paul ordains elders in the churches he founded.

Based on this, the answer to your last question "Was it only in this church that there where bishops and deacons?" Scripture doesn't explicitly say but you can conclude that this structure was in other places.

A bishop was a man who was in charge of the Christians of a certain city. All big cities in the ancient Roman Empire and Sassanian Empire and medieval Europe had bishops. Other Scriptures references:

1 Timothy 3:1 King James Bible (Cambridge Ed.)

This *is* a true saying, If a man desire the office of a bishop, he desireth a good work.

1 Timothy 3:2-7 New King James Version (NKJV)

2 A bishop then must be blameless, the husband of one wife, temperate, sober-minded, of good behavior, hospitable, able to teach; 3 not given

to wine, not violent, not greedy for money, but gentle, not quarrelsome, not covetous; [4] one who rules his own house well, having *his* children in submission with all reverence [5] (for if a man does not know how to rule his own house, how will he take care of the church of God?); [6] not a novice, lest being puffed up with pride he fall into the *same* condemnation as the devil. [7] Moreover he must have a good testimony among those who are outside, lest he fall into reproach and the snare of the devil.

Titus 1:5-11 New King James Version (NKJV) Qualified Elders

[5] For this reason I left you in Crete, that you should set in order the things that are lacking, and appoint elders in every city as I commanded you—
[6] if a man is blameless, the husband of one wife, having faithful children not accused of dissipation or insubordination. [7] For a bishop must be blameless, as a steward of God, not self-willed, not quick-tempered, not given to wine, not violent, not greedy for money, [8] but hospitable, a lover of what is good, sober-minded, just, holy, self-controlled, [9] holding fast the faithful word as he has been taught, that he may be able, by sound doctrine, both to exhort and convict those who contradict.

For more study on this subject, please read the following articles at GotQuestions.org:

http://www.gotquestions.org/qualifications-elders-deacons.html

http://www.gotquestions.org/church-government.html

http://www.gotquestions.org/deacons-church.html

Question: 44

I have developed empirical research findings which, if given to law enforcement officials, would lead to solution of several major conspiracy mysteries. I would have to bear the full expense of presenting these findings which are complex and involved and require me to pay for expensive computer programming work from which I would derive NO PERSONAL BENEFIT. Also, I pretty much know in advance that my work would be exploited to high heavens by everybody and his dog just waiting for this kind of new information to break forth to latch onto. Although my findings would be of great help to society at large with regard to conspiracy, government, and history, I do not consider that people in my position are NOT under any MORAL or ETHICAL obligation to help their future EXPLOITERS AND USERS. What does the bible say about this specific situation of not wanting to be a complete fool besides "love one another" and "love your enemies"?

Answer: Let me start by asking some questions for you to ponder. Will what you are proposing to do or unleash bring glory to God?

Consider if all of your data is accurate? Based on what? Can this data be trusted? What are the consequences of deploying this information?

As you apply the following cycle, does the benefits outweigh the negative possibilities?

Empirical cycle according to A.D. de Groot:

Observation -> Induction -> Deduction -> Testing-> Evaluation.

Do all for the Glory of God!

Consider the following scripture: 1 Corinthians 10:31 New International Version (ESV):

31 So, whether you eat or drink, or whatever you do, do all to the glory of God.

Not all things are beneficial

1 Corinthians 6:12 English Standard Version (©2001)

"All things are lawful for me," but not all things are helpful. "All things are lawful for me," but I will not be enslaved by anything.

1 Corinthians 10:23 English Standard Version (ESV)

Do All to the Glory of God

23 "All things are lawful," but not all things are helpful. "All things are lawful," but not all things build up.

So all because you have something that can benefit some does not necessarily mean that it will be good for society...

Count the cost...

Luke 14:28-30 English Standard Version (ESV)

28 For which of you, desiring to build a tower, does not first sit down
and count the cost, whether he has enough to complete it? 29 Otherwise,
when he has laid a foundation and is not able to finish, all who see it
begin to mock him, 30 saying, 'This man began to build and was not
able to finish.'

Consider the following historical example:

The atomic bomb began with the Manhattan Project. It was tasked to create the bomb beginning in 1939. The scientists who invented the bomb included Robert Oppenheimer, Edward Teller, Rudolf Peierls and many others.

The Origin of the Manhattan Project

Its roots lay in a letter Albert Einstein sent to President Franklin Roosevelt. On August 2, 1939, Einstein sent a letter to the US President stating the Germans were trying to enrich uranium 235. This process would allow them to build an atomic bomb.

This led to Roosevelt's decision to create the Manhattan Project. To purify the uranium, a research center was set up in Oak Ridge, Tennessee. Some of the scientists that figured in this process were Harold Urey, and Ernest Lawrence.

Testing and the Aftermath

Throughout the development and history of the atomic bomb, over $2 billion was spent on the project. Besides Oppenheimer, Peierls, and Teller, other scientists participated. These included David Bohm, Leo Szilard, Neils Bohr, and Eugene Wigner. Otto Frisch, Felix Bloch, Emilio Segre, James Franck, Klaus Fuchs and Enrico Fermi also took part in the Manhattan Project. The headquarters was in Los Alamos.

The project spanned the whole of World War II. The testing day came on July 16, 1945. The gadget (as it was known) was detonated at exactly 5:29, July 16, 1945. The location was the Jemez Mountains in northern New Mexico. The bright light became orange and then turned into a reddish color. Moving upwards at 360 ft per second, the mushroom cloud appeared at 30,000 feet.

Records on the history of the atomic bomb show radioactive glass was created on the ground where it exploded. The explosion was so bright a blind person saw the flash a hundred miles away.

Oppenheimer would go on to say "I am become death". After the testing, a majority of the scientists voiced their opposition to its usage. They made petitions pleading that it not be used. Their protests were ignored.

Hiroshima and Nagasaki: 1945

The atomic bomb was dropped on Hiroshima on August 6, 1945. The bomb was called Little Boy and it was released by the Enola Gay. It was dropped at 8:15 AM and hit the ground with tremendous force.

The history of the atomic bomb shows 66,000 were killed at that moment. Over 70,000 were injured. An area of 1 mile in diameter was completely destroyed. Everything was vaporized or burned. Two miles away there was also heavy damage.

On August 9, 1945 another atomic bomb (plutonium type) was dropped in Nagasaki. Over 25,000 people were killed in an instant. Despite this fact, the two bombs actually used less than a tenth of 1 percent of their power. A day later, Japan surrendered to the Allied Forces.

The bombs didn't just end World War II. It also ushered in the age of atomic and nuclear warfare. The development and history of the atomic bomb would lead to the creation of even more destructive weapons of mass destruction.

Historical example was taken from Article at:

http://www.whoinventedit.net/who-invented-the-atomic-bomb.html

Conclusion:

Discoveries can be use for good and evil. One must count the cost of any invention or action for which may affect another person negatively.

Others will come around afterwards with modifications to the original plan making it better or worse depending on whose view point.

People do not always follow the plan of the originators as seen in the petitions pleading that the atomic bomb not be used.

In my humble opinion, if the research findings will hurt innocent people it is better to not deploy the invention…

You have nothing personally to lose or gain for it, right?

If you ask yourself will this bring glory to God it almost always clears our perspectives.

A challenge proposal for you… Consider using your research methods to enhance the faith and belief of others in the bible and in Jesus Christ.

God will bless and reward your efforts!

Bottom line… Count the cost my friend!

Question: 45

Where do pastors go for advice or counsel, about ministry or otherwise? Can you recommend any good websites or resources for pastors to get good counsel or advice about ministry or otherwise?

Profile: Male 31-45 North America

Answer: Pastors have various options to seek counsel about ministry or otherwise. Scripture supports seeking counsel:

Proverbs 15:22 English Standard Version (ESV)

22 Without counsel plans fail, but with many advisers they succeed.

The first option is always going to God with all of the needs whether it is ministry, personal etc…

A pastor can also contact a close ministry colleague, one that will keep the conversation confidential.

If a pastor is married his spouse can be a valuable resource to bounce ideas off of and vent his confidential frustrations to…

You asked if we can recommend any good websites or resources for pastors to get counsel or advice. Focus on the Family has a ministry that focuses on helping pastors. They use to send out a quarterly CDROM on various pastoral issues. This was discontinued. It was being led by H. B. London who is now retired. The current website is as follows: http://www.thrivingpastor.com/category/pastor-to-pastor/

Focus on the Family also has a Pastor to Pastor Hotline:

Interested in Supportive Direction?

Are you interested in receiving encouragement and supportive direction? Please reach out to Focus on the Family's Pastoral Care Team. They will help you find supportive direction and community resources. Email them at pastors@family.org or call us at 844-4PASTOR Monday through Friday between 6:00 a.m. and 8:00 p.m. Mountain time.

If you are looking for an organization that may be able to offer supportive direction to community resources that minister to pastors and their families, CareGivers Forum is an organization that might be able to offer helpful referral information. This directory is provided by CareGivers Forum, and Focus on the Family's referral doesn't necessarily imply an endorsement by Focus on the Family

http://www.thrivingpastor.com/caregiving-ministries/index.html

Another option:

http://www.thegracewellnesscenter.com/help-for-pastors/?gclid=CJi4wt_lvdICFUodgQodUaQKDw

Counseling For Pastors:

Telephone: +1 724 8637223

Toll Free Number: +1844 744 4335

I hope this helps you in your pursuits!

Question: 46

Dear Brother, What is meant by foreign god and alien god mentioned in Psalm 81:9?

Answer: In context of the scripture, any god who is not the "LORD" who is the God of Israel, they are a foreign or alien god. The true God, maker of Heaven and Earth, has identified himself as one we should all seek, no matter where we live. He established himself as the God of Israel to establish them as a kingdom of priest to show the world how they can embrace him too.

Let's look at how different translations express Psalm 81:9 plus other scripture to draw a conclusion from.

These verses Psalm 81:8-10 summarize God's revelation to Israel at Mt. Sinai, where He gave them the Mosaic Law.

Any other god is man-made whether made from some object or in concept.

Psalm 81:9 English Standard Version (ESV)

9There shall be no strange god among you; you shall not bow down to a foreign god.

Other supporting scriptures:

Exodus 20:3 ESV "You shall have no other gods before me.

Deuteronomy 5:7 ESV You shall have no other gods before me.

Deuteronomy 32:12 ESV The Lord alone guided him, no foreign god was with him.

Psalm 44:20, 21 (ESV)

[20] If we had forgotten the name of our God or spread out our hands to a foreign god, [21] would not God discover this? For he knows the secrets of the heart.

Isaiah 43:12 (ESV)

[12] I declared and saved and proclaimed, when there was no strange god among you;

and you are my witnesses," declares the LORD, "and I am God.

Alien God:

This is not referring to some alien from outer space. It is speaking of a false god from a distant land.

The LORD God wants people to recognize that there is no other God. All others are counterfeits created by man.

In Conclusion:

Friend, the true God would garner in us a similar response found in Revelation 1:10-17 and Ezekiel 1:28.

Revelation 1:10-17 English Standard Version (ESV)

[10] I was in the Spirit on the Lord's day, and I heard behind me a loud voice like a trumpet [11]saying, "Write what you see in a book and send it to the seven churches, to Ephesus and to Smyrna and to Pergamum and to Thyatira and to Sardis and to Philadelphia and to Laodicea."

[12]Then I turned to see the voice that was speaking to me, and on turning I saw seven golden lampstands, [13]and in the midst of the lampstands one like a son of man, clothed with a long robe and with a golden sash around his chest. [14] The hairs of his head were white, like white

wool, like snow. His eyes were like a flame of fire, [15] his feet were like burnished bronze, refined in a furnace, and his voice was like the roar of many waters. [16] In his right hand he held seven stars, from his mouth came a sharp two-edged sword, and his face was like the sun shining in full strength.

[17] When I saw him, I fell at his feet as though dead. But he laid his right hand on me, saying, "Fear not, I am the first and the last,

Ezekiel 1:28 English Standard Version (ESV)

[28]Like the appearance of the bow that is in the cloud on the day of rain, so was the appearance of the brightness all around.

Such was the appearance of the likeness of the glory of the LORD. And when I saw it, I fell on my face, and I heard the voice of one speaking.

The true God is incomparable. No other god measures up to the true God. If the god is not the God of the Christian bible, then they are foreign and alien.

Psalms 81:9 is so important; 'There shall no strange god be in thee; neither shall thou worship any strange god.'

If you study the history of Israel, you will find that when they put away their strange gods, God visited them and there would come a mighty work of restoration, renewal and revival.

Unless we remove these strange gods from our lives, they will ruin our faith.

Question: 47

Is Joel Osteen someone I should listen to?

Profile: Male 31-45 North America

Answer: Hello friend, to determine whether you should listen to Joel Osteen or any pastor you need to test what they are saying in light of scripture...

Does Mr. Osteen or any other pastor teach the bible? Do they twist what is said in the bible to fit their ideals?

According to various sources, Joel Osteen has little theological training, having dropped out of Oral Roberts University in 1982 to run his father's television ministry. Despite this lack of training, Lakewood Church has grown enormously. He teaches his gospel of self-esteem. Osteen also preaches the Word of Faith theology that his father taught. He says, for example, that words have creative power: "Our words are vital in bringing our dreams to pass. It's not enough to simply see it by faith or in your imagination. You have to begin speaking words of faith over your life. Your words have enormous creative power. The moment you speak something out, you give birth to it."

Osteen, like Meyer and others, believes that every day "you should declare good things. Just look in the mirror and say 'I am strong, I am healthy, I'm rising to new levels, I'm excited about my future.' When you say that, it may not be true. You may not be very healthy today, or maybe you don't have a lot of things to look forward to, but the Scripture tells us in Romans we have to call the things that are not as if they already were."

Osteen allots so much power to our words that they can even thwart

God's plans, as nearly happened, he claims, at the angel's announcement of the birth of John the Baptist:

[Zechariah] was so surprised because he and his wife Elizabeth were well up there in years. He said to the angel, "Are you really sure this is going to happen? Do you see how old we are? I just don't think this could be possible."...The angel went on to say "But, Zechariah, because you didn't believe, because you questioned God, you shall remain silent and not be able to speak until the baby is born."...Well, why did God shut his mouth?... He knew Zechariah would go out and start talking to his friends. "Well, they said we're gonna have a baby, but they must have gotten the wrong person. Man, we're way too old!" See, God knows the power of our words. He knows we prophesy our future, and He knew Zechariah's own negative words would stop His plan.

Acknowledging that we may have negative thoughts, he adds, "But let me encourage you: don't make the mistake of verbalizing those thoughts. The moment you speak something out it takes on a whole new meaning. See, one of the main ways we release our faith is through our words. That's how we give life to our faith."

Osteen is giving more power to the creature—us—than to the Creator. As sons and daughters of God, we reflect the communicable attributes of God, such as love and intelligence, but we don't reflect His incommunicable attributes, such as omnipotence. Our words don't contain any magical power that can upset God's plans.

Osteen promises that we can expect to receive preferential treatment in life from God.

God isn't inclined to fall for flattery, resulting in preferential treatment being given to some Christians over other people. This type of thinking is a trait of the North American church, which, for too many years, has expected God to serve it rather than expecting itself to serve God.

Lastly, Osteen holds to the popularly held Word of Faith error that Jesus did battle with Satan in hell. "For three days Jesus fought with the enemy. It was the battle of the ages, light versus darkness, good versus evil. But thank God Satan was no match for Jesus."

Osteen elaborates, "He grabbed Satan by the nap [sic] of his neck and He began to slowly drag him down the corridors of hell. All beat up and bruised because He wanted to make sure that every single demon saw very clearly that Jesus was indeed the undisputed Champion of all time!"

In addition to the fact that Satan isn't in hell, Jesus didn't partially succeed on the cross and then finish the work in hell. He completed the work on the cross and pronounced that the debt had been paid (see, e.g., Rom. 6:10; John 19:30).

http://www.equip.org/articles/christianity-still-in-crisis-

Joel Osteen denies Jesus as the only Path to the Father in the following video:

http://www.youtube.com/watch?v=pKF_QgNezBY

Joel Osteen has developed his own style – sermons are strictly optimistic and address practical, everyday issues, like time management. His critics say it is all too simplistic, that Joel is part of a new trend called prosperity gospel. http://today.msnbc.msn.com/id/6894347

Word-Faith teachers claim that God operates by spiritual law and is obliged to obey the faith-filled commands and desires of believers. He not only reveals prosperity teaching supernaturally to the Word-Faith teachers, but personally and verbally confirms their unique interpretations of Scripture (Copeland, *Laws of Prosperity*, 60-62). http://www.watchman.org/profile/wordpro.htm

What does the bible say regarding False Teachers?

False Teachers

1 John 4:1 English Standard Version (ESV)

Test the Spirits

4 Beloved, do not believe every spirit, but test the spirits to see whether they are from God, for many false prophets have gone out into the world.

2 John 9 English Standard Version (ESV)

9 Everyone who goes on ahead and does not abide in the teaching of Christ, does not have God. Whoever abides in the teaching has both the Father and the Son.

2 John 10 English Standard Version (ESV)

10 If anyone comes to you and does not bring this teaching, do not receive him into your house or give him any greeting,

Matthew 7:15 English Standard Version (ESV)

A Tree and Its Fruit

15 "Beware of false prophets, who come to you in sheep's clothing but inwardly are ravenous wolves.

The following website gives a commentary regarding Mr. Osteen including what happened on the Larry Kings show:

http://www.av1611.org/osteen.html

The Word of Faith movement is deceiving countless people, causing them to grasp after a way of life and faith that is not biblical. At its core is the same lie Satan has been telling since the Garden: "You shall be as God" (Genesis 3:5). Sadly, those who buy into the Word of Faith movement are still listening to him. Our hope is in the Lord, not in our own words, not even in our own faith (Psalm 33:20-22). Our faith comes from God in the first place (Ephesians 2:8; Hebrews 12:2) and is not something we create for ourselves. So, be wary of the Word of

Faith movement and any church that aligns itself with Word of Faith teachings.

Please read the excellent articles posted on GotQuestions.org to further learn about this.

http://www.gotquestions.org/Word-Faith.html

http://www.gotquestions.org/prosperity-gospel.html

http://www.gotquestions.org/name-it-claim-it.html

The "name it and claim it" or "prosperity gospel" is not biblical and is in many ways antithetical to the true gospel message and the clear teaching of Scripture. While there are many different versions of the name it and claim it philosophy preached today, they all have similar characteristics. At its best, this teaching comes from the misinterpretation and misunderstanding of some Scriptures and, at its worst, it is a completely heretical teaching that has the characteristics of a cult.

The roots of the Word of Faith movement and the name it and claim it message have more in common with new age metaphysics than with biblical Christianity. However, instead of us creating our reality with our thoughts, as new age proponents advise, name it and claim it teachers tell us that we can use the "power of faith" to create our own reality or get what we want. In essence, faith is redefined from trusting in a Holy and Sovereign God despite our circumstances to a way of controlling God to give us what we want. Faith becomes a force whereby we can get what we want rather than an abiding trust in God even during times of trials and suffering.

In the word of faith belief system, it is your will (my will) be done not God's…

In my humble opinion, one should avoid Joel Osteen's ministry and others who teach the Word of Faith teachings.

Question: 48

When God made Adam and Eve from what I have read about all this, God likely knew they were going to sin and take us all in to the fall.

If God really wanted to restore things to a tolerable level, you would not have to work so hard to fight unbelief, and doubt.

It is God's will for everyone to be saved but everyone is not saved so even if it is God's will for people to be healed they might not be. Since God knew what was going to happen surely he knows more people would end up in hell than in heaven as the bible says. If I had been God, I would have either destroyed Adam and Eve or started over, doing a better job so they would not sin or just not create man in the first place. To me, it is selfish on God's part to create flawed people or people with the potential to be flawed knowing that means so many would go to hell. It seems like God was so desperate to have people he made us knowing we would screw up and many would go to hell but for some reason either it be ego or whatever he did it anyway. The worse thing about this is we do not get a choice to be born. It seems to me that if we have no choice God has to make sure we get saved, not just make a way to be saved or he should have told us about the choice before birth and gave us the choice to be born or not. My question is based on what I said above, why did God not just forget the whole plan considering the risk for so many people or start over? Somewhere on this site it says something about us being created for God to love or because he loves us but knowing most people will go to hell. If he really loves us, he could have done this better or not done it. I know God did it right in the garden but that does not make any difference. Either he made defective people who would fall into sin so he should not have even done this or knowing what was going to happen he should not have created us. Real love does not create people knowing most of them will go to hell, even

with his efforts to prevent this. It seems that if He does that anyway, and He did, what kind of God is He? The only answer I know of is selfish enough to put God's own needs to have man above man choosing to meet his own needs even if millions of people suffer and die in hell. As God, He has every right to do that but if that is how He is going to be then He is not the God in the bible. This kind of thing is just one of the many mixed messages God shows even in the New Testament where He goes on and on about wanting to be a father and friend but then telling us we have to search for him.

I am trying to come to some understanding of all this, and this problem of making man even though most people will go to hell, even though he has provided a way not to, is hard to understand, and makes God look confusing and too unpredictable. By the way I am not saying people who don't accept Jesus as the payment for sin don't deserve to go to hell because as hard as that is to really understand, it is how God said it is. I just want to know why God made us knowing Billions of people will go to hell. And I am not even going to get into the fact that by making us there would be suffering even with atonement for healing and prosperity, as this all seems to be hard to come by as there are so many conditions to receiving it, like no unbelief, no doubt, and so on. That all being messed up is another reason God should have seen either he made better people or no people.

Profile: Male 46-60 North America

Answer: Thank you for writing and asking your question.

God in His infinite wisdom (Ref: Isaiah 46:10), full of love and grace displayed incredible love in knowing that some of His creation would not choose Him. His love was so strong that he allowed those that He knew would not choose Him to at least experience life. Life no matter how short would offer many instances to experience love, joy, peace etc... This was a huge gift to mankind.

There is an old expression: it is better to have experienced love than not to have loved at all.

God did not want robots. He wanted his people to have the freedom to choose. When we choose to say "I love you Lord" it is so much more meaningful than a doll that you pull a string and it mimics the words "I love you".

If God decided to eliminate Adam and Eve; my family line, my friends, many ministry colleagues, your family line would not have the choice provided to experience life (good or bad) or to choose Jesus as savior for a future promise to experience life in eternity.

Adam and Eve were not out of His control at any time... God was working it all out then and now…

God knew all that would occur and in my opinion has allowed for a sort of filtering process to take place. Those who choose Jesus are heaven bound. Those who refuse to accept Jesus are hell bound. This is their choice…

You mentioned "I am just wanting to know how God made us knowing Billions of people will go to hell"… Let me offer this comment. God loves us so much that He lets us make the choice. He then gives each individual what they want. Eternity with Him or hell without Him…

More on this subject can be read at http://www.gotquestions.org/if-God-knew.html#

As finite human beings, we can never fully understand an infinite God (Romans 11:33-34). Sometimes we think we understand why God is doing something, only to find out later that it was for a different purpose than we originally thought. God looks at things from a holy, eternal perspective. We look at things from a sinful, earthly, and temporal perspective.

Why did God put man on earth knowing that Adam and Eve would sin and therefore bring evil, death, and suffering on all mankind? Why didn't He just create us all and leave us in heaven where we would be perfect and without suffering? These questions cannot be adequately answered this side of eternity. What we can know is whatever God does is holy and perfect and ultimately will glorify Him. God allowed for the possibility of evil in order to give us a true choice in regards to whether we worship Him. God did not create evil, but He allowed it. If He had not allowed evil, we would be worshipping Him out of obligation, not by a choice of our own will.

http://www.gotquestions.org/did-God-create-evil.html

To summarize, God knew that that Adam and Eve would sin in the Garden of Eden. With that knowledge, God still created Adam and Eve because creating them and ordaining the fall was part of His sovereign plan to manifest His glory in all its fullness. Even though the fall was foreknown and foreordained, our freedom in making choices is not violated because our free choices are the means by which God's will is carried out.

Your question above "Why did God not just forget the whole plan considering the risk for so many people or start over? I am quite confident that there are many people who are very glad (me included) that God chose to continue with His plan as I mentioned earlier because we would not be here. Living is a wonderful gift! God loved us before we were born. God knew that there will be people who will not choose him and will cause trouble for the rest who do choose him. God is using all of this to build the faith and trust in His people etc…

Those who do not choose God and live ungodly lives at least are given the precious gift of living life, experiencing all the fruits in it (good or bad), however short it will be.

Romans 1:18-21 English Standard Version (ESV)

God's Wrath on Unrighteousness

[18] For the wrath of God is revealed from heaven against all ungodliness and unrighteousness of men, who by their unrighteousness suppress the truth. [19] For what can be known about God is plain to them, because God has shown it to them. [20] For his invisible attributes, namely, his eternal power and divine nature, have been clearly perceived, ever since the creation of the world, in the things that have been made. So they are without excuse. [21] For although they knew God, they did not honor him as God or give thanks to him, but they became futile in their thinking, and their foolish hearts were darkened.

It is their choice… We all have a choice!

Friend, ask God for the faith required to do life now and for a level of trust in Him that will answer your doubts. Whatever you or I think of in trying to logically reason things out, know that it does not compare to the wisdom of God.

The question God ask Job applies here:

Job 38:4 (ESV)

[4] "Where were you when I laid the foundation of the earth? Tell me, if you have understanding.

Please read all of these chapters: Job 38, Job 39, Job 40, Job 41, and Job 42.

Perhaps your response will be like Job's.

Friend, please understand that God is a multi transcendent being. He is God Almighty! There is no one wiser. He ultimately knows what He is doing!

Additional Optional Readings:

Why does God allow bad things to happen to good people?

http://www.gotquestions.org/bad-things-good-people.html

Romans 1:16-32 (ESV) Topics: "The righteous Shall Live by Faith" & "God's Wrath on Unrighteousness"

Question: 49

Who are the true followers of Christ? Is it the Jehovah's Witness or who? What are the reasons and scriptures backing it? Thank you.

Profile: Male 18-30 Africa

Answer: Dear friend. You asked some very important questions.

First let me say what the followers of Christ are not:

Religious organizations that do not recognize and accept the true deity of Jesus and the Trinity are not to be followed. They do not produce true Christ followers. The Jehovah's Witness organization is a cult type religion that is works oriented and gets the deity of God wrong. Their bible has been constructed to fit their belief system and contains errors.

The most well-known of all the New World Translation (NWT) perversions is John 1:1. The original Greek text reads, "the Word was God." The NWT renders it as "the word was a god." This is not a matter of correct translation, but of reading one's preconceived theology into the text, rather than allowing the text to speak for itself. There is no indefinite article in Greek (in English, "a" or "an"), so any use of an indefinite article in English must be added by the translator. This is grammatically acceptable, so long as it does not change the meaning of the text.

There is a good reason why theos has no definite article in John 1:1 and why the New World Translation rendering is in error. There are three general rules we need to understand to see why.

1. In Greek, word order does not determine word usage like it does in English. In English, a sentence is structured according to word order: Subject - Verb - Object. Thus, "Harry called the dog" is not equivalent

to "the dog called Harry." But in Greek, a word's function is determined by the case ending found attached to the word's root. There are two case endings for the root theo: one is -s (theos), the other is -n (theon). The -s ending normally identifies a noun as being the subject of a sentence, while the -n ending normally identifies a noun as the direct object.

2. When a noun functions as a predicate nominative (in English, a noun that follows a being verb such as "is"), its case ending must match the noun's case that it renames, so that the reader will know which noun it is defining. Therefore, theo must take the -s ending because it is renaming logos. Therefore, John 1:1 transliterates to "kai theos en ho logos." Is theos the subject, or is logos? Both have the -s ending. The answer is found in the next rule.

3. In cases where two nouns appear, and both take the same case ending, the author will often add the definite article to the word that is the subject in order to avoid confusion. John put the definite article on logos ("the Word") instead of on theos. So, logos is the subject, and theos is the predicate nominative. In English, this results in John 1:1 being read as "and the Word was God" (instead of "and God was the word").

The most revealing evidence of the Watchtower's bias is their inconsistent translation technique. Throughout the Gospel of John, the Greek word theon occurs without a definite article. The New World Translation renders none of these as "a god." Just three verses after John 1:1, the New World Translation translates another case of theos without the indefinite article as "God." Even more inconsistent, in John 1:18, the NWT translates the same term as both "God" and "god" in the very same sentence.

The Watchtower, therefore, has no hard textual grounds for their translation—only their own theological bias. While New World Translation defenders might succeed in showing that John 1:1 can be translated as they have done, they cannot show that it is the proper translation. Nor can they explain the fact that the NWT does not translate the same Greek phrases elsewhere in the Gospel of John the same way.

It is only the pre-conceived heretical rejection of the deity of Christ that forces the Watchtower Society to inconsistently translate the Greek text, thus allowing their error to gain some semblance of legitimacy in the minds of those ignorant of the facts.

It is only the Watchtower's pre-conceived heretical beliefs that are behind the dishonest and inconsistent translation that is the New World Translation. The New World Translation is most definitely not a valid version of God's Word.

For more details see the following link:

http://www.gotquestions.org/New-World-Translation.html

Who are the true followers of Christ?

Let see what the bible says:

Christians get their name from being followers and worshipers of Jesus Christ, first called "Christians" in Antioch during Paul's ministry (Acts 11:26). Paul repeatedly made it clear that to be a Christian was to be a witness to men concerning the person of Christ, to be a witness to the words and works of Christ. Jehovah's Witnesses, on the other hand, believe that we are to focus our worship exclusively on God the Father (who is sometimes referred to in the Bible as "Jehovah".) This name, however, was a hybrid name created by Christians by adding vowels to the tetragrammaton "YHWH," which was the original rendering which we now know as "Yahweh" in the Hebrew and "Jehovah" in the Greek. Evangelical Christians understand Jesus to be God in all His fullness, equal in deity, but different in function from that of God the Father. Christians acknowledge that one of the names for God the Father is Jehovah; however, there are many other names and titles which the scriptures use in reference to God the Father.

Jehovah's Witnesses understand Jesus to be Michael the Archangel, and categorically deny His deity. As we shall see, if we understand Jesus to be anything other than God, many verses present obvious contradictions.

However, we know that God's Word is inerrant and does not contradict itself. Therefore, we must understand the truth of God's Word in a way that is consistent and faithful to His revelation. You will notice that these same verses lack any contradiction if we understand Jesus to be God the Son—the fullness of God in bodily form—who surrendered His rights to be the suffering servant and sacrifice for our sin.

Created or Creator?

Jehovah's Witnesses teach that Jehovah created Jesus as an angel, and that Jesus then created all other things.

What do the scriptures say?

(About the Father)

Isaiah 66:2 English Standard Version (ESV)

Now all these things my own hand has made, so that all these came to be…

Isaiah 44:24 English Standard Version (ESV)

24 Thus says the Lord, your Redeemer, who formed you from the womb: "I am the Lord, who made all things, who alone stretched out the heavens, who spread out the earth by myself,

(About Jesus)

John 1:3 English Standard Version (ESV)

3 All things were made through him, and without him was not any thing made that was made.

If all things came into existence through Jesus, He could not have been created because He is included in the "all things."

Status, Names and Titles of Jesus and Jehovah

Isaiah 9:6 English Standard Version (ESV)

6 For to us a child is born, to us a son is given; and the government shall be upon his shoulder, and his name shall be called Wonderful Counselor, Mighty God, Everlasting Father, Prince of Peace.

Revelation 1:8 English Standard Version (ESV)

8 "I am the Alpha and the Omega," says the Lord God, "who is and who was and who is to come, the Almighty."

Revelation 1:17-18 English Standard Version (ESV)

17 When I saw him, I fell at his feet as though dead. But he laid his right hand on me, saying, "Fear not, I am the first and the last, 18 and the living one. I died, and behold I am alive forevermore, and I have the keys of Death and Hades.

Notice that if we understand Jesus to be God incarnate, then all the above verses can be understood to be true and mutually consistent in their claims. They can also be understood clearly with plain reason, taken at face value. However, if we attempt to suggest that Jesus is something less than God—Michael the archangel—then these verses are mutually exclusive and cannot both be true, when taken in their natural context. Therefore, the truth of God's Word necessitates that we must come to another understanding in which all Scripture is unified, interconnected, interdependent, inerrant and true. That unifying truth can be found only in the person and deity of Jesus Christ. May we see the truth revealed in Scripture as it is, not as we would each have it to be and may God receive all the glory.

References:

http://www.gotquestions.org/Jehovah-Witness-Christian.html

True religion is neither rules-based nor ritual-based. True religion is a relationship with God. Two things that all religions hold are that humanity is somehow separated from God and needs to be reconciled to Him. False religion seeks to solve this problem by observing rules and rituals. True religion solves the problem by recognizing that only God could rectify the separation, and that He has done so. True religion recognizes the following:

We have all sinned and are therefore separated from God (Ref: Romans 3:23).

Romans 6:23 English Standard Version (ESV)

23 For the wages of sin is death, but the free gift of God is eternal life in Christ Jesus our Lord.

God came to us in the Person of Jesus Christ and died in our place, taking the punishment that we deserve, and rose from the dead to demonstrate that His death was a sufficient sacrifice (Ref: Romans 5:8 ESV; 1 Corinthians 15:3-4 ESV; 2 Corinthians 5:21 ESV).

If we receive Jesus as the Savior, trusting His death as the full payment for our sins, we are forgiven, saved, redeemed, reconciled, and justified with God (John 3:16 ESV; Romans 10:9-10 ESV; Ephesians 2:8-9 ESV).

True religion does have rules and rituals, but there is a crucial difference. In true religion, the rules and rituals are observed out of gratitude for the salvation God has provided – NOT in an effort to obtain that salvation. True religion, which is Biblical Christianity, has rules to obey (do not murder, do not commit adultery, do not lie, etc.) and rituals to observe (water baptism by immersion and the Lord's Supper / Communion). Observance of these rules and rituals is not what makes a person right with God. Rather, these rules and rituals are the RESULT of the relationship with God, by grace through faith in Jesus Christ alone as the Savior. False religion is doing things (rules and rituals) in order to try to earn God's favor. True religion is receiving Jesus Christ as Savior and thereby having a right relationship with God – and then doing things (rules and rituals) out of love for God and desire to grow closer to Him.

Please be sure to read the information at the following links:

http://www.gotquestions.org/New-World-Translation.html

http://www.gotquestions.org/Jehovah-Witness-Christian.html

http://www.gotquestions.org/true-religion.html

Please read the following information:

http://www.gotquestions.org/what-is-a-Christian.html

Who is a true follower? Here are some more comments:

1. A true follower accepts the Lord Jesus as their savior.
2. Reads the Bible.
3. Attends and serves (volunteers) at a Christian church.
4. Prays regularly.
5. Does what the bible (God's word) says…

Marks of a true Christian can be found in Romans 12:9-21 ESV.

I hope this helps you. I enclosed a lot of information. Take your time reading it and then make your decision. It is my prayer that you choose Christ and avoid the Jehovah's Witness organization.

Go to the following link because it will explain what it means to accept Jesus as your personal Savior?

http://www.gotquestions.org/personal-Savior.html

Question: 50

Do Jehovah Witnesses believe only a limited amount of people will go to heaven and where do they get this from?

Profile: Male 46-60 Europe

Answer: Yes, the Jehovah's Witnesses do believe only a limited amount of people will go to heaven. The Jehovah's Witness gets this information from their false doctrine.

The Jehovah's Witnesses claim that 144,000 is a limit to the number of people who will reign with Christ in heaven and spend eternity with God. The 144,000 have what the Jehovah's Witnesses call the heavenly hope. Those who are not among the 144,000 will enjoy what they call the earthly hope—a paradise on earth ruled by Christ and the 144,000. Clearly, we can see that Jehovah's Witness teaching sets up a caste society in the afterlife with a ruling class (the 144,000) and those who are ruled.

The Bible teaches no such "dual class" doctrine. It is true that according to Revelation 20:4 ESV there will be people ruling in the millennium with Christ. These people will be comprised of the church (believers in Jesus Christ), Old Testament saints (believers who died before Christ's first advent), and tribulation saints (those who accept Christ during the tribulation). Yet the Bible places no numerical limit on this group of people. Furthermore, the millennium is different from the eternal state, which will take place at the completion of the millennial period. At that time, God will dwell with us in the New Jerusalem. He will be our God and we will be His people (Revelation 21:3 ESV). The inheritance promised to us in Christ and sealed by the Holy Spirit (Ephesians 1:13-14 ESV) will become ours, and we will all be co-heirs with Christ (Romans 8:17 ESV).

For the Jehovah's Witness prior to the 1930's it was clearly understood they were to go to heaven. The teaching on the 144,000 the way they believe today did not come from their founder C.T. Russell. Russell taught all the members of the Watchtower were "anointed,' and the 144,000 who were Spiritual Israel having the heavenly hope. The early Watchtower teaching was that all Jehovah's Witnesses go to heaven. There was no paradise earth teaching, no two destinations for their members. Russell actually taught that the calling of the 144,000 was completed in 1881.

It was not until Rutherford introduced changes to their doctrine that there was uncertainty on this matter. From the beginning Russell taught the Jehovah's Witnesses that "...The new covenant is a thing of the future" (*Watchtower* 6/1880 p.110) "...The work of the Christ in the inauguration of the new covenant could not begin until the perfecting of his own body, which is the church... and all of his blood has not yet been shed." (*Watchtower* 4/1/1909 p.4367)

Judge Rutherford took away their pseudo-heavenly hope and had them focus on a earthly paradise. "We understand that this heavenly calling continued down through the centuries, though during the so-called Dark Ages, there may have been times when the numbers of anointed ones were very few. With the reestablishment of true Christianity near the end of the last century, more were called and chosen. But it seems that in the mid-1930's, the full number of the 144,000 was basically completed. Thus there began to appear a group of loyal Christians with the earthly hope. Jesus termed such "other sheep," who unite in worship with the anointed as one approved flock." (*Watchtower* Aug. 15, 1996 p.31)

Joseph Franklin Rutherford (8 November 1869 – 8 January 1942), also known as "Judge" Rutherford, was the second president of the incorporated Watch Tower Bible and Tract Society, and played a primary role in the organization and doctrinal development of Jehovah's Witnesses, which emerged from the Bible Student movement established by Charles Taze Russell.

The Watchtower Societies position is that it has nearly reached completed 144,000 number in 1935. There would only be a few left to complete the number. Jehovah's Witnesses born after 1935 were taught that their only hope in the next life is to be part of the earthly "great crowd."

So let's answer the question "who are the 144,000?" This will depend on which interpretive approach you take to the book of Revelation. With the exception of the futurist approach, all of the other approaches interpret the 144,000 symbolically, as representative of the church and the number 144,000 being symbolic of the totality—i.e., the complete number—of the church. Yet when taken at face value: "Then I heard the number of those who were sealed: 144,000 from all the tribes of Israel" (Revelation 7:4), nothing in the passage leads to interpreting the 144,000 as anything but **a literal number of Jews—12,000 taken from every tribe of the "sons of Israel." The New Testament offers no clear cut text replacing Israel with the church.**

Please read the articles posted below for more details:

http://www.gotquestions.org/Jehovahs-Witnesses.html

http://www.letusreason.org/JW52.htm

Question: 51

Is there proof of time going back other than the bible in Isaiah 38:8?

Profile: Male 31-45 North America

Answer: Thanks for your question. The scripture verse you are referring to is:

Isaiah 38:8 New King James Version (NKJV)

8 Behold, I will bring the shadow on the sundial, which has gone down with the sun on the sundial of Ahaz, ten degrees backward." So the sun returned ten degrees on the dial by which it had gone down.

It is always awesome to read the happenings of God in His word.

There are quite a few hypothesis and skeptic articles in the world regarding this event.

The internet does have some articles trying to explain it. Know that these are speculation at best.

Friend, there is no known proof outside of scripture just speculation.

Except for Joshua's "long day", this is the only other time I know in the Bible where God interfered in time and here, time actually reversed. Well, maybe. It's really tough to be dogmatic here. We just don't know how to interpret this verse for sure. It may not mean that the sun was altered or reversed; it may only mean the shadow cast by the sun reversed. Regardless, <u>this was a miracle.</u> It may have been the reversal of the sun's shadow because the earth's rotation was reversed or perhaps God simply refracted the sun's rays. In truth, we just don't know. There are some things God keeps to Himself.

One final point:

Know that some answers are revealed after some years through archeology and the other sciences… Some will not be known in our lifetime… If we don't have an answer to a biblical passage just wait for the possibility of discovery through archeology and or just trust God for His word is truth. Trust that the bible is true and that an almighty God (the Creator) can do all things! Please read the following scriptures:

2 Timothy 3:16-17 English Standard Version (ESV)

16 All Scripture is breathed out by God and profitable for teaching, for reproof, for correction, and for training in righteousness, 17 that the man of God may be complete, equipped for every good work.

Luke 1:37 English Standard Version (ESV)

37 For nothing will be impossible with God."

May God bless you!

Question: 52

What do demons look like?

Profile: Male Under 18 North America

Answer: I am sure you know that Hollywood paints a different picture of what Satan and the demons look like. In order to answer this we need to check what the bible says…It is the final authority on all matters!

Demons are fallen angels who were pushed out of heaven along with their leader Satan.

What do we know about angels? Not a lot. We know that in the Bible when God sent angels as messengers they were referred to in masculine terms.

A good article to further your study is as follows:

Are angels male or female?

http://www.gotquestions.org/angels-male-female.html

We know that angels are frightening, at least sometimes. Ezekiel gives us a description of the Cherubim in Ezekiel 1:4-28 ESV. A reading of that passage gives us the following characteristics: their basic form is that of a human biped (1:5), but they have four faces (1:6) and four wings (1:6). Their feet look something like those of a calf (cloven hooves?) and are shiny, as if they are made of burnished bronze (1:7). The four wings are spread out, one on each of their four sides. Under each wing is what looks like a human hand (1:8). Their heads have four faces, one on each of the four sides (1:10). One face looked human, one resembled an ox, one a lion, and one an eagle (1:10). As a result of having a face on each side of their bodies, they didn't have to turn to change direction;

no matter which way they decided to go, they were already facing that way (1:9, 12). The sound their wings made was quite loud (1:24). When an angel appears to someone, often one of the first things he has to say is "do not be afraid". After Ezekiel's description, we should not be surprised.

Despite the descriptions in Ezekiel - Genesis 18 ESV and Joshua 5:13-15 ESV, plus most New Testament references indicate that angels most often when sent by God take on human form - or have human form - being indistinguishable from ordinary men. But in any case, 2 Kings 6:16-17 ESV and Numbers 22:21-35 ESV make clear the point that angels are not usually visible to human beings at all.

The good angels serve as God's messengers, to bring information to his servants (Daniel 10:12-14 ESV). They fight for God's people (Joshua 5:13-15 ESV; 2 Kings 6:16-17 ESV), and they protect and help God's people (Psalm 92:11-12 ESV)

The fallen angels (Satan and his demons) are evil and want to destroy God's people.

1 Peter 5:8 English Standard Version (ESV)

8 Be sober-minded; be watchful. Your adversary the devil prowls around like a roaring lion, seeking someone to devour.

Satan is a cherub angel. What do cherubs look like? If you could actually see an angel, they would frighten you to pieces! Satan and likely some of the demons entire body, including their back, their hands, and their wings were completely full of eyes, including the four wheels they had (Ezek.10:12 ESV). Their four faces were faces of a cherub, a man, an eagle, and a lion (Ezek. 10:14 ESV). Similar creatures or angels that may have become fallen had six wings and one looked like an ox, another like a lion, one like a man, and another like that of an eagle (Rev. 4:6-8 ESV). Satan and these fallen angels are spirit beings and so, thankfully, they can not be seen. Fortunately, Satan and his demons are subject to God's sovereignty and can do nothing over and against the will of God.

Read the following for the expanded details:

Ezekiel 10, Ezekiel 28:11-19, Revelation 4:6-8, Revelation 12.

For more study regarding demons please go to the following links at GotQuestions.org:

http://www.gotquestions.org/demons.html

http://www.gotquestions.org/Nephilim.html

http://www.gotquestions.org/sons-of-God.html

http://www.gotquestions.org/Nephilim-demons.html

http://www.gotquestions.org/fallen-angels.html

Question: 53

Go into all the world? Jesus said to the disciples (Mark 16:15). What does all the world mean? The earth as we know it??

Profile: Male Over 60 North America

Answer: Thanks for submitting your question regarding Mark 16:15. Let start by reading the entire verse:

Mark 16:15 English Standard Version (ESV)

15 And he said to them, “Go into all the world and proclaim the gospel to the whole creation.

In this verse Jesus sent His followers into “all the world”. Jesus had a global impact in mind.

Start in the area God provided for you and then look for opportunities to share the good news.

This may include the following:

1. The workplace, made up of business, government, and services.
2. Communities, involving grouping of people such as cities, neighborhoods, and especially families.
3. Systems, such as laws, traditions, and values that support work and community life.
4. Your world (Your sphere of influence)…
5. Supporting a radio or TV broadcast or ministry that reaches out to the world with the gospel…

Through our work, our families, our prayers for the world and its leaders, our activity as good citizens, and our involvement in the structure of society, we present Christ's message and have impact on a world that so desperately needs Him.

For more information regarding this subject please go to the following link: http://www.gotquestions.org/great-commission.html

Question: 54

Thank you for taking time to read this email. I recently ran into a seventh day Adventist at the library near my home. I started talking to her and corrected her on some of her statements. Some of what she said seemed to be scriptural so out of ignorance I agreed. But I worry because according to the Bible I have bidded her "God speed" What should I do if I see her again? I should have known better than to talk to her. I am saved and feel that I did the wrong thing by talking to her?

Answer: Thanks you for writing and asking your question. You appear to be a person who has a caring heart for people and really care to present the word of God in an honoring way.

You are worried that you may cause her to succeed in some way. Don't worry for since you are concerned you are showing your original intentions and truly desire to do God's will.

Let me remind you that God sees the heart. 1 Samuel 16:7 ESV, Proverbs 15:11 ESV, 1 Samuel 16:7 English Standard Version (ESV)

7 But the LORD said to Samuel, "Do not look on his appearance or on the height of his stature, because I have rejected him. For the LORD sees not as man sees: man looks on the outward appearance, but the LORD looks on the heart."

Proverbs 15:11 English Standard Version (ESV)

11 Sheol and Abaddon lie open before the LORD; how much more the hearts of the children of man!

Also remember that God is always good. He will do the right thing with all of us.

Psalm 100:5 English Standard Version (ESV)

5 For the LORD is good; his steadfast love endures forever, and his faithfulness to all generations.

He knows the motives of us all. He also knows not everyone has the ability or the information always available when someone crosses their paths. The information you presented to this seventh day Adventist will be used by God. Our Great God gives everyone a chance to choose Him. God may have or may provide someone else in this person's path to bring correction and redirection. Continue to educate yourself by reading, listening to topics that can improve your knowledge on the subject. Don't worry, keep trying, God is with you. You meant well! God knows this…

What does the bible say about our making mistakes? Consider the following verses:

Isaiah 41:10 ESV

Fear not, for I am with you; be not dismayed, for I am your God; I will strengthen you, I will help you, I will uphold you with my righteous right hand.

Psalm 37:24 ESV

Though he fall, he shall not be cast headlong, for the Lord upholds his hand.

You did nothing wrong in speaking with her. Perhaps in this case you now have the opportunity to grow from the experience.

In the future before you voice your opinions and suggestions, I would suggest you take some time to go and read up about any religion you wish to defend your own faith against. Look at its history, the theology it teaches and especially the qualifications of its original leadership. Then you will have more ammunition and knowledge to use in your discussions. Read your bible daily, dwell on the readings of scripture to aid memorization so you will be able to recall scripture when someone tries to justify their false teachings with supposed verses...

I am so happy to read that you at least tried to guide her. The world needs more people like you!

GotQuestions has some articles regarding the Seventh-Day-Adventist. Please feel free to read the following links

http://www.gotquestions.org/Seventh-Day-Adventism.html

http://www.gotquestions.org/cult-evangelism.html

There is an inexpensive book on the subject at the following website:

http://www.christianbook.com/are-seventh-day-adventists-false-prophets/wallace-slattery/9780875524450/pd/5524451?event=AFFp=1011693&

A suggestion: pray for another opportunity to witness to her or someone else… You could also print the GotQuestions.org articles, and then go to the library and check to see if she is there. If so, give it to her and then either stay and engage conversation or move on…

Thank you for your question. I sincerely hope this helps you. God bless you!

Question: 55

Is it Biblical to say that "if it is meant to be, it will happen"? Are the personal areas of our lives "meant to be"? For example, a girl once told me that if we were meant to be together later, it would happen. Is that Biblical?

Profile: Male 18-30 North America

Answer: This phrase is very similar to the following: what's for you won't go by you? It means that if God intends you to have something, you will get it. In other words "relax, don't scrabble about desperately trying to make things happen; if they are meant to happen they will, and if they aren't they won't".

Also it is similar to The Spanish "que sera sera" - "what will be, will be". This phrase predates Shakespeare's "come what come may".

Is this biblical?

To answer your questions one must put their focus off of what man can do and put it on what God can do. To conform to scripture then perhaps one can say "If it is God's will: it will happen, I will do this or that, or let it be so..."

In our relationship with God we are to make our request known to Him and through faith trust that the best outcome will occur. The outcome may look totally different than what was expected.

Remember what it says in Proverb 16:9 English Standard Version:

9 The heart of man plans his way, but the LORD establishes his steps.

And also what was expressed in the following scriptures:

Psalm 37:23 English Standard Version (ESV)

23 The steps of a man are established by the LORD, when he delights in his way;

Psalm 119:133 English Standard Version (ESV)

133 Keep steady my steps according to your promise, and let no iniquity get dominion over me.

So what I am saying is that a surrendered heart to the Lord will rest in the heavenly arms of Almighty God for His provisions. This includes the good and His allowing bad to occur…

More scripture to ponder:

Proverb 16:1-4 English Standard Version (ESV)

1 The plans of the heart belong to man, but the answer of the tongue is from the LORD.

2 All the ways of a man are pure in his own eyes, but the LORD weighs the spirit.

3 Commit your work to the LORD, and your plans will be established.

4 The LORD has made everything for its purpose, even the wicked for the day of trouble.

God cares for His people and desires to carry out His plans in their lives. Read on…

Jeremiah 29:11 English Standard Version (ESV)

[11] For I know the plans I have for you, declares the LORD, plans for welfare and not for evil, to give you a future and a hope.

Acts chapter 5 mentions what Gamaliel, a teacher of the law thought regarding going up against someone who is following God's plan.

Acts 5:38, 39 English Standard Version (©2001)

[38] So in the present case I tell you, keep away from these men and let
them alone, for if this plan or this undertaking is of man, it will fail; [39]
but if it is of God, you will not be able to overthrow them. You might
even be found opposing God!" So they took his advice.

There are no Bible verses that expressly state that "if it is meant to be, it will happen"? We can take into mind the character of God though. Whatever is meant to be in God's purpose will always find its way. If you put your statement into that form, then you have your answer.

You mentioned that a girl told you that if you were meant to be together later it would happen. My friend, there are no scripture references that expresses it in this manner. You see the human element is in this process. It includes choices (right or wrong).

The free will of humans can stop certain things from occurring especially in a dating relationship.

Know this with certainty; with God all things are possible. With man… forget about it…

Romans 8:28 English Standard Version (ESV)

[28] And we know that for those who love God all things work together for good, for those who are called according to his purpose.

Everything that is "meant to be," in the mind of God, "will be."

You also asked: Are the personal areas of our lives "meant to be"?

Mankind can influence his personal life by the choices he or she makes. This can change the course of ones life slightly, moderately, or dramatically! Example: If a person does something that is hurtful to someone this may affect both his and their life. This is most likely not what a parent had in mind for their child. So was it meant to be? I say no. Was the outcome influenced by a bad decision, yes.

The key to your questions comes to letting your will match God's will. If you do this then in this case whatever is allowed by God will happen.

Read how Isaac met Rebekah… This is a wonderful example of God working behind the scenes establishing a response to the desire of a faithful man "Abraham". Perhaps reading this will witness to you.

Turn in your bible to Genesis 24:1-67 ESV and enjoy the read!

I hope my answer helps you.

"Now this is the confidence that we have in Him, that if we ask anything according to His will, He hears us" (1 John 5:14 ESV).

Question: 56

I was reading the response posted on your website to the question," How do I know which of God's promises are meant for me?" I really would like to know the verses that support the following statement made in the post. "A general promise is one that is given by the Holy Spirit to every believer in every age. When the author penned the promise, he set no limitations on time period or recipient." Sometimes when I read the Bible I wonder if what I'm reading can really be meant for me. From years of living in Christian circles I know that the correct answer to this question should be 'yes', but I don't know how this 'yes' is supported from Scripture.

Answer: Thank you for writing. I pray that the answer provided below will help you in your journey with the Lord.

Many times people try to claim scripture promises that were not meant for us. Every promise in the Bible is not actually meant for everyone. There are conditional promises, as well.

Some promises are just for the people it was mentioned to! We must always remember to read scripture in the context it was intended.

I believe that your question is referring to the following article located at the following url:

http://www.gotquestions.org/God-promises.html

In the article below, examples of scripture were provided to support the statement made.

Note: There are no exact scripture verses that says it the way the writer expressed it in our post: "A general promise is one that is given by the

Holy Spirit to every believer in every age. When the author penned the promise, he set no limitations on time period or recipient."

Friend, the commentary from the writer of the post was made to help explain bible promises in general terms. The meaning is provided, and supported by the scripture examples.

Let me try to explain it in a different way. Please read another article from GotQuestions.org that I included after the article in question. It will further explain how to determine what parts of the Bible apply to us today.

Question: **"How do I know which of God's promises are for me?"**

Answer: There are literally hundreds of promises in the Bible. How can we know which promises apply to us, which promises we can claim? To frame this question another way, how can one tell the difference between general promises and specific promises? A general promise is one that is given by the Holy Spirit to every believer in every age. When the author penned the promise, he set no limitations on time period or recipient.

An example of a general promise is 1 John 1:9, "If we confess our sins, He is faithful and just to forgive us our sins and to cleanse us from all unrighteousness." This promise is based on the forgiving nature of God and is available to all believers everywhere. Another example of a general promise is Philippians 4:7, "And the peace of God, which transcends all understanding, will guard your hearts and your minds in Christ Jesus." This promise is made to all believers who, refusing to worry, bring their requests to God (v. 8). Other examples of general promises include Psalm 1:3; 27:10 ESV; 31:24; John 4:13-14 ESV (note the word "whoever" and "if any man"); and Revelation 3:20 ESV.

A specific promise is one that is made to specific individuals on specific occasions. The context of the promise will usually make clear who the recipient is. For example, the promise of 1 Kings 9:5 is very specific: "I will establish your royal throne over Israel forever." The preceding and following verses make it clear that the Lord is speaking only to King Solomon.

Luke 2:35 contains another specific promise: "And a sword will pierce your own soul too." This prophecy/promise was directed to Mary and was fulfilled in her lifetime. While a specific promise is not made to all believers generally, the Holy Spirit can still use a specific promise to guide or encourage any of His children. For example, the promise of Isaiah 54:10 was written with Israel in mind, but the Holy Spirit has used these words to comfort many Christians today: "my unfailing love for you will not be shaken nor my covenant of peace be removed."

As he was led to take the gospel to the Gentiles, the apostle Paul claimed the promise of Isaiah: "I have made you a light for the Gentiles, that you may bring salvation to the ends of the earth" (Acts 13:47). Isaiah's promise was originally meant for the Messiah, but in it Paul found guidance from the Lord for his own life. When claiming a promise from Scripture, we should keep the following principles in mind:

1) Promises are often conditional. Look for the word "if" in the context.
2) God gives us promises to help us better submit to His will and trust Him. A promise does not make God bend to our will.
3) Do not assume to know precisely when, where, or how the promise will be fulfilled in your life.

How can we know what parts of the Bible apply to us today?

http://www.gotquestions.org/Bible-apply-today.html

Answer: Much misunderstanding about the Christian life occurs because we either assign commands and exhortations we should be following as "era-specific" commands that only applied to the original audience, or we take commands and exhortations that are specific to a particular audience and make them timeless truths. How do we go about discerning the difference? The first thing to note is that the canon of Scripture was closed by the end of the 1st century A.D. What that means is most, if not all, of the Bible was not originally written to us. The authors had in mind the hearers of that day and probably were not aware that their words would be read and interpreted by people all over the world centuries later. That should cause us to be very careful when interpreting the Bible for today's Christians. It seems that much of contemporary evangelical preaching is so concerned with the practical application of Scripture that we treat the Bible as a lake from which to fish application for today's Christians. All of this is done at the expense of proper exegesis and interpretation.

The top three rules of hermeneutics (the art and science of biblical interpretation) are 1) context; 2) context; 3) context. Before we can tell 21st-century Christians how the Bible applies to them, we must first come to the best possible understanding of what the Bible meant to its original audience. If we come up with an application that would have been foreign to the original audience, there is a very strong possibility that we did not interpret the passage correctly. Once we are confident that we understand what the text meant to its original hearers, we then need to determine the width of the chasm between us and them. In other words, what are the differences in language, time, culture, geography, setting and situation? All of these must be taken into account before application can be made. Once the width of the chasm has been measured, we can then attempt to build the bridge over the chasm by finding the commonalities between the original audience and ourselves. Finally, we can then find application for ourselves in our time and situation.

Another important thing to note is that each passage has only one correct interpretation. It can have a range of application, but only one interpretation. What this means is that some applications of biblical passages are better than others. If one application is closer to the correct interpretation than another, then it is a better application of that text. For example, many sermons have been preached on 1 Samuel 17 (the David and Goliath story) that center around on "defeating the giants in your life." They lightly skim over the details of the narrative and go straight to application, and that application usually involves allegorizing

Goliath into tough, difficult and intimidating situations in one's life that must be overcome by faith. There is also an attempt to allegorize the five smooth stones David picked up to defeat his giant. These sermons usually conclude by exhorting us to be faithful like David.

While these interpretations make engaging sermons, it is doubtful the original audience would have gotten that message from this story. Before we can apply the truth in 1 Samuel 17, we must know how the original audience understood it, and that means determining the overall purpose of 1 Samuel as a book. Without going into a detailed exegesis of 1 Samuel 17, let's just say it's not about defeating the giants in your life with faith. That may be a distant application, but as an interpretation of the passage, it's alien to the text. God is the hero of the story and David was His chosen vehicle to bring salvation to His people. The story contrasts the people's king (Saul) with God's king (David), and it also foreshadows what Christ (the Son of David) would do for us in providing our salvation.

Another common example of interpreting with disregard of the context is John 14:13-14. Reading this verse out of context would seem to indicate that if we ask God anything (unqualified), we will receive it as long as we use the formula "in Jesus' name." Applying the rules of proper hermeneutics to this passage, we see Jesus speaking to His disciples in the upper room on the night of His eventual betrayal. The immediate audience is the disciples. This is essentially a promise to His disciples that God will provide the necessary resources for them to complete their task. It is a passage of comfort because Jesus would soon be leaving them. Is there an application for 21st-century Christians? Of course! If we pray in Jesus' name, we pray according to God's will and God will give us what we need to accomplish His will in and through us. Furthermore, the response we get will always glorify God. Far from a "carte blanche" way of getting what we want, this passage teaches us that we must always submit to God's will in prayer, and that God will always provide what we need to accomplish His will.

Proper biblical interpretation is built on the following principles:

1. Context. To understand fully, start small and extend outward: verse, passage, chapter, book, author and testament/covenant.
2. Try to come to grips with how the original audience would have understood the text.
3. Consider the width of the chasm between us and the original audience.
4. It's a safe bet that any moral command from the Old Testament that is repeated in the New Testament is an example of a "timeless truth."
5. Remember that each passage has one and only one correct interpretation, but can have many applications (some better than others).
6. Always be humble and don't forget the role of the Holy Spirit in interpretation. He has promised to lead us into all truth (John 16:13).

As mentioned earlier, biblical interpretation is as much an art as it is science. There are rules and principles, but some of the more difficult or controversial passages require more effort than others. We should always be open to changing an interpretation if the Spirit convicts and the evidence supports.

Question: 57

A guy I go to school with says he is a Christian and says that God has called him to preach. It's nothing wrong with that at all, except he's telling a girl that she is going to hell because her parents had her out of wedlock. He's also calling people rude names. <u>Where in the bible does it say you have to be called by God in order to be a preacher?</u> Thank you!

Profile: Female

Answer: Thanks for writing! I know of no scripture that says this exactly as you have stated it.

Take note that all Christians are to be a kingdom of priest spreading the gospel to the whole world. Mark 16:15 (ESV) God gives all believers spiritual gifts to deploy in the kingdom building efforts (See 1 Corinthians 12).

There are qualifications a person should have to become a pastor.

Two lists of qualifications for pastors are presented in 1Timothy 3:1-7 and Titus 1:5-9.

First Timothy 3:1-7:

* One must seek the office.
* Must be without reproach.
* A husband of one wife.
* Self-controlled
* Sober-minded
* Orderly
* Hospitable
* Able to teach

* Not a drunkard
* Not violent but gentle.
* Not quarrelsome.
* Not a lover of money.
* Must manage his own household well, with all dignity keeping his children submissive.
* Must not be a recent convert.
* Moreover, must be well thought of by outsiders.

Titus 1:5-9:

- Above reproach.
- A husband of one wife,
- His children are believers not open to the charge of debauchery or insubordination.
- Not arrogant.
- Not quick-tempered.
- Not a drunkard.
- Not violent.
- Not greedy for gain.
- Hospitable
- A lover of good.
- Self-controlled
- Upright
- Holy
- Disciplined
* Must hold firm to the trustworthy word as taught.

Based on your comments, the person you go to school with needs seasoning or more training in the word of God. This will come over time. He should have said that all have falling short of the glory of God. We are all sinners in need of a savior. The girl is not going to hell because her parents had her out of wedlock. Every person on this earth is destined to go to hell because of the sin problem we all have. We are all filthy rags in the eyes of a perfect and righteous God. God provided the way to everlasting life through His son Jesus. Everyone who accepts

Jesus as their savior changes their destiny to everlasting life with God. They will be heaven bound with all of their sins forgiven. Jesus paid the sin debt off for all who accepts the free gift.

All believers should read Romans 12:9-21 (Marks of a true Christian) to make sure they are complying…

The guy you mentioned needs to be very careful in how he shares the good news. Name calling is not the proper way to communicate with people. God's word is clear on this.

2 Timothy 2:16 English Standard Version (ESV)

16 But avoid irreverent babble, for it will lead people into more and more ungodliness,

Also, he really needs to be very sure he is feeling called by God to preach. Did anyone affirm this to him? Does the teaching gift reside in him? Is there a burning desire to preach, etc…?

The name calling is revealing a sin issue that he still needs to work on. Perhaps he has repented of this and feels bad for letting the words come out. Extend some grace to him for he is still growing spiritually.

He should become familiar with all of the scriptures presented in this response but especially these three:

James 3:1 English Standard Version (ESV) Taming the Tongue

3 Not many of you should become teachers, my brothers, for you know that we who teach will be judged with greater strictness.

Titus 3:9 English Standard Version (ESV)

9 But avoid foolish controversies, genealogies, dissensions, and quarrels about the law, for they are unprofitable and worthless.

1 Corinthians 10:31 ESV

So, whether you eat or drink, or whatever you do, do all to the glory of God.

Name calling and being rude does not bring glory to God.

Another warning is found in the following:

1 Timothy 6:20-21 English Standard Version (ESV)

[20] O Timothy, guard the deposit entrusted to you. Avoid the irreverent babble and contradictions of what is falsely called "knowledge," [21] for by professing it some have swerved from the faith.

To further clarify, GotQuestions.org has 2 articles posted that speak of a person's calling. I have included them below for your convenience.

http://www.gotquestions.org/call-to-ministry.html

How can I know if I have received a call to ministry?

In the most basic sense, all Christians are called to ministry. The Great Commission (Matthew 28:18-20) applies to all believers. Every Christian is part of the Body of Christ. Fulfilling one's role as part of the Body – no matter what that role is – means ministering to others. However, most people who ask this question are really interested in whether they are called to *vocational* ministry, such as the pastorate. This is an excellent question. Certainly, vocational ministry has unique demands.

In confirming any calling, it is important to first examine your heart and motivation (Jeremiah 17:9). Do you truly feel this call is from God, or is it a personal desire? Or is it an attempt to live up to someone else's expectation of you? If the motivation is pride or people-pleasing, you should give pause. Are you feeling "called" because you think that in order to be "more Christian" you must work in a distinctly "Christian" ministry? Christians are the fragrance of Christ (2 Corinthians 2:15) no matter where they serve. You can be light and salt and "do ministry" outside the church or in a secular job just as well as you can within the church or in a distinctly Christian vocation.

Guilt can sometimes be mistaken as a call to ministry. Many Christians hear that serving God requires sacrifice, which it does. But this does not necessarily mean all Christians are called to the mission field in Third World countries. Yes, living for Christ requires sacrifice, but not misery. There is joy in living out our calling. Paul is a great example of this. He suffered greatly for his ministry, yet he was always content and joyful in Christ (see especially Paul's letter to the Philippians).

After you are certain that your heart is rightly motivated, consider your natural (and spiritual) gifts and strengths. Do these seem to fit with the vocational ministry you are considering? Yes, God is shown strong in our weaknesses and calls us to serve out of His strength rather than our own. But He also gave us gifts and talents to use for Him. It is unlikely that God would call someone who is manually unskilled to be a repairman. Are you gifted in the area in which you think you are called?

Another important consideration is your natural inclination. Someone invigorated by accounting facts, for example, is likely not going to enjoy a position in pastoral care. You may find spiritual gifts tests and even personality tests to be helpful in determining your natural gifting and inclination.

Another area to consider is your experience. God prepares us before launching us into our calling (in the Bible we see this occur with David's training under Saul prior to his taking the throne. Reggie McNeal's *A Work of Heart* does an excellent job depicting this time of preparation). Are there things in your past that God will use to contribute to your work in the call?

Also, you'll want to seek counsel (see Proverbs 11:14 and 15:22). Others can often see strengths and weaknesses in us that we cannot. It is helpful to receive input from trusted, godly friends. It is also helpful to observe others' reactions to you. Do people seem to naturally follow you, or do you often have to force your leadership? Are people naturally open with you and share their concerns? While it is important to seek counsel, it is also important not to rely solely on this. Sometimes our friends and family are wrong (see 1 Samuel 16:7). However, honest feedback from those who love you should help confirm your calling.

Every person has a unique calling from God. The call to vocational ministry, however, is particularly public, and those in public ministry are often both highly regarded and highly criticized. James 3:1 says, "Not many of you should presume to be teachers, my brothers, because you know that we who teach will be judged more strictly." Those in ministry leadership positions are held to high standards because they are guiding others. The books of 1 and 2 Timothy and Titus list requirements for those in church leadership positions.

When determining whether or not you are called to vocational ministry, consider what it will entail, be courageous, and trust God. If God has called you, He will equip you and fill you so that you may be poured out for others (see Matthew 6:33; Hebrews 13:20-21; Ephesians 3:20-21; Psalm 37:23; and Isaiah 30:21).

One more thing… It is important to keep moving. We sometimes refuse to move until we are certain of the call. But it is easier to redirect something already in motion than to get something moving. When we step out in faith – even if our step is not quite in the right direction – God is faithful to guide us.

Also read the following article from GotQuestions.org:

http://www.gotquestions.org/called-to-preach.html

How can I know if I am being called to preach?

There is no doubt that preaching is a noble calling and one which is far more important to God than it is to most people. Preaching is not simply a time-filler in the worship service, nor is it the sharing of personal experiences, no matter how emotional. Nor is it a well-organized "talk" complete with a PowerPoint display designed to give a series of steps to a better life. Preaching, as the Apostle Paul records, is the vehicle by which the life-giving truth of the Gospel of Jesus Christ is conveyed. The words of the preacher are to be faithful to the Word of God, which is "the power unto salvation for everyone who believes" (Romans 1:16). Paul's admonition to the young pastor Timothy was, "In the presence of God and of Christ Jesus... I give you this charge: Preach the Word!" (2 Tim. 4:1-2). So there is no doubt the preaching of the Word is of primary importance to God. So must it be for anyone considering entering the ministry as a preacher.

But how can one be sure he is called to preach? First are the subjective indicators. If a man has the burning desire within him that cannot be denied, that is a good indication of a "calling" by God. The Apostle Paul and the Old Testament prophet Jeremiah experienced the same desire. Paul said, "Yet when I preach the gospel, I cannot boast, for I am compelled to preach. Woe to me if I do not preach the gospel!" (1 Corinthians 9:16). To be "compelled" to preach means to be driven onward by an irresistible and undeniable compulsion to do so. Jeremiah described it as a "burning fire" (Jeremiah 20:8-9) that could not be stifled. Trying to hold it back made him weary.

Second, there are objective indicators of God's calling to preach. If the response to early efforts at preaching are positive, this is a good indication that the prospective preacher has the gift of didaktikos, the gift of teaching from the Holy Spirit (Ephesians 4:11). Every preacher must be first and foremost a teacher of God's Word, conveying it in a clear and concise manner and making personal application to the hearers. The church leadership is usually the best determiners of whether a man has this gift. If they agree that he does, the prospective preacher should then be examined by the leadership as to his character, as outlined in the requirements for elders in 1 Timothy 3 and Titus 1 (for every preacher is also an elder). These two affirmations by the church are another indication of God's calling.

Finally, the whole process should be bathed in prayer every step of the way. If God is truly calling a man to preach, He will confirm it in many ways. Seek His face and ask that doors are opened to more opportunities and more confirmations, both internal and external. Ask also that doors will close if it is not His will to continue. Take heart in the fact that God is sovereignly in control of all things and will work "all things... together for good to those who love God, to those who are the called according to His purpose" (Romans 8:28). If He has called you, that call will not be denied.

I hope this helps you in better understanding a person's call to ministry and what the bible says regarding a Christian's behavior.

Question: 58

What is the difference between being a friend of God and follower of God?

Answer: Let's define the words "friend" and "follower" and piece this together.

The dictionary defines the word "friend" this way:

noun

1. a person attached to another by feelings of affection or personal regard.
2. a person who is on good terms with another; a person who is not hostile.

The dictionary defines the word "follower" as:

noun

1. a person or thing that follows.
2. a person who follows another in regard to his or her ideas or belief; disciple or adherent.
3. a person who imitates, copies, or takes as a model or ideal: *He was little more than a follower of current modes.*
4. an attendant, servant, or retainer.

Switching to a biblical perspective both a friend and follower of God will seek Him. They are considered the people of God.

2Chron 7:14 If My people who are called by My name humble themselves and pray, and seek My face and turn from their wicked ways, then I will hear from heaven, will forgive their sin, and will heal their land.

Both a friend and follower of God should do what is listed below. Note a friend is also a follower but at a deeper level.

1. Seek after humbleness.
2. Seek an ongoing relationship with God through Prayer.
3. Seek the face of God.
4. Seek the way of God.
5. Seek to be right with God.

1. Followers of Jesus are Fishers of men (See Matt 4:19).
2. Followers of Jesus hear His voice and obey (See Matt 4:20), and John 10:27. My sheep hear My voice, and I know them, and they follow Me;
3. Followers of Jesus deny themselves and take up the cross and follow Him (See Luke 9:23).
4. Followers of Jesus are willing to give up everything to follow Him. (See Matt 19:21).
5. Followers of Jesus should never look back (See Luke 9:61-62).
6. Followers of Jesus walk in the Light (See John 8:12).
7. Followers of Jesus are servants of Him (See John 12:26).

Both Friends and followers should be followers of the Way… Acts 9:1-2

Now let's look further into what being a friend of God means.

James 2:23

And the scripture was fulfilled which saith, Abraham believed God, and it was imputed unto him for righteousness: And he was called the friend of God.

In James 2:23 we see one of the highest titles, if not the highest, that can be given to an earthling. "He was a friend of God." In Exodus 33:11, we read of Moses. "And the LORD spake unto Moses face to face, as a man speaketh unto his friend...." However, only Abraham is referred to as a "friend of God" in the entire Bible.

John 15:13-15 "Greater love hath no man than this, that a man lay down his life for his friends. {14} Ye are my friends, If ye do whatsoever I command you. {15} Henceforth I call you not servants; For the servant knoweth not what his lord doeth: But I have called you friends; for all things that I have heard of my Father I have made Known unto you."

Our Lord used the term "friend or friends" in the N.T. He told His disciples that they were no longer slaves, or servants, but were His friends. I believe it is a great privilege to be called the "Friend of God, or Friend of Christ."

(PROV 18:24) "A man that hath friends must show himself friendly: And there is a friend that sticketh closer than a brother."

Friendship in this connotation is speaking of intimacy. More than just a close acquaintance… "One who is attached to another by affection..." So, we must understand that there was a reason why Abraham was called "The Friend of God." It is possible to be a child of God and not be a friend of God.

A person can follow God without ever getting close in relationship with Him. The difference between a follower and a friend is as follows:

Intimacy - Getting close in your relationship with God. In this situation you are not following God because he is the boss but there is more meaning to your emotional connection to Him.

Like Abraham, a friend submits to God's direction.

(HEB 11:8) "By faith Abraham, when he was called to go out into a place which should after receive for an inheritance, obeyed; and he went out, not knowing whither he went."

1 TH 5:22) "Abstain from all appearance of evil."

Abraham was called the "Friend of God" because he was willing to be separated from the ungodly city of Sodom.

If we expect to be the "Friend of God", we must follow the example of Abraham.

Abraham was willing to stand on the dependability of God Gen. 15:1-6.

The true friend of God is the Christian that is willing to stand on the Word of God.

ROMANS 4:20-21) "He staggered not at the promise of God through unbelief; but was strong in faith, giving glory to God; {21} And being fully persuaded that, what he had promised, He was able also to perform."

Abraham stood on the promise of the dependability of God.

Abraham was willing to sacrifice his dearest to God Gen. 22:1-6.

A faith that has not been tested is faith that cannot be trusted.

God has already shown Himself a friend to us.

To begin the journey of becoming friends with God one must do the following:

Begin first of all by confessing that you are a sinner.

Accept Jesus as your Savior.

Trust Christ for your salvation.

Trust Him with your life.

Be willing to follow His direction.

Totally surrender to Him.

The believer as a friend of God will strive to develop the friendship with God. Friendships with people come as a result of getting to know another individual through communication. It is no different with God. The only way to get to know God better is through the communication He has given us regarding Himself. This is found only in the Bible – both the Hebrew Scriptures and the New Testament writings. We must read His word daily. Doing this strengthens the friendship. Therefore, the friend of God (the one who has made peace with God through faith in the work of His Son) will get to know the Scriptures which tell us of the character and nature of our God and His act of reconciliation that benefits the redeemed (2 Tim 3:15, 16). A friend of God stays in community with God through prayer as often as possible. This includes listening for His promptings…

Conclusion:

The difference between a friend of God and a follower of God comes down to the intimacy level. A friend of God works on the friendship.

A friend of God knows Him at a higher level, more than just carrying out His commands robotically or through habit. It is about connecting with God in a more personal, loving manner. Always seeking Him and involving God in everything that is done.

Perhaps a friend should try to please God like another individual in scripture at Genesis 5:21-24: A brief commentary regarding Enoch: he walked with God and God took him….

another individual through communication. It is no different with God. The only way to get to know God better is through the communication He has given us regarding Himself. This is found only in the [illegible] the Hebrew Scriptures and the New Testament writings. We must read [illegible] daily. Doing this strengthens the relationship. The closer the friend of God (the one who has made peace with God through faith in the sacrifice of His Son) gets to know the Father, the appreciation of the character and nature of our God and the act of reconciliation [illegible]

[illegible]

Question: 59

If a Christian leader is separated from their spouse, should they continue in leadership?

Profile: Male 46-60 Europe

Answer: This situation depends on what the issues are. This is crucial in determining the leader's status. In trying to understand this we must ask why they are separated. If a Christian leader is separated due to no fault of their own, and can still function well as a leader, and the Elders or church board agree to keep the leader active, then they should continue in the leadership role. This is also, first a matter of prayer requesting guidance from the Lord who knows all things.

One example that I can think of for a person to continue functioning in the leadership role is as follows:

The leader's spouse cheated on them with someone and refuses to change their ways and work on the marriage. The spouse then wants out of the marriage to be with the new person thus abandoning the marriage. In this scenario the leader should not be removed due to the sins of the spouse.

If the leader is a person who is caught up in a pattern of sin (ie... sexual, abuse, addictions etc...) the leader should step aside or be removed from the leadership role. In this case the leader disqualifies themselves by his/her actions. (1Timothy 3:1-7 and Titus 1:5-9). We want to be loving to them, but if and when they disqualify themselves, action must be taken. This disqualification from leadership does not mean exclusion from fellowship. Disqualification by sexual sin does not mean exclusion from fellowship in the church, who should forgive and welcome them in the grace of Jesus, and provide counseling for them and their family.

We need to keep in mind that sexual sin is not an "ordinary" sin. The Bible seems to "elevate" the seriousness of sexual sin, when Paul says, "All other sins a person commits are outside the body, but whoever sins sexually, sins against their own body" (1 Cor 6:18), because our body is a temple of the Holy Spirit (1 Cor 6:19).

Full repentance and forgiveness is needed.

Reasons for allowing a Christian leader to lead after a sexual sin:

According to reports, it has been "common" for leaders to continue in their positions of leadership in the church after sexual transgression. Common justifications include:

- "God forgives all sin, including sexual sin,"
- "He repented,"
- "He served so well for so long,"
- "He has great gifts that can greatly benefit the church,"
- "Now he can understand sinners better."

There are ample biblical arguments for each of the above justifications.

We have to remember that we all have fallen short of the Glory of God. We are all sinners needing forgiveness. If true repentance is exhibited reconciliation can occur.

Let us take a look at a few of the guidelines for Biblical Leadership.

The bible gives us attributes we should all have especially our leaders. For all of us we need to follow what is in the following scripture verses:

1 Corinthians 13:4-7 English Standard Version (ESV)

4 Love is patient and kind; love does not envy or boast; it is not arrogant
5 or rude. It does not insist on its own way; it is not irritable or resentful
6 it does not rejoice at wrongdoing, but rejoices with the truth. 7 Love
bears all things, believes all things, hopes all things, endures all things.

Leaders need to make sure that they meet the following qualification in 1 Timothy 3:1-7 not just prior to qualifying for the position but all during:

1 Timothy 3:1-7 English Standard Version (ESV)

Qualifications for Overseers

3 The saying is trustworthy: If anyone aspires to the office of overseer, he desires a noble task. [2] Therefore an overseer must be above reproach, the husband of one wife, sober-minded, self-controlled, respectable, hospitable, able to teach, [3] not a drunkard, not violent but gentle, not quarrelsome, not a lover of money. [4] He must manage his own household well, with all dignity keeping his children submissive, [5] for if someone does not know how to manage his own household, how will he care for God's church? [6] He must not be a recent convert, or he may become puffed up with conceit and fall into the condemnation of the devil. [7] Moreover, he must be well thought of by outsiders, so that he may not fall into disgrace, into a snare of the devil.

If it is concluded that the Christian leader should be disqualified, the ministry must take action. 1Timothy 5:19-20 tells us the elder does not have special privileges when it comes to sin and error.

[19] Do not admit a charge against an elder except on the evidence of two or three witnesses. [20] As for those who persist in sin, rebuke them in the presence of all, so that the rest may stand in fear. [21] In the presence of God and of Christ Jesus and of the elect angels I charge you to keep these rules without prejudging, doing nothing from partiality.

1 Tim. 5:19-21 (ESV)

This applies to church leaders. See definitions below:

Definitions:

Pastor: One who leads and instructs a congregation.

Overseer: An elder, bishop, presbyter, or supervisor in charge of a congregation (Acts 20:8).

Elder: 1. In the O.T. an older member of a tribe or clan who was a leader and official representative of the clan (Num 22:7). 2. In the N.T. a local church leader who served as a pastor and teacher (1 Tim 5:17).

In conclusion, the answer to the question you ask has many answers depending on why the leader is separated. All individuals involved in this needs to proceed biblically in resolving the matter.

Christian leaders who have failed big can truly repent, recommit and surrender all to the Lord and try again under certain circumstances. God can remove or restore a leader's role if it is His will. It has happen in past…

Question: 60

Is the Old Testament accepted by all religions as historical fact (with some variations)?

Profile: Female Over 60 North America

Answer: Unfortunately not all religions accept the Old Testament as historical. Some religions mistakenly believe that it was altered by man.

For example, Muslims believe in the Torah as revealed to Moses and the Psalms as revealed to David. The OT that exists today does not qualify for this recognition by Muslims because they believe and are told in the Qur'an that they have been altered by the hands of man. They believe that God revealed the Qur'an and promised to protect it from alteration. So they accept some things in the OT that agrees with the Qur'an.

One who studies deeper on the issue of the Qur'an's accuracy should be sure to read the article posted at: http://www.gotquestions.org/errors-Quran.html

Many religious texts claim to convey a divine message. The Bible, however, stands alone in that *God left absolutely no room for doubt as to whether or not this is His written Word.* If anyone undertakes an honest effort to examine the facts, he will find the Bible most assuredly has God's signature all through it. The very same mouth that spoke all of creation into existence also gave us the Bible.

Most of the historical record for the start of the Christian faith is recorded in the New Testament accounts, the history of Christianity actually began with prophecy in the Old Testament. There are over 300 prophecies (predictions) that span over a period of 1000 years that are recorded in the Old Testament concerning the coming of a Jewish Messiah. A study of Jesus' life, death and background will show that He was undoubtedly the fulfillment of these Messianic prophecies. Thus, even long before Jesus walked the earth, His mission was made known to mankind through the Word of God.

The Christian faith, unlike any other religion, hinges on historical events, including one of pivotal importance. If Jesus Christ died and never rose to life, then Christianity is a myth or a fraud. In 1 Corinthians 15:14, Paul exhorts his readers to grab hold of this central truth: "And if Christ be not risen, then is our preaching vain, and your faith is also vain." The evidence for the resurrection is the key to establishing that Jesus is indeed who He claims to be. It is the historical validity of this central fact that gives Christians genuine and eternal hope amidst a hurting world.

The Bible has many confirmations in sciences such as biology, geology, astronomy, and archaeology. The field of biblical archaeology has absolutely exploded in the last century and a half, during which time hundreds of thousands of artifacts have been discovered. Archaeology continues to bolster the Bible's historicity. As Dr. Henry M. Morris has remarked, "There exists today not one unquestionable find of archaeology that proves the Bible to be in error at any point."

Other religions can not claim this truth or the following scriptural truth:

2 Timothy 3:16 English Standard Version (ESV)

16 All Scripture is breathed out by God and profitable for teaching, for reproof, for correction, and for training in righteousness,

The Old Testament was breathed out by God and is definitely a historical fact whether other religions accept it or not. The facts are there for all to observe.

Question: 61

How should a Christian respond if a friend or even a stranger "comes out of the closet" and admits they are homosexual or bisexual?

Answer: This depends on how this information was presented... Was this revealed in an audience of others?

Are they seeking validation? Are they seeking help in changing and showing a willingness to change? Did they come out boldly without caring whether it is right or wrong? Was this a "by the way I am ....!"

The important thing to remember is to go slow in responding so you can be praying for godly wisdom and listening to the Holy Spirits promptings. Not all responses fit all situations. Ask God to open the person's heart to hear the truth as presented in the bible and not the twisted lie that the world is pushing on mankind. The believer should not be combative, hateful or accepting of this sinful act. A sin is a sin no matter what type of action it is.

There are many verses in the bible that say we are to hate sin. Jesus also stated love your neighbor as yourself and we find recorded in Romans 5:8 "But God demonstrates his love for us in this that while we were still sinners Christ died for us." So we find in the bible that God hates sin but he loves the sinners and desires for all people to come to His Son for salvation. If we are to be followers of the Messiah then we should also love the sinner and hate the sin.

John 3:16-17 English Standard Version (ESV) For God So Loved the World

16 "For God so loved the world, that he gave his only Son, that whoever believes in him should not perish but have eternal life. 17 For God did

not send his Son into the world to condemn the world, but in order that the world might be saved through him.

If the person is seeking help, confirm this with them by asking them if they would like to change the sexual desires he/she has been dwelling on or in…

Give them the hope that is found in God's word. Encourage them by informing them that there are many in the world who successfully turned from being homosexual or bisexual.

It is not how God made them. It is a choice just like other sins.

Mankind have in our make up the lean towards doing certain sinful things if they give into the desire.

Speak the truth in love…

Ephesians 4:15 English Standard Version (ESV)

15 Rather, speaking the truth in love, we are to grow up in every way into him who is the head, into Christ,

So how should a Christian respond? Well, consider this answer:

First of all, Jesus (who created us and therefore owns us and has the authority to determine right and wrong), as the God-man, *did* deal directly with the gay issue for example marriage, in the Bible's New Testament, in *Matthew 19:4–6*: "And He answered and said to them, 'Have you not read that He who made them at the beginning "made them male and female," and said, "For this cause a man shall leave father and mother and shall cling to his wife, and the two of them shall be one flesh?" So then, they are no longer two but one flesh. Therefore what God has joined together, let not man separate."

Christ quoted directly from the book of Genesis (and its account of the creation of Adam and Eve as the first man and woman—the first marriage) as literal history, to explain the doctrine of marriage as being one man for one woman. Thus marriage cannot be a man and a man, or a woman and a woman. The book of Genesis is real history. Jesus dealt quite directly with the gay marriage issue when he explained the doctrine of marriage.

Not only this, but in *John 1* we read: "In the beginning was the Word, and the Word was with God, and the Word was God. The same was in the beginning with God. All things were made by him; and without him was not any thing made that was made" (KJV).

Jesus, the Creator, is the Word. The Bible is the written Word. Every word in the Bible is really the Word of the Creator—Jesus Christ.

Therefore, in *Leviticus 18:2,* Jesus deals directly with the homosexual issue, and thus the gay marriage issue. This is also true of *Romans* 1:26–27 *and* 1 Timothy 1:9–10.

Because Jesus in a real sense wrote all of the Bible, whenever Scripture deals with marriage and/or the homosexual issue, Jesus himself is directly dealing with these issues.

God is the ultimate authority on this and all issues. We must obey God rather than men. Acts 5:29 English Standard Version (ESV)

If the person is willing to change tell them that God can take the desire away and replace it... He or she will need Christ inside to be made new. Tell them the gospel...

God can change a person's life if they are willing and surrender to Him. They need to accept Jesus as their savior. Ask them if they are willing to accept Jesus as their savior right now. If yes, lead them in a prayer.

Tell them if they want to receive the salvation that is available only through Jesus; place your faith in Him. Fully trust His death as the sufficient sacrifice for your sins. Completely rely on Him alone as your Savior. That is the biblical method of salvation. If you have received

Jesus as your Savior, by all means, say a prayer to God. Tell God how thankful you are for Jesus. Offer praise to God for His love and sacrifice. Thank Jesus for dying for your sins and providing salvation for you.

2 Corinthians 5:17 English Standard Version (ESV)

17 Therefore, if anyone is in Christ, he is a new creation. The old has passed away; behold, the new has come.

The Christian should study the articles (see below) posted on Gotquestions.org to further educate them on the topic of homosexuality from a biblical perspective:

http://www.gotquestions.org/homosexuality-Bible.html

http://www.gotquestions.org/bisexual-bisexuality.html

http://www.gotquestions.org/born-gay.html

http://www.gotquestions.org/gay-Christian.html

http://www.gotquestions.org/Bible-lesbian.html

http://www.gotquestions.org/love-sinner-hate-sin.html

Question: 62

Why did John the Baptist simply tell the tax collectors "Collect no more than is appointed to you" (Luke 3:12-13), yet Jesus told a tax collector to leave everything and follow Him? Why do the tax collectors have a bad image?

Profile: Male Under 18 North America

Answer: To answer this let's look briefly at some of the biblical history of tax collectors.

In Roman Palestine, tax collectors were particularly hated. One reason is they collaborated with the foreign oppressors. The Roman system of "tax farming" made tax collectors especially despised. The Romans wanted to collect as much tax as they could without tying up their own personnel. So they recruited locals and gave them a percentage of what was collected. The more they could wring out of the people, the more they could keep. So these tax collectors profited off their countrymen's misfortune. In so doing, they helped raise the funds necessary to finance the brutal repression of the chosen people by the pagans. In this they were beyond stench to all decent, God-fearing people. They were hated and looked upon as traitors by their fellow citizens. (Ref: Matt 5:46). The actions of many of the Tax collectors caused this bad image.

Luke 3:12, 13 English Standard Version (ESV) 12 Tax collectors also came to be baptized and said to him, "Teacher, what shall we do?" 13 And he said to them, "Collect no more than you are authorized to do."

John the Baptist informed the tax collectors to collect no more than what was appointed because it was well known what the collectors were doing. John was trying to convince them to change and do the right thing. They needed to repent of this sin. They still needed to work. This was their occupation. With this repentance, it would go well with them and God's people.

Jesus told a tax collector to leave everything and follow Him because he had a calling on this person's life. We know this person to be Matthew (Levi) referenced in Luke 5:27-32.

He collected taxes around Capernaum in Galilee. He made his money by squeezing from the public every last penny he could and keeping whatever was more than he agreed to pay the government. He "Matthew Levi" was to become a disciple that God was going to use to spread the gospel...

Not all Tax collectors continued living a life that ripped off the God fearing people. Read the story of Zacchaeus in Luke 19. In Short, when Jesus came to Jericho, Zacchaeus just had to "see what he was like." In John 6:44, Jesus says "no one can come to me unless the Father draws Him." Jesus saw past Zacchaeus' crimes to his heart, which was open to the grace that prompted him to climb that tree. Jesus inviting himself to the tax-collector's home meant an offer of forgiveness, mercy, acceptance by God. The tug that Zacchaeus felt inside was the grace of God drawing him to his Son. Zacchaeus became a changed man...

God is so amazing for He desires to save those who turn to Him and choose to follow Him.

Luke 19:10 English Standard Version (ESV) 10 For the Son of Man came to seek and to save the lost."

Even tax collectors!

Question: 63

Is Christian rap and light rock bad, or is it just a way to praise God? Also, clapping during songs, is this a sin or not?

Profile: Male Under 18 North America

Answer: Let's see what the bible has to say regarding your question.

In the New Testament, the apostle Paul instructs Christians to encourage one another with music: "Speak to one another with psalms, hymns and spiritual songs" (Ephesians 5:19). So, while the primary purpose of music does seem to be worship, the Bible definitely allows for other uses of music.

One can express themselves in various styles of music (Christian rap and light rock) as long as the message is God honoring. Please read on...

The Bible nowhere condemns any particular style of music. The Bible nowhere declares any particular musical instrument to be ungodly. The Bible mentions numerous kinds of string instruments and wind instruments. While the Bible does not specifically mention drums, it does mention other percussion instruments (Psalm 68:25; Ezra 3:10). Nearly all of the forms of modern music are variations and/or combinations of the same types of musical instruments, played at different speeds or with heightened emphasis. There is no biblical basis to declare any particular style of music to be ungodly or outside of God's will.

The content of the lyrics must be considered. This is extremely important! While not specifically speaking of music, Philippians 4:8 is an excellent guide for musical lyrics: "Finally, brothers, whatever is true, whatever is noble, whatever is right, whatever is pure, whatever is lovely, whatever is admirable—if anything is excellent or praiseworthy—think about such things." If we should be thinking about such things, surely those are the things we should invite into our minds through music and lyrics. Can the lyrics in a secular song be true, noble, right, pure, lovely, admirable, excellent, and praiseworthy? If so, then there is nothing wrong with a Christian listening to a secular song of that nature.

The best kind of music is that which praises and glorifies God. Talented Christian musicians work in nearly every musical genre, ranging from classical to rock, rap, and reggae. There is nothing inherently wrong with any particular style of music. It is the lyrics that determine whether a song is "acceptable" for a Christian to listen to. If anything leads you to think about or get involved in something that does not glorify God, it should be avoided.

Clapping:

Every instance of dancing that is not considered sinful was done in worship or praise to God.

The following scriptures offer some examples of people who danced and used the tambourine (a clapping style instrument) to praise God.

Exodus 15:20 English Standard Version (©2001)

Then Miriam the prophetess, the sister of Aaron, took a tambourine in her hand, and all the women went out after her with tambourines and dancing.

1Samuel 18:6 It happened as they were coming, when David returned from killing the Philistine, that the women came out of all the cities of Israel, singing and dancing, to meet King Saul, with tambourines, with joy and with musical instruments.

2 Samuel 6:14-16

14 And David danced before the LORD with all his might; and David was girded with a linen ephod.

15 So David and all the house of Israel brought up the ark of the LORD with shouting, and with the sound of the trumpet.

16 And as the ark of the LORD came into the city of David, Michal Saul's daughter looked through a window, and saw King David leaping and dancing before the LORD; and she despised him in her heart.

Every instance of dancing that is not considered sinful was done in worship or praise to God. Here are some more principles to keep in mind in considering dancing: Ecclesiastes 3:4—There is an appropriate time to dance (and by implication an inappropriate time to dance). Psalm 149:3; 150:4—Both passages mention that we can praise or worship God through dance. 1 Corinthians 6:19-20—Our bodies belong to God, and they are the temple of the Holy Spirit. So everything we do must be honoring to Him.

Dancing to bring inappropriate attention to yourself or your body therefore would be sinful. In 1 Corinthians 7:1-3, the writer says, "It is good for a man not to touch a woman" (NASB, KJV). Paul was acknowledging that men have a very strong sex drive that is easy to set off. Because of this, many styles of pair dancing outside of marriage can be very tempting, especially to the man. "Flee (as in "run away from") the evil desires of youth" (2 Timothy 2:22). Any dancing that stirs up sinful desires in us or in others is sinful. Matthew 18:6—Doing something that might cause someone else to stumble into sin is considered absolutely inexcusable. Dancing in a way that would cause someone else to lust would fall under this guideline. 1 Thessalonians 5:22—This is a great rule of thumb if we're not sure if a dancing situation is acceptable.

"Avoid every kind of evil." If it even looks like it could be sinful, don't do it.

In the end, there is a lot of dancing that is inappropriate for believers who should be seeking to glorify God with their lives and especially with their bodies. Yet the Bible acknowledges that we can dance in a way that does not tempt others, does not tempt ourselves, and brings glory to God.

Scripture commands that we worship God, that we exalt His name and offer Him our praise. There is biblical precedent for both the lifting of hands and the clapping of hands as an act of worship. Psalms 47:1 says, "Clap your hands, all you nations; shout to God with cries of joy." In this instance, both clapping and shouting out joyful worship to God are urged.

Clapping is not sinful…

Consider reading the following articles at GotQuestions.org to further explain this topic:

Should a Christian listen to secular music?

http://www.gotquestions.org/secular-music.html

What does the Bible say about dancing? Should Christians dance?

http://www.gotquestions.org/Christian-dance.html

Should we raise our hands/clap our hands during worship?

http://www.gotquestions.org/worship-hands.html

Question: 64

But in Luke 19, could we not infer that Zacchaeus left his profession? Shouldn't we take Jesus' words priority over the words of John the Baptist?

Profile: Male Under 18 North America

Answer: Thanks for writing GotQuestions.org again seeking follow up to your previous question.

Friend, it is always a good practice to read the bible in context and not add to what is being conveyed. The bible showed how Zacchaeus became a changed man through his encounter with Jesus. He made restitution fourfold to all those he had cheated even though levitical law only required full restitution plus a twenty percent penalty (Leviticus 6:1-5).

Scripture does not say that Zacchaeus left his profession but indicated that he changed how he practiced it. While acting in the role as a tax collector he paid back the people.

Yes, we must always put priority in the words of Jesus over anyone but in this instance there is no disagreement. John was trying to get the tax collectors to do the right thing. Zacchaeus encounter with Jesus led to Zacchaeus doing the right thing. The same objective was being pursued by John the Baptist and Jesus.

God bless you and your study of His word.

Question: 65

Speaking with an Atheist they feel that the Old Testament law is eternal. I pointed to them that there are many verses that says Jesus ended the law, but they won't accept the New Testament and feel Jesus undermined the law and did not fulfill the law, and that Paul's teaching about the law contradicts the Old Testament. The atheist question was that he might believe if there are any foreshadowing's in the Old Testament or prophecy that Jesus would end the law? Are there such verses?

Profile: Male 18-30 North America

Answer: Thanks for writing to GotQuestions.org. In discussing any scripture with anyone we must always prepare ourselves as you are doing.

Let us look at what the word of God has to say regarding the law.

This assumption of the Atheist is grounded in a misunderstanding of the words and intent of some passages. Christ did not suggest here that the binding nature of the law of Moses would remain forever in effect. Such a view would contradict everything we learn from the balance of the New Testament (Romans 10:4; Galatians 3:23-25; Ephesians 2:15).

In the book of Matthew it clearly mentions that Jesus did not come to get rid of the law. He came to fulfill them. In doing so Jesus did not undermine the law. Paul's teaching did not contradict the Old Testament. See the following scriptures to support this:

Matthew 5:17

Matthew 5:17 English Standard Version (©2001)

"Do not think that I have come to abolish the Law or the Prophets; I have not come to abolish them but to fulfill them.

Jesus revered the law, loved it, obeyed it, and brought it to fruition. He fulfilled the law's prophetic utterances regarding Himself (Luke 24:44). Christ fulfilled the demands of the Mosaic Law, which called for perfect obedience under threat of a "curse" (see Galatians 3:10, 13). In this sense, the law's divine design will ever have an abiding effect. It will always accomplish the purpose for which it was given.

Note: Paul mentions in Romans that they were upholding the law...

Romans 3:31 Do we, then, nullify the law by this faith? Not at all! Rather, we uphold the law.

I see no contradictions...

As for foreshadowing in the Old Testament or prophecy that Jesus would end the law, the only information in the bible that I could find is that sacrificing animals as a blood sacrifice for sins could never make perfect those who draw near. It is impossible for the blood of goats and bulls to take away sin. It was leading to the one who can take away their sins...

The Law was a foreshadow of things to come...

The following scripture compares the Law's requirement of blood sacrifice of animals to the final and once for all blood sacrifice of God's Sacrificial Lamb - Christ Jesus. Only through the blood of Jesus can we know we are forgiven by God!

Hebrews 10:1-4 (English Standard Version)

Christ's Sacrifice Once for All:

10 For since the law has but a shadow of the good things to come instead of the true form of these realities, it can never, by the same sacrifices that are continually offered every year, make perfect those who draw
near. 2 Otherwise, would they not have ceased to be offered, since the worshipers, having once been cleansed, would no longer have any
consciousness of sins? 3 But in these sacrifices there is a reminder of

sins every year. [4] For it is impossible for the blood of bulls and goats to take away sins.

So it pointed to a better way. A change… Fulfillment of prophesy… Jesus Christ!

An exposition of Romans 10:4; which says: "Christ is the end of the law so that there may be righteousness for everyone who believes," will help in understanding what is means that Christians are not under the law. The apostle Paul clarifies the effects of original sin in Romans 2:12; stating "All who sin apart from the law will perish apart from the law, and all who sin under the law will be judged by the law." All men stand condemned before God, whether they are Jews or not, or to put it another way, whether they have the Law of God or not. Paul also states "For all have sinned and fall short of the glory of God" (Romans 3:23).

If we are without Christ, we are justly condemned in God's sight by the Law that was given to His servant Moses.

Christians are under the New Covenant. Note: A few of the Old Testament laws are ratified in the new covenant and some are not.

The moral laws continue, for they are reaffirmed in the New Testament. (ie... you shall not kill, you shall not commit adultery, no lying or stealing).

Romans 3:19-20 English Standard Version (ESV)

[19] Now we know that whatever the law says it speaks to those who are under the law, so that every mouth may be stopped, and the whole world may be held accountable to God. [20] For by works of the law no human being will be justified in his sight, since through the law comes knowledge of sin.

Let me put it a different way. The law shows us how sinful we really are. These laws are violated daily all over the earth…

Once a person becomes saved through faith in Jesus Christ, a lot changes… The person becomes a new creation filled with the Holy Spirit. Desiring to follow God and live by His word. He is under the New Covenant.

Romans 7:4-6 English Standard Version (ESV)

4 Likewise, my brothers, you also have died to the law through the body of Christ, so that you may belong to another, to him who has been raised from the dead, in order that we may bear fruit for God. 5 For while we were living in the flesh, our sinful passions, aroused by the law, were at work in our members to bear fruit for death. 6 But now we are released from the law, having died to that which held us captive, so that we serve in the new way of the Spirit and not in the old way of the written code.

Romans 8:1 English Standard Version (ESV) - Life in the Spirit -

There is therefore now no condemnation for those who are in Christ Jesus.

So, again, moral laws continue from the law but a saved individual has hope in the saving work of Jesus Christ.

Jesus fulfilled all aspects of the law…

Christ became the end of the Law by virtue of what He did on earth through His sinless life and His sacrifice on the cross. So, the Law no longer has any bearing over us because its demands have been fully met in the Lord Jesus Christ. Faith in Christ who satisfied the righteous demands of the Law restores us into a pleasing relationship with God and keeps us there. No longer under the penalty of the Law, we now live under the law of grace in the love of God.

Please spend time reading all of the following links to learn more about the law. These articles will go into more details. We have a lot of excellent information that will guide you in this very important topic.

What does it mean that Jesus fulfilled the law, but did not abolish it?

http://www.gotquestions.org/abolish-fulfill-law.html

Do Christians have to obey the Old Testament law?

http://www.gotquestions.org/Christian-law.html

What does it mean that Christians are not under the law?

http://www.gotquestions.org/not-under-the-law.html

Does God require Sabbath-keeping of Christians?

http://www.gotquestions.org/Sabbath-keeping.html

What is the curse of the law?

http://www.gotquestions.org/curse-of-the-law.html

There is also an article at letusreason.org that can be of help as well:

Do Not Think That I Came to Destroy the Law but to Fulfill it.

http://www.letusreason.org/7thAd26.htm

Question: 66

Why couldn't the Holy Spirit come before Jesus returned to heaven?

Profile: Female Over 60 North America

Answer: First, let's answer this from a big picture point of view... The Holy Spirit did come to the earth before Jesus returned to heaven. In Genesis 1:2 speaks of the Spirit of God hovering over the face of the waters. Also, the Holy Spirit also came upon some in the Old Testament at special times and then would leave. The Holy Spirit's ministry through individuals in the Old Testament was not the same as it was from the Day of Pentecost onwards. In the Old Testament He 'came upon' a few notable characters for particular reasons. Neither did He remain with those individuals throughout their lives. Just before His ascension into Heaven, the Lord Jesus Christ promised that the coming Holy Spirit would abide permanently with His followers. We speak of Old Testament characters being blessed by the Holy Spirit 'coming upon' them, this is very different from being 'baptized with (or in) the Spirit. He moved upon them, guiding, directing and encouraging for a specific purpose. For example, the story of Gideon illustrates the fact that the Holy Spirit came upon certain people to give wisdom or strength (Judges 6-7). It appears that He ministered through national leaders such as Moses, Joshua, Samuel, and the judges and kings, and the prophets. There are many other characters such as David, Ezekiel and Daniel that were dynamically used by the Spirit of God.

Let me offer another time the Holy Spirit arrived before Jesus returned to heaven. This was when Jesus was conceived by the Holy Spirit (Luke 1:35 ESV).

35 And the angel answered her, "The Holy Spirit will come upon you, and the power of the Most High will overshadow you; therefore the child to be born will be called holy—the Son of God.

There are different roles in the Trinity. The Father points to the Son, Jesus points to the Father, the Holy Spirit points the way to Jesus.

God is a God of order. He ordered the steps needed to redeem mankind. The Holy Spirit was to dwell with believers thus fulfilling the verse that says I will never leave you nor forsake you. Once baptized, believers are sealed with the Holy Spirit who then dwells in them.

After Jesus ascension the Holy Spirit was going to play a big part in pointing the way for people to be saved.

In John 16:8-11 speaks of The Holy Spirit will convict the world.

Jesus is the One who baptizes with the Holy Spirit, and the disciples had to wait in Jerusalem until He sent the Spirit from heaven. (John 1:26, 33-34).

In the text, Jesus gives us three reasons the Holy Spirit coming to the world is a good thing.

First, Jesus says that the Holy Spirit will be God's instrument of salvation by convicting people of their sin. We usually talk about the work of the Holy Spirit in the life of people who are already Christians. But the first work of the Holy Spirit is actually in the lives of unbelievers, people who have yet to place their faith in Jesus as their Savior.

To convict the world of sin simply means God, through the work of the Holy Spirit, will move in peoples' hearts and minds to convince them that they are sinners in need of a Savior.

Let's look at 2 more points:

1. **The necessity of Jesus' departure**

Jesus told the apostles in John 16:7, "It is expedient for you that I go away; for if I go not away, the Comforter will not come unto you; but if I depart, I will send him unto you." The Spirit couldn't be sent until

Christ returned to heaven. The disciples had to wait ten days between the ascension and the day they received the Spirit, the day of Pentecost (Acts 2:1). Pentecost is Greek for "the fiftieth day." It was when the Jewish people celebrated the Feast of harvest, and fell on the fiftieth day after the Feast of Passover. It also refers to the fifty-day period between Christ's resurrection and the sending of the Spirit.

2. **The necessity of the Spirit's arrival**

Since the apostles had to wait to receive the Holy Spirit before they could do the Lord's work, it shows us that it's impossible to carry on His work in our own power. You can make elaborate plans for ministry and give eloquent sermons, but without the Spirit's power, your work will be fruitless. The apostles themselves knew they needed the Spirit's power. When Christ first commissioned them to spread the gospel, He said, "It is not ye that speak, but the Spirit of your Father who speaketh in you" (Matt. 10:20). In Luke 12:12 the apostles were told there would come a day when the Spirit would speak through them. John 14:17 says that the Holy Spirit was already with the disciples, but that later on He would be in them. (Prior to the sending of the Spirit in Acts 2, people weren't indwelt by the Holy Spirit. Instead, God sent the Spirit on specific occasions to do a special work through someone as I mentioned above. For example, the Holy Spirit descended on King Saul [1 Sam. 11:6] and departed from him [1 Sam. 16:14]).

In conclusion, scripture does not explicitly say why the Holy Spirit could not come in the role He fulfilled post ascension before Jesus returned to heaven. So we can not be dogmatic about it. Please consider this: There was no need for the Holy Spirit to come in this capacity for the people had the law and the prophets who pointed the way to the coming Messiah. Once the Messiah arrived the next phase in the process was needed. It simply must not have been God's will to send His Spirit in the role needed post ascension.

Question: 67

How do I respond to an email from a dear Mormon friend that promotes Mormonism?

Profile: Male Over 60 North America

Answer: The first thing I would recommend is studying the many articles about Mormonism at the following GotQuestions.org website:

http://www.gotquestions.org/search.php?zoom_sort=0&zoom_query=witnessing+to+a+mormon

There is so much wrong with this religion that it would be best to read all of the articles and then pray. Ask God to open up your friend's heart to read some of the Mormon articles that are posted. You decide which links to send him.

What your friend has to realize is that he should not be blinded by the good works they are doing. People who are not involved in organized religion also do good things for the poor, etc… Our works will not get us into the kingdom… Bottom line, we are all filthy rags to a just and Holy God. Without accepting the true deity of God which includes Jesus, who is not the spirit brother of Lucifer; he is not saved but lost. What Jesus do they accept as their savior? It is not the same by Christian definitions…

Check out the following article:

http://www.equip.org/articles/is-jesus-christ-the-spirit-brother-of-satan-

He also made the statement that they must be doing something right since the quantity of Mormon ward increased over the years. Friend, one cannot say because there are more Mormons now, so that constitutes truth. Many people will believe a lie and increase in numbers. Look at all the people who were yelling crucify him (against Jesus)... Look at the many people caught up in the word of faith movement... This is false teaching and has hooked many...

Focus on what the Mormon core beliefs are and how it compares to our bible. Some suggestions:

Go to the following URL's to listen to or download MP3 files regarding this crucial topic. You might want to send them to your friend. The texts are also located here:

I am a Mormon. Why should I consider becoming a Christian?

http://www.gotquestions.org/Mormon-Christian.html

What is Mormonism? What do Mormons believe?

http://www.gotquestions.org/Mormons.html

Read these articles too:

Who was Joseph Smith?

http://www.gotquestions.org/Joseph-Smith.html

What is Mormonism? What do Mormons believe? http://www.gotquestions.org/Mormons.html

Mormonism is a cult and is not Christian. Be mindful that if your friend is closed to open dialogue regarding this religion, no matter what you present he will not accept it.

Let's pray that God will be able to get his attention to the truth of His word, recorded in the bible, so that he will reject the Mormon teachings...

Question: 68

A Pagans Rant I (trouble believing...)

I'm the Pagan with Faith & Hope & Love. I do have questions that I could use your help on. My basic understanding into the many paradoxes within the bible has led me to believe something is missing... The truth has been white-washed, tainted by corruption, for some to have control over others.

I do believe in Jesus". But I strongly feel his teachings have been corrupted. I'm looking for 'Truth'!

Answer: Please let me start by saying do not believe the lie that Satan have been telling people for years.

As you have indicated that you are a Pagan, know that being a Pagan is a serious matter when it comes to your eternity. You matter to us so please continue to have an open dialog with us for you matter to God.

The truth is in scripture. The Bible was protected by God for many years. Please tell me what corruptions you are referring to. From the time God told Moses to write in a book and store it in the Tabernacle the Lord has guided and watched over His word as He instructed the additional writers.

God is a God of order. Order is found in scripture.

There has been and will continue to be people who will twist scripture for various reasons including manipulating others into believing their way...

This behavior is not only with the bible but with any book. Ask God to open your heart, open your eyes, and open your mind to receive His truth about the bible and about Christianity.

Question: 69

A Pagans Rant II (trouble believing...)

I'll start our dialogue by stating, "I do believe in Jesus". But I strongly feel his teachings have been corrupted.

I'm looking for 'Truth'! I do not believe all that I see or hear or read anymore; no more lies, partial truthfulness, or dishonesty. And like anyone, I turned to the bible...But I needed more. I don't sense the peaceful outlook I once felt.

To me, Religion has to do with Gods and Devils, because certain beliefs tell mankind his place in relation to the world. You know, like turning us into cowards and not letting us be our own moral heroes.

"The Devil Preaching, Hell Scaring System", you're scared straight into Heaven. It's a very wise policy to frighten and control men into seeing a devil, where there is none. It's the fear of this Devil and of endless punishment that converts people, not the Love of God.

Jewish (Hebrew/Israelite) history shows no conception of a devil or of a place called Hell, in the Old Testament, as being provided or prepared for the wicked. The Book of Job may even be inappropriately translated; not to mention the fact, how does one know what was said between God and Satan in heavenly places anyway.

Answer: First, it sounds like one issue is with your understanding of divine inspiration, God's protection of His word, and the Holy Spirit's influence in the communication of His word.

First, I want to address the fact that there are false religions, false teachers out there preaching a false doctrine confusing and misleading many.

There are also very fine Christian Churches honoring God and teaching proper doctrine.

Sir, as I have been doing ministry for a while, I have noticed that people are getting saved not just by the fear of hell as you have mentioned but also for the love that they saw in God. Yes, God's love shown in their circumstances and in their lives. In human make up, there are various motivations that get people's attention. Some require the hard hitting approach to get their attention so there are Pastors who take this approach, and there are those who do not require this approach.

The nature of biblical inspiration: The bible claims to be the word of God, a message with divine authority. The bible writers say they were moved by the Holy Spirit to utter His very words – the message came by revelation so that what they wrote was breathed out (Inspired) by God Himself. The scriptures confirm what the writers claimed. 2 Peter 1:20-21 2, Timothy 3:16 etc…

Over the course of History God has protected His word from those who tried to discredit it and take it out of circulation by destroying as many bibles as they could get to. Last time I checked, the bible is on the best seller list. Recall that Jesus went so far as to declare that even parts of letters are inspired: "I tell you the truth, until heaven and earth disappear, not the smallest letter, not the least stroke of a pen, will by any means disappear from the Law until everything is accomplished" (Matt 5:18).

God established laws for our benefit. His word provides rules to live by. Jesus has confirmed this by not coming to get rid of the law (His word) but to uphold it. The Fulfillment of the Law 17"Do not think that I have come to abolish the Law or the Prophets; I have not come to abolish them but to fulfill them (Matthew 5:17-20).

Note: A lawless world would be hell to live in... In history, some have twisted what the bible was actually saying to promote their evil ways... (KKK, Prosperity Gospel etc...). We have to beware of them...

Teaching regarding Hell

The Old Testament teaches life after death, and that all people went to a place of conscious existence called Sheol. The wicked were there (Psalm 9:17; 31:17; 49:14; Isaiah 5:14), and so were the righteous (Genesis 37:35; Job 14:13; Psalm 6:5; 16:10; 88:3; Isaiah 38:10).

The New Testament equivalent of Sheol is Hades. Prior to Christ's resurrection, Luke 16:19-31 shows Hades to be divided into two realms: a place of comfort where Lazarus was and a place of torment where the rich man was. The word hell in verse 23 is not "Gehenna" (place of eternal torment) but "Hades" (place of the dead). Lazarus's place of comfort is elsewhere called Paradise (Luke 23:43). Between these two districts of Hades is "a great gulf fixed" (Luke 16:26).

Jesus is described as having descended into Hades after His death. (Acts 2:27, 31; cf. Ephesians 4:9). At the resurrection of Jesus Christ, it seems that the believers in Hades (i.e., the occupants of Paradise) were moved to another location. Now, Paradise is above rather than below (2 Corinthians 12:2-4).

Today, when a believer dies, he is "present with the Lord" (2 Corinthians 5:6-9). When an unbeliever dies, he follows the Old Testament unbelievers to Hades. At the final judgment, Hades will be emptied before the Great White Throne, where its occupants will be judged prior to entering the lake of fire (Revelation 20:13-15).

Scripture does not tell us the geological (or cosmological) location of hell. Hell is a literal place of real torment, but we do not know where it is. Hell may have a physical location in this universe, or it may be in an entirely different "dimension." Whatever the case, the location of hell is far less important than the need to avoid going there.

Is the devil real?

All evil happening in the world is the result of the evil Satan introduced to humans and the devil is still at work as a roaring lion traveling the earth with his demons tempting people. Confusing them, blinding them of things of God etc…

Scripture mentioned the devil in Genesis and other places in the bible.

Question: "Is the devil / Satan a person or a force / personification of evil?"

Answer: Although he has persuaded many people that he doesn't even exist, Satan definitely is a real, personal being, the fountainhead of all unbelief and of every kind of moral and spiritual evil in the world. He is called by various names in the Bible, including Satan (meaning, "adversary"—Job 1:6; Romans 16:20; etc.), the devil (i.e., "slanderer"—Matthew 4:1; 1 Peter 5:8; etc.), Lucifer (Isaiah 14:12), the serpent (2 Corinthians 11:3; Revelation 12:9; etc.), and many others.

To the Christian, the existence of Satan as a real person is proven by the fact that the Lord Jesus Christ recognized him as such. He referred to him frequently by name (e.g., Luke 10:18; Matthew 4:10; etc.) and indeed called him "the prince of this world" (John 12:31; 14:30; 16:11).

The Apostle Paul called him the "god of this world" (2 Corinthians 4:4) and the "prince of the power of the air" (Ephesians 2:2). The Apostle John said, "The whole world is under the control of the evil one" (1 John 5:19) and that he is the one "that leads the whole world astray" (Revelation 12:9). These could hardly be the descriptions of a force or a mere personification of evil.

The Scriptures teach that, before man and the world were created, God had created an "innumerable company of angels" (Hebrews 12:22), a heavenly host of spiritual beings, of great strength and intelligence. The highest of these beings are the cherubim, who are attendants at the very throne of God, and the "anointed cherub" at that throne was originally

Satan himself (Ezekiel 28:14). He was "full of wisdom and perfect in beauty."

God did not create Satan as an evil being, however. The angels, like man, were created as free spirits, not as unthinking machines. They were fully able to reject God's will and rebel against His authority if they should chose to do so.

The root of all sin, in both man and angels, is the twin sin of unbelief and pride—the refusal to submit to God's will as revealed by His own Word and the accompanying assertion of self-sufficiency which enthrones the creature and his own will in the place of God. This was the original sin of Satan, rejecting God's Word and trying to become God himself. He said in his heart, "I will ascend into heaven, I will exalt my throne above the stars of God . . . I will be like the most High" (Isaiah 14:13, 14). Again, these could hardly be the actions or motivations of an impersonal force.

Jesus also told us of some of the characteristics of Satan. Christ said he was a murderer from the beginning, not holding to the truth, for there is no truth in him, and that when he speaks he lies, he speaks his native language, for he is a liar and the father of lies (John 8:44).

It is crucial that Christians recognize the reality of Satan in this world and understand that he prowls around like a roaring lion looking for someone to devour (1 Peter 5:8). It is impossible to overcome sin and temptation from the devil by ourselves, but Scripture tells us how to be strong. We need to put on the full armor of God daily to be able to stand our ground against temptation (Ephesians 6:13) from the very personal being, Satan.

In the Old Testament of the Bible, The Book of Job origin range from 1500 B.C. to 600 B.C., and the author is unknown, but it is assumed that the story of Job takes place sometime between Noah and Moses, and it is considered one of the earliest books of the Old Testament.

The author of the Bible book of Job is not fully known but traditionally we think it was written by Moses. Read the following to begin to see why this is a possibility:

If Job was the son of Issachar (Gen 46:13), then we have a clue that may help us with this.

And the sons of Issachar; Tola, and Phuvah, and Job, and Shimron.

Gen 46:13.

It is better to keep within the Bible itself for the settlement of its problems; and to treat the whole Book as the context of all its parts.

There is no reason why Job should not be the son of Issachar, and no better evidence is forthcoming for a different view.

The three friends of Job were descendants of Esau; they would therefore be contemporaries. Eliphaz of Teman, in Idumea, was a son of Esau, and had a son called Teman, from whom his country took its name (Gen 36:10-11). The country was noted for its "wise men" (Jer 49:7); and is mentioned with Edom (Amos 1:11-12). Compare (Jer 25:23) where both are connected with Buz, the brother of Uz (Gen 22:21).

Bildad the Shuhite. Shuah was the sixth son of Abraham by Keturah (Gen 25:2); and is mentioned in connection with Esau, Edom, and Teman (Jer 49:8). Zophar the Naarnathite. Naamah (now *Na'aneh*, six miles south of Lod, in the lowlands of Judah).

If Job was the son of Issachar (Gen 46:13), he would have gone down to Egypt with his father. Issachar was forty at "the going down to Egypt ". (See Appendix 50, III, p. 52 Companion Bible).

If Job was the third son (Gen 46:13), he would have been about twenty at that time (1706 BC).

We are told that he lived 140 years after his "double" blessing (Job 42:10). If that "double" blessing included length of years, then his age would have been 70 + 140 = 210 (i.e. three seventies of years). His lifetime would be from 1726-1516 BC.

According to this, he was born the year after Joseph was sold, and died 119 years after the death of Joseph (in 1635 BC). When Joseph died, Job was ninety-one. If his "double" blessing did include length of years, then his affliction took place twenty-one years previously, when he was seventy. His removal from Egypt to Uz must therefore have taken place earlier still.

When Job died (1516 BC) Moses was fifty-five, and had been in Midian fifteen years (twenty-five years before the Exodus).

This would account for Job being a worshipper of the God of Abraham, and explains how Moses could have been the author of the book, and perhaps an eye- and ear-witness of the events it records in Midian.

We believe in the inspired word of God and that God provided the information on what happened with the conversation with Satan to one of his prophets (Job and Moses).

I hope this was not too much information but in order to try to answer your inquiry much information was required.

Question: 70

A Pagans Rant III (trouble believing...)

Do I comprehend you and your point of view properly? You are advising and instructing me to: read and believe-in one of the most bigoted, racist and gender-bias books ever published. This book was written for only one group of people and all the other people were to be wiped out, killed or destroyed. From, the pen on the paper, Moses told of the history of Adam and Abram and the written word continued with the start of the ministry of Jesus, because even he stated that he came to help one group of people and save the lost tribe of Hebrews, an example being the story of the woman at the well, by the way her name was Photini. Are these facts written down in the book=YES! So please, "No-Let-me-translate-another-verse", okay. The book does contain inspiring words from truly inspirational people. A Catholic Nun, states the book should be taken as an inspirational motivator for proper civil conduct. She also says "I'm Bad" because my thinking challenges the order of things. I hate simple solutions for simple minds. The Greek Poet Virgil, 60 B.C, wrote a poem that some scholars say the Book of Revelation's is a common copy of the lyricist visions of Hades and includes other Greek Myths.

Now, a news highlight, the fastest growing population in the world is the Muslim Culture and it's estimated that the Religion of Islam will control Europe and the African Continent within our lifetime.... That's so nice, a one world religion.

Answer: This email will be tough to read for I felt it needed to be said at this point in our communication. Please know that it is being written from someone who sincerely wants to help you in understanding the truth.

It is good that you are trying to get information but I feel you are really not interested in the truth and you have already made your mind up as your responses are indicating. You matter to us so we continue to bring the truth of Christ to you. Are you really interested in the truth?

The bible is not the most bigoted, racist and gender-bias book that was ever published as you have strongly mentioned! If the passages are read in context it is clear what was being communicated and why. You cannot have people living wickedly, going against what God has communicated, without punishment being enacted by a Just and Holy God. This is the God that Christians are following.

I do not understand why there is so much venom against the Christian faith. You have Christianity and the Bible all wrong. It is unfortunate that you have become so blinded by the evil one that you see the wrong belief system as truth. Jesus came to seek and save the lost. He came to make himself available for all in the world who will accept Him as their savior. Whoever will believe in Him will have eternal life.

The source where you are getting your information against the Bible and Christianity is not accurate. Sir, why do you hold so strongly to them? I think you really need to spend your time and energy challenging what you currently believe and the people who are writing these incredibly inaccurate data. Be highly critical and dogmatic with this challenge and you may see the falseness in the Pagan and false belief system.

Why on earth would you be happy with Islam becoming the one world religion is besides me... Strange how you are rooting for a cult religion (Islam) that is not based in the truth but you totally disregard the message of hope in the bible. Read the following information to get educated on Islam:

Islam is certainly supported by some inconvenient truths that our culture seems determined to ignore:

- Devout Muslims have a sacred responsibility, according to the command of Allah through his prophet Muhammad, to "slay the idolaters wherever you find them (Sura 9:5)." Over 100 verses in the Koran call for the death of infidel Christians and Jews. We have seen the tragic fruit of this ideology both on 9/11 and at Fort Hood. Islam is not, in fact, a religion of peace but of violence, death and war.

- Islam, through the example of Muhammad, sanctions the marriage of girls who are but children. Muhammad himself began having sex with his youngest wife Aisha when she was just nine years old (Bukhari, Vol. 8). In year 2010 a 12-year-old girl in Saudi Arabia went to court to divorce her 80-year-old husband. In the West, these are acts of pedophilia and utterly at odds with the Christian principle that the sexual purity of young females is to be protected until they are mature enough to voluntarily and freely enter into marriage.
- Christians are granted only second class status under Islam, and are given only three choices where Islam reigns: conversion, submission or death. Conversion from Islam to Christianity remains a capital offense in many Muslim countries. In supposedly free Egypt, Coptic Christians are even today routinely harassed, persecuted and killed by Islamic fundamentalists. Freedom of religion, a profoundly American value, is utterly absent in Islam. Further, this practice is directly at variance with the fundamental concept in American jurisprudence that we are all, everyone of us, equal under the law.
- Women under the iron fist of Islam are given "horrid" treatment. In many Islamic countries, women are not allowed to receive an education or even show their faces in public. Husbands are taught in the Koran that they may literally beat their wives into submission, completely contrary to the Christian admonition that husbands are to "love their wives as Christ loved the church." The blatant and deadly sexism in Islam is contrary to the fundamental Christian precept that men and women are full equals before the true God in spiritual worth, value and significance.
- The practice of honor killings is widespread in the Islamic world. According to the U.N., over 5,000 women a year are brutally murdered under the flag of Islam, in many cases because they

> have brought "dishonor" to their families by becoming the tragic victims of rape. The "horrid" practice of honor killings sadly has come to the U.S. A Muslim husband decapitated his wife in New York, while a Muslim father in Texas shot his two teenage daughters to death in the back of a taxi cab and another Muslim father in Arizona ran his daughter down with the family SUV. The crime in the latter two cases was that their daughters had become too "Westernized." This practice is utterly at odds with the Christian teaching that fathers are to nurture and protect their children.

I will pray for your heart to change towards hearing the truth. Until then, you are already set strongly in your position on what you believe. No matter what I offer, you will counter it with your strong beliefs. There are many problems with your views on scripture and your lean towards the pagan religion.

Do you own a bible or are you just listening to other pagan leaders and reading false doctrine? I challenge you to pray to the Christian God asking Him to reveal Himself to you in ways that you can understand. Then pray to Him as you read the bible from the beginning to the end with your heart being open to what is being communicated. Check your prejudices and hate for the bible at the door each time you read the bible. I guarantee that it will change your life. Are you up for the challenge?

Jesus is God. The bible is God's word. To not trust in His word is a serious matter. No other person in history measures up to Jesus. Mohammed, Buddha etc… cannot measure up to Jesus. Jesus never sinned and He conquered the grave!

Continue your research but eventually you must choose who you will follow…Satan and his lies or God.

You cannot serve two masters. Please make the right choice. Choose Jesus and read the book that God gave to mankind, the Holy bible.

Question: 71

A Pagans Rant IV (trouble believing...)

They say, the ultimate vision within Christianity is a Judgment Day, our final purpose; an eagerly awaited day of reckoning with the impending slaughter of the multitude; while hopefully we're elected, among the chosen few, to be rapturously delivered unto heaven, only to look back at the many others screaming from a lake of fire for all eternity.

What kind of radical people are these redeemed soldiers of Christ; lovers of mercy and forgiveness, faithful humanistic reformers to the 'Divine Spirit of God'. What a vision of an after-life to look forward too, to watch other people suffer. I'd be suffering too, just looking at them. I feel some reason to believe that we have missed an important clue in our system of "Savior Enlightenment"....

I think of 'Religion' as a living-force in society that does produce humanities greatest horrors; "A Golden Age of Holy Slaughter"; where violence and repression are claimed as a 'Divine Mandate' to massacre rival denominations, like performing an act of moral cleansing in God's name. The devotees of Christianity and Islam have been butchering each other for countless centuries. Protestants and Catholics, Jew and Muslims have a long history of violent bloodletting murder.

We base our faith in a process called: 'Selective Perception', with intercession by a supernatural force. I disapprove of those who pretend to discern 'God's Holy Wisdom', as teaching us a lesson; God's divine intervention in all natural disasters, moving unseen in mysteriously wondrous ways and all beyond our puny comprehension. We have the habit of treating fortunate human outcomes as proof of God's direct love; being faithful to support

and confirm our religion by our successes or our happy outcomes. I believe people are turning to God only in their time of greed. They say God will tend to our monetary needs; if we can only believe with unquestioning faith.

When it comes to marketing, no commodity can compare to that of religion. Religious promoters dish-up, dangle and sell not only God, but godly artifacts that promise you the world. They promise you everything in the next life too. Even missionaries impose their competitiveness and selfish value systems of global industrial capitalism in their efforts to convert. The message most God-peddlers use is based on a prosperity gospel or prosperity theology, calling upon divine promises for material acquisition. Self-appointed Holy hucksters, who are speaking on God's behalf, offer a sure ticket to paradise to spend an afterlife romping joyfully with angels. God is now a product with no guarantee, no warranty and no refund, because if the customer is disappointed they can only blame themselves for having such little faith. Organized religion, too often, serves as a demonic tool by using armed force and state power to acquire other denominations and gather their wealth unto themselves.

If any religion allows one form of persecution, any type of slavery, mental or physical, or keeps people in ignorance with sexual and emotional abuse for material exploitation; I can not accept that religion.

I want to entertain every belief openly and any disbeliefs with total impunity. Ideas do affect our history by defining our reality and inspiring social action. Most of the people I know turn to Religion for solace and inner peace. Some seek to expand their consciousness and obtain the promised protections against the terrors of life. We're searching for a haven in a cruel and heartless world. We want to pursue the 'Hopefulness' in which the better angels of our human natures shall prevail and track down God's demons and finally put them to rest. You might think I'm not saved, you're wrong. I want

people to know the truth about why they're not saved, when they really think they are.

Answer: The vision within Christianity as you state is based on the response of choices. One chooses to be or not to be a Christian. Everyone is given the choice at some time in their life, and those who are not capable of making a choice, God looks at the heart. Where is your heart?

Everyone responds to a consequence of our own or of some one else's choices. If someone chooses to do a terrible thing, they must pay the consequence.

You state we base our faith on selective perception. Yes, we base our faith on God's perception, because man does not know what is best without direction/intervention from God. God has been trying to teach us from the beginning of time. Our problem is that we don't listen or follow his teachings much of the time. Through God's grace, He doesn't give up on trying to teach us. Through God's grace, we don't receive all the consequences that we deserve. When we realize how much of God's grace we receive, we respond in love by wanting to share what we have received. If there are those who don't want to hear about God's grace, we pray for them and go to others who are looking for peace in their lives. Some people like being where they are.

People are a work in progress. There are so many areas that people need to work on to be the people God wants them to be. That's why we look to God and the word of God for guidance. Any time there is something that one hears, it should match up with the Bible as the person asks God to reveal to him/her.

If you look in the Bible, you will see that it states that not all who call upon the Lord are believers in Christ and his teachings. There are false teachers. There are true teachers of the Bible. If you focus on man, you will be disappointed. If you trust in God, you will be strengthened.

The reference in the Bible to slavery is like our modern work environment. Our master is our boss, our supervisor. References to discipline are not to lead to physical or emotional abuse, although there are people who will use this to their advantage. This is due to man's sinful heart, not God's guidance. Christ followers who truly follow Christ would not want any of these situations to happen.

Have you seen people with peace? Some people have peace. One cannot expand consciousness and obtain protection because we are not God who controls the world. People who are Christ followers in persecuted countries don't have a haven, but they have peace. No, we don't want to track down God's demons and finally put them to rest. That is what the Lord will do. We have the hope that whatever happens, God gives us peace until He returns, individually or in a group.

You may be seeing that some people are not saved, but some are.

You want to entertain every belief. This is your choice. Entertaining every belief means no commitment to any belief. This is also your choice. Choose wisely whom you will serve. If you make no decision on any particular belief, you have made a choice.

We pray that you see who God is in your situation.

Question: 72

Should we imitate the widow in Mark 12:41-44 when it comes to giving, and should we imitate Stephen when it comes to being bold?

Profile: Male 18-30 Asia

Answer: Thanks you for writing! Answer is yes to both of your questions.

The scripture verses you are referring to is Mark 12:41-44 and Acts 6:1-8:3 (ESV).

The Widow's Offering

41 And he sat down opposite the treasury and watched the people putting money into the offering box. Many rich people put in large sums. 42 And a poor widow came and put in two small copper coins, which make a penny. 43 And he called his disciples to him and said to them, "Truly, I say to you, this poor widow has put in more than all those who are contributing to the offering box. 44 For they all contributed out of their abundance, but she out of her poverty has put in everything she had, all she had to live on."

In imitating the widow it is her heart that we should all seek to imitate. She saw the value in investing in the kingdom to the point that she gave all she had. She demonstrated a certain level of faith not seen to often. She must have believed that our God shall supply all of our needs.

We should give all we can to the kingdom building efforts. Not just money but our time, and talents... Let me also say that giving is not always tied to money. We should give our time, talents and use our spiritual gifts to the kingdom building efforts out of full love for the LORD. Charity need not always be in the form of money or what we would consider a typically "charitable" act. When Peter and John met a crippled beggar, rather than give the man coins, Peter said, "Silver or gold I do not have, but what I have I give you. In the name of Jesus Christ of Nazareth, walk" (Acts 3:6). Charity is giving of whatever resources we have in order to meet the need of another.

Steven is a wonderful example of being bold. This is not always an easy thing to accomplish. It can come with persecution, ridicule etc…

You can read more about Stephen's Boldness in Acts 6:1-8:3.

Stephen was one of the seven leaders that were chosen to guarantee fairness. He was known as one with spiritual qualities of grace, faith, wisdom, and power because of the presence of the Holy Spirit in his life. Stephen was an outstanding leader, teacher and a great debater…You need to read his message in chapter seven delivered in his own defense. He was an orator. And he was the first member of the early church that gave his life as a martyr.

Question: 73

Question concerning tithing when spouse does not agree

My wife and I are fairly new Christians and my question is concerning tithing. I recently accepted a new position and my wages increased. I spoke with my wife and told her that I wanted to increase my donations to the church to 10% of my new wages, I understand that 10% is old law and we are not required to follow but I have always felt that 10% was a good baseline. Anyway, when I spoke to my wife about this she exploded and said that I was being irresponsible and not thinking of my family's needs. This happened about a month ago and since that time she has refused to speak to me. I fear that this issue may result in our divorce if I were to move forward and up my donations to 10%. I don't want a divorce but I feel that I am being greedy by not donating at least 10%. So do I keep my promise to God to love, honor and obey my wife or do I honor God by giving at least 10% of my income? Thank you

Answer: Hello Sir. It is good that you have a heart to give to the kingdom of God. Never lose that willingness.

With that said, know that God loves a cheerful giver (2 Cor 9:7). It would be very hard to be a cheerful giver knowing that it is tearing you and your wife apart. Brother, it is very, very important as you and your wife grow together to listen to one another. If your spouse feels that there are specific things that your family needs and you are disregarding them this can be very frustrating to her. It's like her words don't matter. Talk to her, and be loving… Not talking to each other for almost a month is totally unhealthy for your relationship. It gives the devil time to cause havoc…

Take the lead today to ask her to sit down (Just the two of you) and talk this issue out. You really need to be a good listener at this crucial time.

Let her say all that she needs to say, without arguing, even if some words are hurtful, and attacking. Take it on the chin brother. She had a month to build up an additional explosion. After the explosion, apologize for not hearing her strong need for financial contentment in the areas discussed. Now come up together with a plan you can both agree on and charge forth to accomplish it.

As for increasing the tithe, I do not think this is the time to do this. Try to get your house in order where you are both comfortable. You are both growing in Christ at a different rate. Respect where she is regarding the tithing issue. As she grows, and the financial stress decreases, she may start to see it your way.

Brother, it appears to me based on your email that there is more going on here. To not speak for a month is so sad! Get to the root cause and save your marriage. Again, giving needs to be done cheerfully… This can not be done in your current situation. For your wife to explode means she kept in a lot of frustration. Both should apologize for any wrong doing… Talk it out… Be gentle to her if she asks you to vent and get your frustrations out.

Tell her that you love her and don't want to fight. Say I just want to love you. Tell her this in a calm, loving, trusting voice. Tell her you want things to improve. Hopefully she still has some love for you deep within.

Marriage counseling would be a great thing for you and your wife. It would afford the opportunity for more venting and correction to take place thus leading towards a healing in your marriage.

Don't let the sun go down in your anger.

Ephesians 4:26 English Standard Version (ESV) 26 Be angry and do not sin; do not let the sun go down on your anger,

Try as best as possible to correct the issues before you guys turn in at night.

Both of you need to keep your promise to God and keep your marriage, rebuild it from despair. It can be done… It does take two plus prayer.

Remember this" God hates divorce" Malachi 2:16.

Conclude your time of discussion taking one another's hand and pray to God. I recommend that both of you pray…

Home work assignment for both of you: read Philippians 4:8 and apply this whenever you both think of each other.

Philippians 4:8 English Standard Version (ESV)

8 Finally, brothers, whatever is true, whatever is honorable, whatever is just, whatever is pure, whatever is lovely, whatever is commendable, if there is any excellence, if there is anything worthy of praise, think about these things.

PS. Forgive one another…

Please let us know how things turn out. God's best to you and your wife sir!

Question: 74

I happened to view YouTube of Nigerian Prophet TB Joshua and deep in my heart feel uncomfortable and unbelievable of what I had seen of his miracle healings, seemed too theatrical to me. Is his ministry false and is he a false Christian prophet?

It scares me that I may be right, hopefully not.

Profile: Male 46-60 Asia

Answer: There is not a lot of information on the internet but I will try to answer your question regarding TB Joshua. It appears to me that he is not really going out on the limb when he says someone is going to die. The people are already sick, or up in age. As for the Russian air plane accident there is not enough information that says when he predicted the incident.

We do know this however, to determine a false prophet in Christianity, you need only to look at a set of standards by which one can judge according to the Bible, as taught and lived by the prophets, Jesus Christ, and His disciples.

If any persons or organizations claiming to serve Jesus Christ offend in these standards, then one ought to walk away from them and pay them no further mind...or money; they are false teachers. That is assuming one desires to embrace truth and not be deceived or serve to deceive others. Some Christian organizations have adopted non Christian doctrines, but these doctrines have no foundation in Jesus Christ or in Scripture, though teachers have many ways to rationalize and make the Bible say whatever they wish. Blind people calling themselves "Christians" follow blind teachers who call themselves "Christians," and both fall into the ditch.

Please read the following GotQuestions article regarding prophets:

http://www.gotquestions.org/prophets-today.html

Are there true prophets today? If the purpose of a prophet was to reveal truth from God, why would we need prophets if we have the completed revelation from God in the Bible? If prophets were the "foundation" of the early church, are we still building the "foundation" today? Can God give someone a message to deliver to someone else? Absolutely! Does God reveal truth to someone in a supernatural way and enable that person to deliver that message to others? Absolutely! But is this the biblical gift of prophecy? No.

Whatever the case, whenever a person claims to be speaking for God (the essence of prophecy) the key is to compare what is said with what the Bible says. If God were to speak through a person today, it would be in 100% complete agreement with what God has already said in the Bible. God does not contradict Himself. 1 John 4:1 instructs us, "Dear friends, do not believe every spirit, but test the spirits to see whether they are from God, because many false prophets have gone out into the world." 1 Thessalonians 5:20-21 declares, "Do not treat prophecies with contempt. Test everything. Hold on to the good." So, whether is it a "word from the Lord" or a supposed prophecy, our response should be the same. Compare what is said to what the Word of God says. If it contradicts the Bible, throw it out. If it agrees with the Bible, pray for wisdom, and discernment as to how to apply the message (2 Timothy 3:16-17; James 1:5).

There is also an article at the following url:

Is God restoring the offices of apostle and prophet in the church today?

http://www.gotquestions.org/apostles-prophets-restored.html

Jesus made it clear that the false prophets would be easily identified by their fruits, saying that a good tree cannot bring forth bad fruit.

Check the history of what was said by Nigerian Prophet TB. Did he mention specifics names or speak in generalities before the deaths? Anyone can do this... Is he following scripture in his daily walk and teachings?

Also consider this: How is what he is saying bringing glory to God?

One other thing I saw on the internet is the local news reported that Nigerian Prophet TB Joshua was banned from Cameroun for False Miracles... The Cameroonian government has blacklisted Prophet Temitope Balogun Joshua of the Synagogue Church of All Nations, saying that he is an agent of satan hoodwinking unsuspecting members of the public with "diabolical miracles".

http://news2.onlinenigeria.com/headlines/158961-prophet-temitope-balogun-joshua-banned-from-cameroun.html

The following list the Biblical test a friend and I used to determine if a person is a prophet in the true sense of the word.

1. Has he confessed Jesus Christ as Lord and Savior?
2. Does he read the Bible and pray every day?
3. Does his life showcase fruit consistent with being a Christian?
4. If married, does he treat his wife well?
5. Does he tithe and give money to the poor?
6. Does his prophecies come to pass?
7. Does he give God the glory when the prophecies come to pass?
8. Does he point people to Jesus?

Answer these questions and then you will be on your way to answering your question.

Nigerian Prophet TB Joshua docs have some false predictions and negativity on his record. See the following article:

http://tbjoshuawatch.wordpress.com/

Based on the information on the internet Nigerian Prophet TB Joshua is someone to avoid following. He has some false predictions, it is being reported that he is worshipped, and there are allegations of sexual abuses, etc…

In time, more information will be available to help more people needing answers. We will certainly know him and others by their fruits.

Question: 75

Can you provide information on Jenetzen Franklin? Is he a false prophet?

Profile: Female 46-60 North America

Answer: Thanks for writing GotQuestions.org.

No information is available for Jenetzen Franklin. Perhaps you mean Jentezen Franklin.

To answer your question, I will try to piece together what information exists regarding Jentezen Franklin and provide required learning URL's to round out how I arrived at my conclusion. Please read all of the GotQuestions.org articles referenced so that you will be totally equipped to give an answer to your question if called upon in life.

Jentezen Franklin is a Word of Faith teacher who gathered together on TBN for one week telling you to "sow a seed" or "sow a seed faith promise" or "sow a faith promise seed" etc… however you slice it, it's the same thing! The whole idea here is for you to "go to the phone and give". This is your act of obedience to the Lord and if you hesitate, you are in rebellion! They don't come out and say that directly, well at least some of them don't, but that is usually what is meant here.

Jentezen leads a church and is a guru of a fasting movement that has way too much talk about financial rewards as a result of fasting.

For a biblical perspective on fasting please go to the following URL's:

http://www. gotquestions.org/fasting-Christian.html

http://www.gotquestions.org/prayer-fasting.html

http://www.gotquestions.org/Daniel-fast.html

Friend, to determine a false prophet in Christianity, you need only to look at a set of standards by which one can judge according to the Bible, as taught and lived by the prophets, Jesus Christ, and His disciples.

If any persons or organizations claiming to serve Jesus Christ offend in these standards, then one ought to walk away from them and pay them no further mind...or money; they are false teachers. That is assuming one desires to embrace truth and not be deceived or serve to deceive others. Some Christian organizations have adopted non Christian doctrines, but these doctrines have no foundation in Jesus Christ or in Scripture, though teachers have many ways to rationalize and make the Bible say whatever they wish. Blind people calling themselves "Christians" follow blind teachers who call themselves "Christians," and both fall into the ditch.

Please read the following GotQuestions article regarding prophets:

http://www.gotquestions.org/prophets-today.html

Are there true prophets today? If the purpose of a prophet was to reveal truth from God, why would we need prophets if we have the completed revelation from God in the Bible? If prophets were the "foundation" of the early church, are we still building the "foundation" today? Can God give someone a message to deliver to someone else? Absolutely! Does God reveal truth to someone in a supernatural way and enable that person to deliver that message to others? Absolutely! But is this the biblical gift of prophecy? No.

Whatever the case, whenever a person claims to be speaking for God (the essence of prophecy) the key is to compare what is said with what the Bible says. If God were to speak through a person today, it would be in 100% complete agreement with what God has already said in the Bible. God does not contradict Himself. 1 John 4:1 instructs us, "Dear friends, do not believe every spirit, but test the spirits to see whether they are from God, because many false prophets have gone out into the world." 1 Thessalonians 5:20-21 declares, "Do not treat prophecies with contempt. Test everything. Hold on to the good." So, whether is it a "word from the Lord" or a supposed prophecy, our response should be the same. Compare what is said to what the Word of God says. If it contradicts the Bible, throw it out. If it agrees with the Bible, pray for wisdom and discernment as to how to apply the message (2 Timothy 3:16-17; James 1:5).

There is also an article at the following url:

Is God restoring the offices of apostle and prophet in the church today?

http://www.gotquestions.org/apostles-prophets-restored.html

Jesus made it clear that the false prophets would be easily identified by their fruits, saying that a good tree cannot bring forth bad fruit.

Check the history of what was said by Jentezen Franklin. Is he following scripture in his daily walk and teachings?

Also consider this: How is what he is saying bringing glory to God?

The following list the Biblical test a friend and I used to determine if a person is a prophet in the true sense of the word.

1. Has he confessed Jesus Christ as Lord and Savior?
2. Does he read the Bible and pray every day?
3. Does his life showcase fruit consistent with being a Christian?
4. If married, does he treat his wife well?
5. Does he tithe and give money to the poor?
6. Does his prophecies come to pass?
7. Does he give God the glory when the prophecies come to pass?
8. Does he point people to Jesus?

Answer these questions and then you will be on your way to answering your question.

At http://www.deceptioninthechurch.com/buyamiracle.html there is an article that mentions the following:

In the book of Acts, chapter eight, we have a very insightful incident that happened to Peter and John in Samaria. Peter and John were laying their hands on the Christian believers and they were receiving the Holy Spirit as a result.

There was a certain man, Simon, who had just become a believer, and after he had seen this gift of God that was given to the new believers he asked Peter and John if he could also have this gift of God by giving them money. Peter answered Simon, "Thy money perish with thee, because thou hast thought that the gift of God may be purchased with money. Thou hast neither part nor lot in this matter: for thy heart is not right in the sight of God."

This has particular significance today because so many "Christian" television stations use the very tactic that Simon used to get people to give money during their telethons. These false teachers lure babes in Christ into believing that we could actually buy a miracle from God. They teach that we give to God expecting a blessing, miracle, healing, or a 100 fold return on our investment.

This article also mentioned that TBN, Daystar, and LeSea all use this tactic. Their favorite false teachers that play the role of Simon are; John Avanzini, Steve Munsey, Benny Hinn, Rod Parsley, Paula White, Joyce Meyer, T. D. Jakes, **Jentezen Franklin**, Mark Chironna, Paul Crouch, etc…

As mentioned previously Jentezen Franklin is the guru of fasting. He has written two books on it and is the one who championed "The Daniel Fast". His statements about why we fast include fasting to get a blessing, to earn God's favor, to get a public reward, to get our greatest breakthrough, to "release" a hundredfold return.

So the lesson from "The Daniel Fast" by Jentezen Franklin is that we fast to get something.

Friend, I do not believe we should fast for the reasons he mentions.

Secondly, if we fast, Franklin says, it causes God to "release" these things into our lives. My understanding is that fasting is a private expression of a deeply felt spiritual need and a way to humble oneself before Almighty God.

All of this elevates fasting to an importance the bible does not give it nor did Jesus give it.

As for Jentezen's Franklin teachings, they are false doctrine too. He said in one sermon as he appealed for money, lots of it for over ten minutes, over sentimental music blared from loudspeakers, "I've never come to Hillsong Conference where I haven't sown at least a $1000 seed…"

Yet the bible says, "So when you give to the needy, do not announce it with trumpets, as the hypocrites do in the synagogues and on the streets, to be honored by men. I tell you the truth, they have received their reward in full." See Matthew 6:2:

Matthew 6:2 English Standard Version (ESV)

2 "Thus, when you give to the needy, sound no trumpet before you, as the hypocrites do in the synagogues and in the streets, that they may be praised by others. Truly, I say to you, they have received their reward.

Franklin goes on, "$1000 seed...into this place, because if I sow now, the rain of now will fall on my life." NAME IT CLAIM IT! Tithe big, you get big. And what is "the rain of now"? His hands were fluttering down as rain, and the audience looked up as if expecting manna or money to fall from the sky right then.

He is a Word of Faith preacher and we know those are false. The Word of Faith crowd is big on "if you do this, you get this." "If you do this it will cause God to move." They talk about 'releasing' power into your life, but in fact the only thing we have the power to release is a burp after dinner. He elevates to us more power than we have and diminishes Jesus in the process.

He said, "When I feel myself growing dry spiritually, when I don't sense that cutting-edge anointing, or when I need a fresh encounter with God, fasting is the secret key that unlocks heaven's door and slams shut the gates of hell. The discipline of fasting releases the anointing, the favor, and the blessing of God in the life of a Christian."

Don't gloss over this…

It is the most abhorrent statement imaginable. It is sacrilege. Jesus has the key to heaven and hell. Nothing we do unlocks it. How sacrilegious to say that any activity we do unlocks heaven or shuts hell. This is totally wrong!

Revelation 1:18 English Standard Version (ESV)

18 and the living one. I died, and behold I am alive forevermore, and I have the keys of Death and Hades.

Jentezen Franklin is a word of faith teacher.

The Word of Faith doctrine "puts confidence in the nature of faith rather then in the object of faith. It assumes that there's something inherent in believing that enacts [or "releases"] something when it isn't true at all.

It is not the nature of faith that is effective. It is the object of faith. It is my faith in God that gets results not my faith in my faith." It is God's will be done not mine…

I do not recommend that you listen to or follow him and others in the Word of Faith Movement. This is false doctrine.

For more teaching on the word of faith movement please go to the following GotQuestions.org articles:

http://www.gotquestions.org/Word-Faith.html

http://www.gotquestions.org/prosperity-gospel.html

http://www.gotquestions.org/name-it-claim-it.html

May God bless you in the study of His word!

Question: 76

Question: Did Jesus ever receive worship while on earth?

Male over 60 years old… USA

Answer: Friend, I know that you disagreed with me while I spoke with you but please read my answer and study it for truth matters!

Answer: Yes. Read Matthew 2:11 and the scriptures that follow:

Matthew 2:11 English Standard Version (ESV)

11 And going into the house they saw the child with Mary his mother, and they fell down and worshiped him. Then, opening their treasures, they offered him gifts, gold and frankincense and myrrh.

Matthew 14:33 English Standard Version (ESV)

33 And those in the boat worshiped him, saying, "Truly you are the Son of God."

John 9:1-38 English Standard Version (ESV)

Jesus Heals a Man Born Blind:

Read this true story to see the background information but take note of the ending at John 9:38

John 9:38 English Standard Version (ESV)

38 He said, "Lord, I believe," and he worshiped him.

In Revelation, an angel instructed the apostle John to only worship God (Revelation 19:10). Several times in Scripture Jesus receives worship

(Matthew 2:11; 14:33; 28:9, 17; Luke 24:52; John 9:38). He never rebukes people for worshiping Him. If Jesus were not God, He would have told people to not worship Him, just as the angel in Revelation did. There are many other verses and passages of Scripture that argue for Jesus' deity.

For more study regarding this please read the article "Is Jesus God? Did Jesus ever claim to be God?" at the following website:

http://www.gotquestions.org/is-Jesus-God.html

Question: 77

Where in the bible does it say Jesus is God?

Male over 40, USA

Answer: You have asked a question that will help many. Let us dive into God's word now…

The Word "became flesh" in John 1:1.

In John's gospel it says "In the beginning was the Word, and the Word was with God, and the Word was God". In this John is introducing Jesus with a word or a term that both his Jewish and Gentile readers would have been familiar with. The Greek word translated "Word" in this passage is Logos, and it was common in both Greek philosophy and Jewish thought of that day. For example, in the Old Testament the "word" of God is often personified as an instrument for the execution of God's will (Psalm 33:6; 107:20; 119:89; 147:15-18). So, for his Jewish readers, by introducing Jesus as the "Word," John is in a sense pointing them back to the Old Testament where the Logos or "Word" of God is associated with the personification of God's revelation. And in Greek philosophy, the term Logos was used to describe the intermediate agency by which God created material things and communicated with them. In the Greek worldview, the Logos was thought of as a bridge between the transcendent God and the material universe. Therefore, for his Greek readers the use of the term Logos would have likely brought forth the idea of a mediating principle between God and the world.

Please read the full article at the following url:

http://www.gotquestions.org/Jesus-Word-God.html

Take for example, Jesus' words in John 10:30, "I and the Father are one." We need only to look at the Jews' reaction to His statement to know He was claiming to be God. They tried to stone Him for this very reason. "… you, a mere man, claim to be God" (John 10:33). The Jews understood exactly what Jesus was claiming—deity. Notice that Jesus does not deny His claim to be God. When Jesus declared, "I and the Father are one" (John 10:30), He was saying that He and the Father are of one nature and essence. John 8:58 is another example. Jesus declared, "I tell you the truth, before Abraham was born, I am!"

The response of the Jews who heard this statement was to take up stones to kill Him for blasphemy, as the Mosaic Law commanded them to do (Leviticus 24:15).

John reiterates the concept of Jesus' deity: "the Word was God" and "the Word became flesh" (John 1:1, 14). These verses clearly indicate that Jesus is God in the flesh. Acts 20:28 tells us, "Be shepherds of the church of God, which he bought with his own blood." Who bought the church—the church of God—with His own blood? Jesus Christ. Acts 20:28 declares that God purchased His church with His own blood. Therefore, Jesus is God!

In Revelation, an angel instructed the apostle John to only worship God (Revelation19:10). Several times in Scripture Jesus receives worship (Matthew 2:11; 14:33; 28:9, 17; Luke 24:52; John 9:38). He never rebukes people for worshiping Him. If Jesus were not God, He would have told people to not worship Him, just as the angel in Revelation did. There are many other verses and passages of Scripture that argue for Jesus' deity.

Please read the full article at the following url:

http://www.gotquestions.org/is-Jesus-God.html

Please take time out and study the following passages:

Jesus Christ, the Son, is declared to be God.

His deity is proven by the divine names given to Him, by His works that only God could do (upholding all things, Col. 1:17; creation, Col. 1:16, John 1:3; and future judgment, John 5:27), by His divine attributes (eternality, John 17:5; omnipresence, Matt 28:20; omnipotence, Heb. 1:3; omniscience, Matt. 9:4), and by explicit statements declaring His deity (John 1:1; 20:28; Titus 2:13; Heb. 1:8).

Thanks for asking Lord of Hope Ministries this very important question.

May this answer move you and many others closer to our Lord and Savior Jesus Christ!

Question: 78

Why did Jesus say you call me Good? No one is good except God. This statement tells me he is not God.

Male over 40, USA

Answer: You are referring to Luke 18:18-19 or Mark 10:17-22.

Luke 18:18-19 English Standard Version (ESV)

The Rich Ruler

18 And a ruler asked him, "Good Teacher, what must I do to inherit
eternal life?"
19 And Jesus said to him, "Why do you call me good? No
one is good except God alone.

This verse regarding the rich ruler needs to be taken in the context intended. This verse is used by people who try to say that Jesus is not God. They have not interpreted the verse correctly. This must be read in the context of scripture.

Is Jesus here rebuking the man for calling Him good and thereby denying His deity? No. Rather, He is using a penetrating question to push the man to think through the implications of his own words, to understand the concept of Jesus' goodness and, most especially, the man's lack of goodness. The young ruler "went away sad" (Mark 10:22) because he realized that although he had devoted himself to keeping the commandments, he had failed to keep the first and greatest of the commandments—love the LORD your God with all your heart and with all your soul and with all your strength (Matthew 22:37-38). The man's riches were of more worth to him than God, and thus he was not "good" in the eyes of God.

Jesus fundamental lesson here is that goodness flows not from a man's deeds, but rather from God Himself. Jesus invites the man to follow Him, the only means of doing good by God's ultimate standard. Jesus describes to the young ruler what it means to follow Him—to be willing to give up everything, thus putting God first. When one considers that Jesus is drawing a distinction between man's standard of goodness and God's standard, it becomes clear that following Jesus is good. The command to follow Christ is the definitive proclamation of Christ's goodness. Thus, by the very standard Jesus is exhorting the young ruler to adopt, Jesus is good. And it necessarily follows that if Jesus is indeed good by this standard, Jesus is implicitly declaring His deity.

Jesus question to the man is designed not to deny His deity, but rather to draw the man to recognize Christ's divine identity.

Such an interpretation is substantiated by passages such as John 10:11 wherein Jesus declares Himself to be "the good shepherd." Similarly in John 8:46, Jesus asks, "Can any of you prove me guilty of sin?" Of course the answer is "no." Jesus was "without sin" (Hebrews 4:15), holy and undefiled (Hebrews 7:26), the only One who "knew no sin" (2 Corinthians 5:21).

The logic can thus be summarized as follows:

1: Jesus claims only God is good.
2: Jesus claims to be good.
3: Therefore, Jesus claims to be God.

For the full article on this topic please go to the following url:

http://www.gotquestions.org/good-God-alone.html

Question: 79

Is it true that we are an image not a man?

Profile: Male, over 40, USA

Answer: This statement I heard a Christian Science gentlemen say to another person. He was very emphatic about it. Just to be clear on this topic, one must read the bible in context. If anyone is getting this from a religious organization that has been classified as a cult, throw away that teaching. Make crumbs of it. It is false doctrine. One example of this is in the Christian Science belief system. In reality it is neither Christian nor Science.

The bible makes it clear… Let's read Genesis 1:26-27. It gives a clear overview regarding how mankind was made.

Genesis 1:26-27 English Standard Version (ESV)

26 Then God said, "Let us make man[a] in our image, after our likeness. And let them have dominion over the fish of the sea and over the birds of the heavens and over the livestock and over all the earth and over every creeping thing that creeps on the earth."

27 So God created man in his own image, in the image of God he created him; male and female he created them.

Footnotes:

a. Genesis 1:26 The Hebrew word for **man** (adam) is **the generic term for mankind** and becomes the proper name Adam.

God created **MAN** in His own image, in the image of God He created him **male and female** He created them.

So you are not an image walking around. You are not a hologram.

We are male and female (mankind), not imagekind.

For better clarification consider this: Having the "image" or "likeness" of God means, in the simplest terms, that we were made to resemble God. Adam did not resemble God in the sense of God's having flesh and blood. Scripture says that "God is spirit" (John 4:24) and therefore exists without a body. However, Adam's body did mirror the life of God insofar as it was created in perfect health and was not subject to death.

The image of God refers to the immaterial part of man. It sets man apart from the animal world, fits him for the dominion God intended him to have over the earth (Genesis 1:28), and enables him to commune with his Maker. It is a likeness mentally, morally, and socially.

For a deeper study regarding this topic please read the article at the following URL:

http://www.gotquestions.org/image-of-God.html

Question: 80

Please show me a scripture where David worships God using instrumental music.

Answer: Thanks for submitting your question. There are scripture verses that support using musical instruments in worship. Over 60 Old Testament verses refer favorably to worshiping God by using instruments.

See below for your answer:

Instrumental music as a means of praising God:

2 Samuel 6:5, 21

5 And David and all the house of Israel were celebrating before the LORD, with songs and lyres and harps and tambourines and castanets and cymbals.

21 And David said to Michal, "It was before the LORD, who chose me above your father and above all his house, to appoint me as prince over Israel, the people of the LORD—and I will celebrate before the LORD.

Israel played before the lord on instruments.

1 Chronicles 23:5 – English Standard Version (ESV)

5 4,000 gatekeepers, and 4,000 shall offer praises to the LORD with the instruments that I have made for praise."

They praised the lord with instruments which David made for giving praise (NKJV).

2 Chronicles 7:6 – English Standard Version (ESV)

[6] The priests stood at their posts; the Levites also, with the instruments for music to the LORD that King David had made for giving thanks to the LORD— for his steadfast love endures forever—whenever David offered praises by their ministry; opposite them the priests sounded trumpets, and all Israel stood.

The Levites had instruments of music, which David had made to praise the lord. David offered praise by their ministry.

2 Chronicles 29:25 – English Standard Version (ESV)

[25] And he stationed the Levites in the house of the LORD with cymbals, harps, and lyres, according to the commandment of David and of Gad the king's seer and of Nathan the prophet, for the commandment was from the LORD through his prophets.

The Levites were arranged with cymbals, stringed instruments, and harps. This was commanded of the Lord.

There is no inscription for this psalm, so we cannot be certain who wrote it (though many think that David was the author):

Psalm 71:22 English Standard Version (ESV)

[22] I will also praise you with the harp for your faithfulness, O my God;

I will sing praises to you with the lyre, O Holy One of Israel.

Psalm 33:2 English Standard Version (ESV)

[2] Give thanks to the LORD with the lyre; make melody to him with the harp of ten strings!

We know instruments were used in the time of David (1 Chronicles 15:16, 28, 16:4-5, Psalms 150, etc.). They were also used at Solomon's Temple (2 Chronicles 5:11-14), and they were used at the rebuilt Temple after the Babylonian captivity (Ezra 3:10, Neh. 12:31-37).

Instrumental music was acceptable in worship during this time because it was authorized by God.

"Raise a song and strike the timbrel, the pleasant harp with the lute. Blow the trumpet at the time of the New Moon, at the full moon, on our solemn feast day. For this is a statute for Israel, and a law of the God of Jacob." (Psalms 81:2-4 NKJV)

I hope that this helps you in the study of God's word.

Question: 81

What do Native Americans believe in? Do they worship wolves, tigers, and animal spirits? What is that tribal stuff all about?

Answer: The question you asked may contain many answers if you are speaking over the course of time. I will pull my research information together to piece together my answer. The answer to question #1 is contained throughout my answer.

Traditional Native American religions in the United States exhibit much diversity, largely due to the relative isolation of the different tribes that were spread out across the entire breadth of the North American continent for thousands of years, allowing for the development of different beliefs and practices between tribes.

Question #3, you ask "What is that tribal stuff all about?" In the United States, a Native American tribe is any extant or historical tribe, band, nation, or other group or community of Indigenous peoples in the United States. Tribes are often associated with territory in the form of a reservation.

A Native American tribe often is self-governing to roughly the same extent as a city or county.

Native American religion is closely connected to the land in which Native Americans dwell and the supernatural. While there are many different Native American religious practices, most address the following areas of supernatural concern: an omnipresent, invisible universal force, pertaining to the "three 'life crises' of birth, puberty, and death", spirits, visions, and the shaman and communal ceremony.

Shamans: Although the term "Shaman" has its origins in Siberia, it is often used by anthropologists throughout the world to refer to Aboriginal healers. Spirits may be encouraged to occupy the Shaman's body during public lodge ceremonies. Drum beating and chanting aid this process. The spirits are then asked to depart and perform the needed acts. Other times, Shamans enter into a trance and traverse the underworld or go great distances in this world to seek lost possessions or healing.

Native American spirituality is often characterized by animism or panentheism, with a strong emphasis on the importance of personal spirituality and its inter-connectivity with one's own daily life, and a deep connection between the natural and spiritual 'worlds'. Their lives were steeped in religious ceremonies often directly related to farming and hunting. Now I will answer question #2, "Do they worship wolves, tigers, and animal spirits? Spiritual power, they believed, suffused (To spread through or over) the world, and sacred spirits could be found in all kinds of living and inanimate things-animals, plants, trees, water, and wind. Through religious ceremonies, they aimed to harness the aid of powerful supernatural forces to serve the interests of man. In some tribes, hunters performed rituals to placate the spirits of animals they had killed.

Panentheism (from Greek πᾶν (*pân*) "all"; ἐν (*en*) "in"; and θεός (*theós*) "God"; "all-in-God") is a belief system which posits that the divine (be it a monotheistic God, polytheistic gods, or an eternal cosmic animating force) interpenetrates every part of nature and timelessly extends beyond it. Panentheism differentiates itself from pantheism, which leaves open the possibility that the divine is not a distinct being or beings but is synonymous with the universe.

In panentheism, the universe in the first formulation is practically the whole itself. In the second formulation, the universe and the divine are not ontologically equivalent. In panentheism, God is viewed as the eternal animating force behind the universe.

Native American religions tend not to be institutionalized but rather experiential and personal. This has been a source of a great deal of misunderstanding. Individual asceticism through sweat lodge ceremonies and other events along with rituals that appear to resemble idol worship make understanding their faith and religion problematic at best. Native American religions tend to be carried out mainly in a family or tribal location first and are better explained as more of a process or journey than a religion. It is a relationship experienced between Creator and created. For Native Americans, religion is never separated from one's daily life unlike Western cultures where religion is experienced privately and gradually integrated into one's public life. Conversation about theology and religion, even within their society, is extremely limited but to live and breathe is to worship. For Native Americans, a relationship with God is experienced as a relationship with all of creation which interestingly, is ever present and does not require an institution or building. To them all of creation has life. Rocks, trees, mountains, and everything that is visible lives and is part of creation and therefore has life which must be respected. Achiel Peelman suggests that, "strictly speaking, Amerindians do not believe in God but know God as an intrinsic dimension of all their relations." God is known indirectly through an awareness of the relationships or links between various aspects of both the physical and supernatural realms. Spirituality of the Native Americans makes no distinction between these realms; the living and dead, visible and invisible, past and present, and heaven and earth.

Most adherents to traditional American Indian ways do not see their spiritual beliefs and practices as a "religion"; rather, they see their whole culture and social structure as infused with 'spirituality' - an integral part of their lives and culture.

The following are the major Native American religions:

Christianity
Longhouse Religion
Waashat Religion or Dreamer Faith
Indian Shaker Religion
Drum Religion
Earth Lodge Religion

Ghost Dances
Ghost Dance Religion
Bole-Maru Religion
Dream Dance
Feather Religion
Peyote Religion

I hope that this information was helpful to you.

Question: 82

I have been trying to break an emotional attachment that I have with my ex-girlfriend. I have dated her for almost 3 years, and have bonded with her. We have done things that should not be done outside of marriage, but not all the way. We have forgiven each other, and I know that the Lord has forgiven me as well. My question is, "how do you break an emotional attachment?" I love her as I love my wife, which is why I have trouble letting her go. It hurts even more now that she flirts with other men. I feel as if she cheats on me when I know that we are no longer together. Please help me. I have prayed to God many times and I feel as if he directed me to your ministry.

Profile: Male 18-30 North America

Answer: Hello Sir! I want to first thank you for writing to us expressing your heart in this matter.

Before I address this, I need to let you know that there is a confusing comment expressed in your question that needs to be cleared up. You said this: "I love her as I love my wife". Forgive me, but I have to ask you, are you married and were cheating on your spouse for 3 years? Or are you saying that you loved your ex-girlfriend as if she were your wife?

Another question, Are there any children caught up in the middle of this break up?

My response can vary drastically depending on your answer to this.

Let me assume that you are not married, have no children in the middle of this, and address your question from this standpoint.

Please know that I am only making a suggestion in my response to you so please think about it and determine how you will proceed.

A broken heart can happen when we lose a love one. This emotional pain happens when you are deeply disappointed or grieved over a life circumstance. The Bible has many verses that can encourage the brokenhearted. I placed some encouraging Bible verses for the brokenhearted later in my response.

How do you break an emotional attachment?

In private, pray a lot! Cry out to God and let the tears flow if they start up… Ask the Lord to change your heart regarding your previous relationship so that the break up has less and less effect on you each day. You will get stronger!

After a romantic breakup, a couple's emotional attachment fades over time. The length of time depends on the individual. Sometimes, though, feelings can linger longer for one of the individuals. You can free yourself from emotional ties once you and your ex have gone your separate ways by working to move past the relationship and by taking care of yourself. Stop being concerned with who she flirts with. You two are no longer an item. Set her free in your mind. She needs to live her life too! Yes, it probably stings big time!

On a personal note, years ago an ex-girlfriend and I broke up and in a very short time frame she was kissing big time, her new man, in a car right by the employee entrance where I use to work. I had to walk by the car to enter the building. Ouch!!!!

Friend, the Lord sees all… In my case, after about 2 years of random dating, nothing serious, working on self improvement, serving the kingdom, the Lord brought me a woman in my life that I ended up marrying. It has now been (in year 2013) 13 years of marriage and counting… She is wonderful!!!

If you desire to marry someday God knows this… Honor God in how you live your life!

Taste and see that the Lord is good! Psalm 34:8.

See if the following can help you as well:

1. Establish boundaries. Don't see or call your ex-girlfriend or try to remain "friends." This often just masks an unwillingness to break an emotional bond. Enforce ground rules if you must see each other. Co-parenting is a special challenge. Do not permit your ex to enter your home without permission or to stay overnight. Stay neutral in your communications.

2. Limit talk about your ex-girlfriend with mutual friends. Tell your friends you prefer not to hear about your ex right now. Assure them this is a temporary situation and that in time you will be able to resume normal conversations. If they are believers you could ask them to pray regarding the break up.

3. Pack up, throw out or sell items that remind you of your ex-girlfriend. "Out of sight, out of mind" is the right adage in this case. Gather up and pack gifts, mementos and photos and decide what to do with them. Some people find it cathartic to chuck these things in the trash. Others store them or sell them. You may be able to sell them and buy something you really like or go on a fun trip with the proceeds.

4. Do what you enjoy. Do the things you rarely did because your ex-girlfriend disliked them. One of the benefits of breaking up is not having to compromise. Head to a sports arena and watch a football, baseball, basketball, hockey or other game. Perhaps staying up late and watching movies brings excitement to you. Avoid the romantic movies if you are not ready for them otherwise you may need a box of Kleenex near by.

5. Don't envy those in romantic relationships. It's hard to revel in being single when the media barrages people with images of impossibly happy couples. While a good relationship is a joy, single people also live happy lives. Consider not dating for a while. Make a list of the benefits of being single and promise yourself to enjoy your status without reservation, at least for a time. Take time to improve yourself by working on what can make you better in life and a better person for your future relationship.

Go to the gym and exercise regularly. Exercise can help in improving how a person feels…

6. Consider a move. Sometimes the place we live reminds us of a past relationship and makes it impossible to get over an emotional attachment. Moving is a big step, but it might prove beneficial. Weigh the pros and cons of moving to a new town. If you decide to move, consider an area where you'll meet other singles living happily. It can be a great start to a new life.

Seek counseling if you find yourself totally unable to get over an old flame or is constantly depressed about a failed relationship.

Friend, you can overcome this issue prayerfully, taking one day at a time, getting involved in projects, serving others at a church or ministry, adding new friends to your world etc…

Shift your focus:

Read the Bible and worship the Lord more than you have in the past! When the longings to be connected come upon you worship the Lord. He cares for you. Sing along to worship CD's, watch worship DVD's or Worship videos on the internet. It will make a big difference in your emotional healing.

Colossians 3:16 English Standard Version (ESV)

16 Let the word of Christ dwell in you richly, teaching and admonishing one another in all wisdom, singing psalms and hymns and spiritual songs, with thankfulness in your hearts to God.

Heart Break Example in Scripture:

David, a man after God's own heart, suffered many heartbreaking circumstances. Each time, he recovered and was an even stronger man of God. Psalm 34 gives an example of how David overcame heartbreak by calling on the Lord. Notice the first step: "I sought the Lord, and he answered me and delivered me from all my fears" (Psalm 34:4). David knew "the Lord is near to the brokenhearted and saves the crushed in spirit" (Psalm 34:18). Finally, he expressed a confidence in the love of God that every believer should have: "Many are the afflictions of the righteous, but the Lord delivers him out of them all" (Psalm 34:19).

Please read the full article at the following link: http://www.gotquestions.org/heartbreak.html

Encouragement:

Please know this, if you are a person who has accepted Jesus Christ as your savior you are a very precious child of God. He loves you very much! You matter to God and He knows the plans He has for you. Trust God and serve Him… God knows what you need. God will take care of you according to His will…

Jeremiah 29:11 English Standard Version (ESV)

11 For I know the plans I have for you, declares the LORD, plans for welfare and not for evil, to give you a future and a hope.

Matthew 6:33 English Standard Version (ESV)

33 But seek first the kingdom of God and his righteousness, and all these things will be added to you.

If you have not accepted Jesus as your savior, please go to the following link to get answers and move forward regarding Salvation:

http://www.gotquestions.org/questions_salvation.html

Let the following words of scripture fill your heart and mind. These are for the Broken Hearted:

Psalm 34:18 (ESV)

The LORD is near to the brokenhearted and saves the crushed in spirit (Psalms 34:18).

It is encouraging to read what King David wrote in the previously quoted psalm. We can be healed and delivered from a broken heart. The Lord is Strong; Do not Fear.

Psalms 73:26 (ESV) My flesh and my heart may fail, but God is the strength of my heart and my portion forever.

Isaiah 41:10 (ESV) Fear not, for I am with you; be not dismayed, for I am your God; I will strengthen you, I will help you, I will uphold you with my righteous right hand.

Matthew 11:28-30 Come to me, all who labor and are heavy laden, and I will give you rest. Take my yoke upon you, and learn from me, for I am gentle and lowly in heart, and you will find rest for your souls. For my yoke is easy, and my burden is light."

John 14:27 Peace I leave with you; my peace I give to you. Not as the world gives do I give to you. Let not your hearts be troubled, neither let them be afraid.

2 Corinthians 12:9 But he said to me, "My grace is sufficient for you, for my power is made perfect in weakness." Therefore I will boast all the more gladly of my weaknesses, so that the power of Christ may rest upon me.

Trust the Lord for Deliverance and Healing

Psalms 55:22 Cast your burden on the LORD, and he will sustain you; he will never permit the righteous to be moved.

Psalms 107:20 He sent out his word and healed them, and delivered them from their destruction.

Psalms 147:3 He heals the brokenhearted and binds up their wounds.

Proverbs 3:5-6 Trust in the LORD with all your heart, and do not lean on your own understanding. In all your ways acknowledge him, and he will make straight your paths.

1 Peter 2:*24* He himself bore our sins in his body on the tree, that we might die to sin and live to righteousness. By his wounds you have been healed.

1 Peter 4:19 Therefore let those who suffer according to God's will entrust their souls to a faithful Creator while doing good.

Look Forward and Believe

Isaiah 43:18 Remember not the former things, nor consider the things of old.

Mark 11:23 Truly, I say to you, whoever says to this mountain, 'Be taken up and thrown into the sea,' and does not doubt in his heart, but believes that what he says will come to pass, it will be done for him.

Romans 5:1-2 Therefore, since we have been justified by faith, we have peace with God through our Lord Jesus Christ. Through him we have also obtained access by faith into this grace in which we stand, and we rejoice in hope of the glory of God.

Romans 8:28 And we know that for those who love God all things work together for good, for those who are called according to his purpose.

1 Corinthians 13:7 Love bears all things, believes all things, hopes all things, endures all things.

2 Corinthians 5:6-7 So we are always of good courage. We know that while we are at home in the body we are away from the Lord, for we walk by faith, not by sight.

Philippians 3:13-14 Brothers, I do not consider that I have made it my own. But one thing I do: forgetting what lies behind and straining forward to what lies ahead, I press on toward the goal for the prize of the upward call of God in Christ Jesus.

Hebrews 11:1 (KJV) Now faith is the substance of things hoped for, the evidence of things not seen.

Revelation 21:3-4 And I heard a loud voice from the throne saying, "Behold, the dwelling place of God is with man. He will dwell with them, and they will be his people, and God himself will be with them as their God. He will wipe away every tear from their eyes, and death shall be no more, neither shall there be mourning, nor crying, nor pain anymore, for the former things have passed away."

Friend, you are not alone. Many people deal with emotional attachments in various ways. I will pray for you to feel better! You matter! Think on these Christian Quotes for the Brokenhearted:

"The church is not a select circle of the immaculate, but a home where the outcast may come in. It is not a palace with gate attendants and challenging sentinels along the entrance-ways holding off at arm's-length the stranger, but rather a hospital where the broken-hearted may be healed, and where all the weary and troubled may find rest and take counsel together." ~ **James H. Aughey**

"Leave the broken, irreversible past in God's hands, and step out into the invincible future with Him." ~ **Oswald Chambers**

Scripture Verses to ponder as you walk with God:

Zephaniah 3:17 English Standard Version (ESV)

17 The Lord your God is in your midst, a mighty one who will save;

he will rejoice over you with gladness; he will quiet you by his love;

he will exult over you with loud singing.

Colossians 2:5 English Standard Version (ESV)

5 For though I am absent in body, yet I am with you in spirit, rejoicing to see your good order and the firmness of your faith in Christ.

Ephesians 5:18-20 English Standard Version (ESV)

18 And do not get drunk with wine, for that is debauchery, but be filled
with the Spirit, 19 addressing one another in psalms and hymns and
spiritual songs, singing and making melody to the Lord with your heart,
20 giving thanks always and for everything to God the Father in the name
of our Lord Jesus Christ,

Romans 8:14 English Standard Version (ESV)

14 For all who are led by the Spirit of God are sons of God.

1 John 1:9 English Standard Version (ESV)

9 If we confess our sins, he is faithful and just to forgive us our sins and to cleanse us from all unrighteousness.

Romans 6:11-14 English Standard Version (ESV)

11 So you also must consider yourselves dead to sin and alive to God in Christ Jesus.

12 Let not sin therefore reign in your mortal body, to make you obey
its passions. 13 Do not present your members to sin as instruments for
unrighteousness, but present yourselves to God as those who have been
brought from death to life, and your members to God as instruments for
righteousness. 14 For sin will have no dominion over you, since you are
not under law but under grace.

John 3:3 English Standard Version (ESV)

3 Jesus answered him, "Truly, truly, I say to you, unless one is born again he cannot see the kingdom of God."

Closing comments:

May our Great and Awesome Lord guide you through this season in your life!

Please remember to help someone else you encounter some day who may struggle in this way.

You are getting equipped right now to be a light for others. Smile for you are in good hands!

May you receive the joy that can only flow from the Masters hand!

Question: 83

1. Is it right for the Pastor to bow down to the altar in a church? 2. Please share your biblical experience on this practice.

Profile: Male Over 60 North America

Answer: Thanks for writing to GotQuestions.org.

The answer to your questions depends on a lot of factors.

An altar is used in many religions. An altar is any structure upon which offerings such as sacrifices are made for religious purposes. Altars are usually found at shrines, and they can be located in temples, churches and other places of worship.

Today they are used particularly in Christianity, Buddhism, Hinduism, Shinto, Taoism, as well as in Neopaganism and Ceremonial Magic. Judaism did so until the destruction of the Second Temple. Many other faiths also made use of them, including Greek and Norse religion.

Without knowing what religion you are referring to I am forced to ponder the questions listed below. Afterwards, I will unpack my answer in brief.

1. What religion is it?
2. Is the religion or sect considered a cult?
3. Is the pastor actually bowing to the altar as if to worship it?
4. Did the Pastor reveal verbally what he was actually doing?
5. Is this Altar being used as in idol worship?
6. Is the Pastor bowing in front of a table designated for communion, where he is picturing in his mind God and not the table or bread and wine?
7. Is the altar getting more attention than God?
8. What is the Altar?

The bible, which is the final authority, instructs us that God should always be given honor and glory in all that we do!

Honoring and bowing down to any object is committing idolatry. For example, the cross is a symbol of what Jesus did for us but is not something that deserves our bowing down to, worship and praise. The only one worthy and deserving the bow, honor, and praise is the Lord!

Please read: Exodus 20:4-5 English Standard Version (ESV)

[4] "You shall not make for yourself a carved image, or any likeness of anything that is in heaven above, or that is in the earth beneath, or that is in the water under the earth. [5] You shall not bow down to them or serve them, for I the LORD your God am a jealous God, visiting the iniquity of the fathers on the children to the third and the fourth generation of those who hate me,

An example in scripture that shows how bowing really should be use is found below:

Thus when Cornelius met Peter, he fell at his feet in reverence. Peter would not allow this kind of "honour" and he made him get up: "Stand up; I myself am also a man" (see Acts 10:25,26). Similarly, when John fell down to worship at the feet of an angel, the angel rebuked him: "See that you do not do that. For I am your fellow servant, and of your brethren the prophets, and of those who keep the words of this book. Worship God" (see Revelations 22:8,9). Clearly the honour and praise we give to men and angels could easily deteriorate into idolatry.

Please take some time to read the following articles posted at GotQuestions.org that really clarifies the subject regarding idolatry. See if they shed some light as to whether the pastor was right in what he was doing. You know more of the situation…

What is the significance of high places in the Bible?

http://www.gotquestions.org/high-places.html

What are some modern forms of idolatry?

http://www.gotquestions.org/idolatry-modern.html

What is the definition of idolatry?

http://www.gotquestions.org/idolatry-definition.html

God defines idolatry as the making of images, bowing down and serving them. God does not prohibit art or sculpture.

For example, God commanded the making of golden cherubim's and a bronze serpent (Exodus 25:18-20, Numbers 21:8-9). But the people of Israel were not called to bow down before them or serve them. God never intended that the cherubim's should be venerated by praying and bowing down before them, and indeed they were hardly ever seen by the people of Israel as they were hid in the Holy of Holies.

Similarly the bronze serpent was a picture of Christ dying on the cross (Numbers 21:8,9; John 3:14,15), but the people of Israel were never told to pray or bow down before it. When in course of time they did that, the godly king Hezekiah smashed it to pieces (2 Kings 18:3, 4).

Consider the respect factor:

Bowing - a way of showing respect

Abraham "bowed himself to the people of the land" (Gen. 23:7); so did Jacob to Esau (Gen. 33:3); and the brethren of Joseph before him as the governor of the land (Gen. 43:28).

Bowing is also frequently mentioned as an act of adoration to idols (Josh. 23:7; 2 Kings 5:18; Judg. 2:19; Isa. 44:15), and to God (Josh. 5:14; Psalms. 22:29; 72:9; Micah 6:6; Ps. 95:6; Eph. 3:14).

Respect can clearly be misused when it comes to the actions of bowing…

Friend, if the pastor is clearly bowing to an image, a structure, and praying to it he needs to stop immediately. This is idolatry!

I don't know the pastor's motives. If he was not bowing in worship to it, perhaps he was showing respect to God and not praying to the Altar. In conclusion, consider this:

If the Pastor was kneeling down, but mentally and in his heart he was not worshiping, sending praise and prayers to the altar, like if he would bow at any other location to show humility towards God, then this in my opinion does not fit the idolatry paradigm.

In trying to determine the pastor's actions you might not be able to tell whether the pastor's focus was really on God and not on the objects around him. Know this, if there are carved images, statues, pictures etc… that he is clearly bowing to then this is idolatry. This is wrong… It should not be done!

Personally, as a pastor, I would not bow as if to an item. The congregation usually contains people who are at different levels of their spiritual development where it can confuse some… It may also unbeknownst to the pastor endorse an idolatrous practice for those coming from this type of religious experience, thus leading some down the dark awful path of idolatry…

Follow up communication to question 83:

Thank you for your reply. My Church is Lutheran.

I do take part in the service --1. Assistant Minister, 2. Help with Communion etc... of which the Pastor bow down to the altar before going up and after coming down. I used to bow down too, but sometime now I refuse to bow down. I assist the same way. No one even the Pastor did not ask me why.

I took some of the answers from the bible and prepared for the time.

PS. Pastor Roscoe if there is any more light on the matter I would appreciate it. Also, sometimes I think of going to another church.

Yours Truly.

Profile: Male Over 60 North America

Hello Minister, Thanks for clarifying some points to your previous question. In addition to what was already answered, read the following:

In some Lutheran churches this process of bowing is required when approaching the altar. They sincerely believe that they are doing the right thing. During prayer the clergy turn and face the altar since it represents Christ. So when bowing to the altar they believe a person is essentially bowing to Christ. His throne so to speak is the altar. Since the altar is a symbol of the constant presence of God, and since it serves as the focus of devotion in the church (except during the reading of the Gospel when the focus of attention shifts to the book), for Lutherans it is appropriate to salute the altar with a profound bow when first entering and last leaving the sanctuary and to bow moderately whenever crossing, approaching, or leaving the midst. In going to and from the altar, or when otherwise walking about, the officiants' hands should also be folded reverently.

There appears to be to much focus on the Altar. A man made structure not ordained by God. Why can't they just in their minds revere God without the imagery?

1. Pray for discernment as to what is really going on when the pastor bows to the Altar.
2. Once you are sure of the Lords answer, pray for wisdom and courage to approach the pastor in a one on one meeting. This is to be non confrontational. Friendly… Let him know that you are having some difficulty with seeing him or people bowing to the Altar. You respect him highly and did not want this issue between you. Ask if he can explain what is going on within his mind when he bows? What's the thought process… When

it is time for you to share your viewpoint, share with him the scriptures regarding idolatry. If he dismisses it as not being idolatry yet he is actually bowing and giving reverence to the altar he just may be blind to this entire process. You may end up saying that you respectfully disagree but will take the matter to prayer. At the right stopping point in the conversation, thank him for spending time with you.

3. If your conscious is speaking loudly to you, pay attention to it as you already are doing. Know this; symbols are powerful things because of the meaning people attach to them. Perhaps God can speak through you to the pastor.
4. Attending that particular church is optional unless you were put there for such a time as this! In this case, you may be planting the seed of wisdom before leaving to pursue fellowship in a church that does not follow this practice.

Some scriptures to ponder:

1 Corinthians 10:31 English Standard Version (ESV)

31 So, whether you eat or drink, or whatever you do, do all to the glory of God.

Leviticus 26:1 English Standard Version (ESV)

Blessings for Obedience

26 "You shall not make idols for yourselves or erect an image or pillar, and you shall not set up a figured stone in your land to bow down to it, for I am the LORD your God.

Exodus 20:4 English Standard Version (ESV)

4 "You shall not make for yourself a carved image, or any likeness of anything that is in heaven above, or that is in the earth beneath, or that is in the water under the earth.

Exodus 20:3 English Standard Version (ESV)

3 "You shall have no other gods before me.

In conclusion:

How is bowing to an image giving glory to God? No matter how it is sugar coated or explained, the image is not God. Bowing to it is forbidden in scripture.

You choosing to go to a different church is certainly an option… Pray about it… If you leave this church, go in peace. If you stay and can effectively promote changing this practice, praise the Lord!

May God guide you brother with keeping His will, and honoring Him in all that you do!

Question: 84

Question: 1. I dedicated my life to the Lord on Jan. 4th, 1974. 2. I was raised in foster homes - one of which I was severely beaten and molested. 3. I have and continue to suffer from Bi-polar disorder. 4. I am a retired Secondary School English teacher. Getting to my question, for years I have suffered from BP. When I am down, I hate myself, feel unworthy, unloved, of no value or use to God. I know that God does not see me this way but I do. I deliberately withdraw from people during those times because I usually end up saying hurtful things that I don't mean to say but despite the fruits of the Spirit, I have difficulty exercising self-control. I am constantly asking for forgiveness from those I have hurt. I then take on a defeatist attitude saying to myself, "It doesn't matter because I ask for the Lord's forgiveness then the next time it happens I hate myself and go through the same forgiveness process again. Most of the time I go without food because I can't afford to buy anything... The Lord says He will provide but when I go two or three days without, I believe that I have done something wrong that I haven't asked His forgiveness for. I search my mind and my heart to see if there is something there. Does God still care?

Profile: Male Over 60 North America

Answer: Dear friend. Thanks for taking the time to write to Gotquestions.org.

Sorry it has been a tough ride for you for such a long time. Troubling issues happens to the best of us! Our Lord did say in this life we will have trouble…

John 16:33 (ESV)

33 I have said these things to you, that in me you may have peace. In the

world you will have tribulation. But take heart; I have overcome the world."

Know that your email to us may be a start of something new for you. Are you up for taking my suggestions to heart? It is all up to you.

God still cares about you! He never stopped loving you! He knows His plans for you.

God loves us because GOD IS LOVE (see 1 John 4:8-10). He loves us in spite of us being unlovable at times. The beauty of God's love is that He loves the unlovable. He loves us because of his character, not because of ours. Praise the Lord! Because therein is security. If God's love for me depended on my character or anything within me, it might constantly change. But because God is love and God is immutable, He changes not. His love for us is never ending (see Romans 8:37-39).

For further study regarding God's love please read the article at gotquestions.org:

Does God love me?

http://www.gotquestions.org/does-God-love-me.html

God can use you to help others who are struggling with the same issues.

Having this disorder means you have a concern that is negatively impacting how you live your life. Left unresolved, this concern can cause a person significant distress and problems in their relationships and life.

Did you ever get counseling or treatment for the beating and molestation that occurred in the foster care system? This devastating issue in your life has had a hold on you for such a long time. It was an evil act that should not happen to you or anyone else.

I am not a medical professional but let me give you more of my thoughts for you to consider. This trauma may have brought on much trouble such as the Bi-polar on you. You had to protect yourself some how during that evil experience and perhaps your mind tilted and you got stuck in a mode of the continuous cycle of " I am down, I hate myself, feel unworthy, unloved, of no value or use to God etc.." because of what some evil individual did to you. These self defeating thoughts repeated often enough become a habit and the new normal for a person. Don't believe the lie regarding your value to God and to others!

Know this and really hang on to this:

1. You did not deserve this action!
2. You are not at fault!
3. A sick individual misused his or her power to force their will on you!
4. You are not unworthy! You are not unloved! You are precious to God!
5. You matter to God! You matter in the big scheme of things!
6. Do not believe the lie that Satan may be reminding you every day... Whatever it is... The devil is a liar!
7. Whatever took place during the attack does not mean that you are now the same as the perpetrators!
8. Began redirecting your mind to God's view of you every time evil creeps into your thoughts, reminding you of your supposed value... For example here is what Gods word says:

Psalm 139:14 English Standard Version (ESV)

[14] I praise you, for I am fearfully and wonderfully made.

Wonderful are your works; my soul knows it very well.

The next important step is to read and memorize Philippians 4:8

Philippians 4:8 English Standard Version (ESV)

[8] Finally, brothers, whatever is true, whatever is honorable, whatever is

just, whatever is pure, whatever is lovely, whatever is commendable, if there is any excellence, if there is anything worthy of praise, think about these things.

Print the scriptures I mention in my response and carry them with you. Memorize them... Read them every time battles within you occur.

When your mind starts drifting towards depressing thoughts focus your mind on Philippians 4:8. Pray and ask God to help you think on these things. Ask yourself is it honorable? Is it just? Etc... If not, force your mind to think of honorable actions, just acts, pure commendable thoughts etc... Pray asking God to help you with this... Do this everyday for 3 months time... Remember we are trying to break the negative thought habits that have been in place for many years...

Know that God knows what occurred and will care for you and enact justice.

Get help from a Christian counselor. There is nothing wrong with getting help. Proper treatment can yield promising results emotionally if addressed appropriately and for the proper length of time.

Proverbs 15:22 English Standard Version (ESV)

22 Without counsel plans fail, but with many advisers they succeed.

The first option is always going to God with all of your needs.

You mentioned that you deliberately withdraw from people at times because you usually end up saying hurtful things that you don't mean. Does this include church attendance?

Are you connected to a particular church? A lot of churches have a ministry where they have food shelters or can refer a person to one. The food is free to the person in need.

Are you isolating yourself from the care that God has put in place while you are trying to not say hurtful things to others? This can be an endless loop…

It is time right now to stop doing this. Yes you, my friend. Stop isolating yourself…

Pick up the phone and call out for help. I included a phone number below to a place that can help you with the Bi-polar disorder.

Brother, we were all created to be in community with other believers and following the LORD.

I do not know what state or country you are from but please consider looking into this.

God has provided a way but it may not have been realized until now. Be bold and make the phone call and don't quit in the process. Stick to it and pray often.

There are also government programs that can assist you with getting food.

Brother, are you hurting? Are you looking for counseling or are in need of some answers?

I urge you to contact New Life counseling ministry and request help:

Call Center Phone: 800-NEW-LIFE (639-5433)

New Life Live! Radio Program

Phone: (800) 229-3000

Fax: (949) 494-1272

http://newlife.com/contact

http://newlife.com/

Additional information to consider:

Rule out Underlying Causes

Finding relief from the symptoms associated with mood disorders is a process that starts with addressing various physical issues. The biggest step many of us can take toward mental health involves getting our bodies into the best shape possible. This requires skilled sleuthing by the patient and experienced practitioners. The goal? To identify and eliminate common underlying causes of mental illness, such as environmental toxins, medications, diseases, low or imbalanced hormones, food allergies, parasites, and candida yeast.

- **Get a complete physical**, and ask your healthcare provider to review all your prescriptions and any illnesses you may have for mood disorder side effects. Look into some or all of the tests below, using the knowledge of your history and symptoms to gauge which of them will most likely identify potential culprits.
- **Make sure you're taking the basics**. These include high potency vitamin (with vitamin B), or with B Complex vitamin, mineral, and amino acid supplements and fish oils to ensure the brain has adequate supplies of the raw materials it needs to function properly and override genetic errors or digestive flaws.
- **Avoid unhealthy foods and lifestyle choices**. Start by eliminating the "bad" fats. Fried foods, hydrogenated oils, and trans fats clog up the body's intricate systems and contribute to systemic inflammation. Replace these bad actors with the "good" fats required for health, such as fish, olive, vegetable, nut, and seed oils.
- **Cut out any and all substances that affect your mind**. This may sound like a no-brainer, but stop using street drugs, alcohol, and tobacco, and either cut way back or eliminate caffeine, refined sugar, chocolate, artificial sweeteners, and monosodium glutamate.

Some mood disorders, those triggered by emotional trauma or produced by abnormal brain-wave patterns, remain immune to biological remedies. However, two nondrug therapies, Eye Movement Desensitization & Reprocessing (EMDR) and neurofeedback have shown remarkable rates of success.

As you go through your day remember these verses:

Deuteronomy 31:6 (ESV)

6 Be strong and courageous. Do not fear or be in dread of them, for it is the LORD your God who goes with you. He will not leave you or forsake you."

For further study see the following articles at Gotquestions.org:

What does the Bible say about being bipolar / manic depression?

http://www.gotquestions.org/bipolar-manic-depression.html

What does the Bible say about depression? How can a Christian overcome depression?

http://www.gotquestions.org/depression-Christian.html

Conclusion:

Brother, pray continually! God does care and He loves you!

Worship God continually, especially every time you start going to the negative thoughts... Fix your eyes and mind on Jesus.

Cry out to God daily. Keep asking God to heal you.

Jeremiah 17:14 English Standard Version (ESV)

Heal me, O LORD, and I shall be healed; save me, and I shall be saved, for you are my praise.

Know this too brother. God puts a limit on our struggles:

1 Corinthians 10:13 English Standard Version (ESV)

13 No temptation has overtaken you that is not common to man. God is faithful, and he will not let you be tempted beyond your ability, but with the temptation he will also provide the way of escape, that you may be able to endure it.

Trust God with the future that awaits you.

Jeremiah 29:11 English Standard Version (ESV)

11 For I know the plans I have for you, declares the LORD, plans for welfare and not for evil, to give you a future and a hope.

If fear rushes upon you read the following:

Isaiah 41:10 English Standard Version (ESV)

10 Fear not, for I am with you; be not dismayed, for I am your God;

I will strengthen you, I will help you, I will uphold you with my righteous right hand.

Let the words in Psalm 91 comfort you as you move forward.

Psalm 91 Read this chapter in the bible regarding "My Refuge and My Fortress". Hang onto theses words…

Take heart. Jesus said "I have overcome the world".

Stay in God's word daily… Confess your sins to the Lord daily…

Let the words of the bible book of Revelation 21:1-27 encourage you.

Spend time reading all of the scriptures suggested in my reply, especially when you are feeling down… If you can print them and keep them with you that would give you quick access to them.

This life is not all we have. Look forward my friend. Look forward!

May God help change your life more than ever before as you dwell in the study of His word.

I will pray for you!

Question: 85

My big problem, which I need help on, is learning how to love, and how to accept love if it is given to me...

I have found a Bible-believing, born-again Christian counselor and shared with him many things I had written to you about. Regarding food, because of the excruciating pain I have from my knees and am having them replaced in early 2013, I find it difficult to get around. I was at a food bank the other day. A woman, who works at a Men's Mission, volunteered to take me home plus will go to other food services to help me. I have not returned to church for five weeks now. I am afraid to. I stay in my apartment only going out if absolutely necessary - to see counselor, and for physiotherapy on my knees. I have talked with the counselor about the Bi-polar situation. We are going to work on that. My big problem, which I need help on, is learning how to love, and how to accept love if it is given to me...With the Lord, I have head knowledge but have difficulty having heart knowledge. I pray and pray. I continually ask for forgiveness thinking that He really doesn't love me yet his Word says he does and asks me why He allowed Jesus to die on the cross. I am so afraid that He is going to reject me and send me to the lake of fire when I die. It must sound to you that I have lived a very rotten life for me to even think that this was going to happen to me, but I haven't. Each day I have to look at the scars all over my body. I can't get rid of the hatred and ridicule and abuse I have in my mind when I remember the people who knew what was going on and didn't do anything about it. I can't forget the pain. I have 3 children I love and who love me.

Profile: Male Over 60 North America

Answer: Greetings! Glad you have stepped up to the plate and are on the journey to healing. Remember to keep at it even if and when it gets difficult. Press on to the finish line. Pray continually!

You mentioned that you need to learn how to love and accept love if it is given to you.

In my opinions this is probably what you need to do:

You have to improve in loving and possibly forgiving yourself. It is not easy to receive love if you feel unworthy of it. You mention "Each day I have to look at the scars all over my body". Friend, do you know God does not see you in this way…

Read the following to see what I mean:

1 Samuel 16:7 English Standard Version (ESV)

7 But the LORD said to Samuel, "Do not look on his appearance or on the height of his stature, because I have rejected him. For the LORD sees not as man sees: man looks on the outward appearance, but the LORD looks on the heart."

Yes, you have scars but you are more than your scars. Do you hear me? You are more than your scars! Never forget this!

What is the condition of your heart? This makes a person the real deal!

If you can still find it, there was a Billy Graham Movie called "Scars That Heal" from year 1993, World Wide Pictures, Inc. Perhaps watching this may be helpful…

If there are reasons that you are not forgiving yourself discuss this with your counselor. You need to trust yourself. Afterwards your confidence will be more enhanced to aid the process of trusting those who should be trusted.

Please read the following article for a biblical perspective on trust:

What does the Bible say about trust?

http://www.gotquestions.org/Bible-trust.html

Another exercise for you: Each day, look in the mirror and tell yourself you matter.

1. Read the bible everyday.
2. Say "I matter", I matter to God!

Do this for 3 months.

As you live find ways to make God smile... One way is by using your spiritual gift serving in the church...

What is love?

The bible devotes a chapter to describing what love is... Through out scripture we learn from the very best lover. Proven over the course of time... God has this perfect love that is unmatched, period!

Please read:

1 Corinthians 13 English Standard Version (ESV)

The Way of Love

13 If I speak in the tongues of men and of angels, but have not love, I
am a noisy gong or a clanging cymbal. [2] And if I have prophetic powers,
and understand all mysteries and all knowledge, and if I have all faith,
so as to remove mountains, but have not love, I am nothing. [3] If I give
away all I have, and if I deliver up my body to be burned,[a] but have not
love, I gain nothing.

[4] Love is patient and kind; love does not envy or boast; it is not arrogant [5]
or rude. It does not insist on its own way; it is not irritable or resentful;[b]

[6] it does not rejoice at wrongdoing, but rejoices with the truth. [7] Love
bears all things, believes all things, hopes all things, endures all things.

[8] Love never ends. As for prophecies, they will pass away; as for tongues,
they will cease; as for knowledge, it will pass away. [9] For we know in
part and we prophesy in part, [10] but when the perfect comes, the partial
will pass away. [11] When I was a child, I spoke like a child, I thought like
a child, I reasoned like a child. When I became a man, I gave up childish
ways. [12] For now we see in a mirror dimly, but then face to face. Now I
know in part; then I shall know fully, even as I have been fully known.

[13] So now faith, hope, and love abide, these three; but the greatest of
these is love.

Footnotes:

a. 1 Corinthians 13:3 Some manuscripts *deliver up my body* [to death] *that I may boast*
b. 1 Corinthians 13:5 Greek *irritable and does not count up wrongdoing*

You mentioned that you have 3 children who love you and you love them. This is wonderful! Treasure this!

You have said "I am so afraid that He is going to reject me and send me to the lake of fire when I die."

Friend, as long as you are a born again believer the lake of fire is not waiting for you. The lake of fire is awaiting the devil, his demons and the non-saved. The people who abused you are on a path to the lake if they do not turn to Christ. God is a just God and knows everything about you and all of us. He will do right! Never worry, our God will do the right thing! As a saved child of God your sin debt was paid by Jesus on the cross.

Psalm 94:14 English Standard Version (ESV)

14 For the LORD will not forsake his people; he will not abandon his heritage;

Good to hear that a lady offered to help you with the food issue. This is another example of putting yourself in community with others so God can work in their hearts. Don't stay long in isolation. Go back to church...

Proverbs 10:3 English Standard Version (ESV)

3 The LORD does not let the righteous go hungry, but he thwarts the craving of the wicked.

Make sure you continue to present all of your troubling issues to the counselor so you can get the help that can only come while meeting and discussing them in person.

May God help you with your knees and any other health problem...

May God bless your efforts! May you feel His love more and more each day to the point that you become so filled with over flowing love that you can't wait to pass it on to others!

You are loved.

Question: 86

Having Doubt

People at church and my close friends tell me that I'm bearing fruit and that they can see evidence of Christ in my life. I know that there has been a clear time in my life when I turned to Him in repentance and accepted Him as my Savior. Yet I still constantly doubt my salvation and sometimes even the authenticity of the Word of God. I have grown up in church but also around many unbelievers. Sometimes I am tempted into thinking that the Bible just brings "false hope" for something more and that it's too good to be true, even though I know that there is no way we're here without God. I often question whether I am actually following Him or the ways of this world. I have great grief as well because I always tend to overlook the verses speaking of joy and focus on the ones where He talks about how He never truly knew us. My hearts honest desire is to be with Him in His Kingdom someday, but can I possibly be saved if I still doubt what He and the Bible says? P.S. I know this is a long question and that there are answers to similar questions out there. I do apologize for the length and greatly appreciate your support and effort.

Answer:

Hello friend, thank you for writing us to express your concerns and doubts…

I am going to try to answer you without knowing your regular habits that support growing in the faith.

Are you reading the bible everyday?

Are you spending time with the Lord?

Are you attending church?

Are you becoming more loving?

Etc…

Your question revolves around the following topics:

1. Eternal Security
2. Biblical Inspiration
3. Trust in God
4. Marks of a true Christian

Eternal Security:

If you had a particular time in your life when you truly surrendered your life to Christ, then your eternity is in the protections of our Great God. Nothing can take you out of His strong hand. A true follower will want to live their life honoring and trusting God daily.

His followers would want to read His word the bible taking in all of it as they live their life.

When people come to know Christ as their Savior, they are brought into a relationship with God that guarantees their eternal security. Jude 24 declares, "To Him who is able to keep you from falling and to present you before His glorious presence without fault and with great joy." God's power is able to keep the believer from falling. It is up to Him, not us, to present us before His glorious presence. Our eternal security is a result of God keeping us in His grip, not us maintaining our own salvation.

For more on this topic please go to the following url:

http://www.gotquestions.org/eternal-security.html

Biblical Inspiration

When a believer has been saved the Holy Spirit resides in them to guide them. When you make a decision that is against God, the Holy Spirit convicts…

The bible becomes easier for them to understand for the Spirit of truth will guide them.

God's word is truth regardless of what the world is shoveling out there. There are a lot of websites and people who are all about trying to discredit the bible but when you really look at the issues they bring up they end up with egg in their faces. For the many websites that attack the bible there are many who have answers to all of these supposed errors and attacks…

Perhaps your doubts are because you have heard some negative incorrect comments and did not have an answer for them.

If you are struggling with believing the bible because of what I just mentioned, or want to start erasing the doubt in the bible please go to the following website to read these very important articles:

Does the Bible contain errors, contradictions, or discrepancies?

http://www.gotquestions.org/Bible-errors.html

Is the Bible truly God's Word?

http://www.gotquestions.org/Bible-God-Word.html

What does it mean that the Bible is inspired?

http://www.gotquestions.org/Bible-inspired.html

Why is the Bible called the Holy Bible?

http://www.gotquestions.org/Holy-Bible.html

Spend time addressing your doubts. There are answers for many issues that cause doubt.

The bible is a book that has transformed countless lives and cultures throughout the last 2000 years. No matter how its opponents try to attack, destroy, or discredit it, the Bible remains; its veracity and impact on lives is unmistakable. The accuracy which has been preserved despite every attempt to corrupt, attack, or destroy it is clear testimony to the fact that the Bible is truly God's Word and is supernaturally protected by Him. It should not surprise us that, no matter how the Bible is attacked, it always comes out unchanged and unscathed. After all, Jesus said, "Heaven and earth will pass away, but my words will never pass away" (Mark 13:31). After looking at the evidence, one can say without a doubt that, yes, the Bible is truly God's Word.

Trust in God

It goes without saying that we cannot trust someone we don't know, and therein lies the secret of learning to trust God. When someone says, "Trust me," we have one of two reactions. Either we can say, "Ok, I'll trust you," or we can say, "Why should I?" In God's case, trusting Him naturally follows when we understand why we should.

Please read the following article that articulates this topic very well:

How can I learn to trust in God?

http://www.gotquestions.org/trust-God.html

At this point I have suggested some articles for you to read. Please understand that I sincerely would like to help you resolve this important matter in your life. It will require that you spend time immersing your thoughts on these articles and making a decision.

There are also good Christian apologetic websites out there that can assist your learning.

You have to decide to step forward and say I choose to believe God (who is all truth) no matter what doubts pop into my head. If there are people spreading false information to you daily that is affecting you negatively towards the faith, see if you can remove yourself from it. If not, write down what they may be saying to trip you up and seek answers.

Another thing, the devil is seeking to devour people. He is a liar. He is out to spread doubt about God and His word to as many people as he and his demons can….

Nothing in the bible is too good to be true. It does not give false hope. It is all in how you choose to look at things. Humans look at things from a limited view point. God sees the big picture and allows things to occur according to His will. You see a sovereign and majestic God has spoken and His words are in the bible. It is impossible for God to lie, so what you see in the bible actually happened and the predictions will occur. Hang in there, for if your faith is in the God of the Christian bible it is in the only true God.

2 Timothy 3:16 English Standard Version (ESV)

16 All Scripture is breathed out by God and profitable for teaching, for reproof, for correction, and for training in righteousness,

Hang on to Jesus. Anything that tempts or suggests that any of His ways are false is a lie most likely from the evil one or a person who is lost spiritually.

To refresh your thinking please read the following articles at the following URLS:

Is the Bible truly God's Word?

http://www.gotquestions.org/Bible-God-Word.html

How do I know the Bible is not just mythology?

http://www.gotquestions.org/Bible-mythology.html

It is time to build your faith right now! Make sure that you are not being a lone ranger Christian. Stay connected to other believers. If you are attending a church that is not teaching you scripture and promoting growth in God's word you may want to consider changing churches.

My friend, you mentioned that you are not sure if you are following God or the ways of the world. If you are not sure if you are following the Lord, the bible teaches us how to do so. Be sure to read your bible for a life time….

See if you are following God in the way the 2 scriptures I listed below describes to us:

Marks of a True Christian

Romans 12:9-21 English Standard Version (ESV)

Marks of the True Christian

9 Let love be genuine. Abhor what is evil; hold fast to what is good. 10
Love one another with brotherly affection. Outdo one another in showing
honor. 11 Do not be slothful in zeal, be fervent in spirit,[a] serve the Lord.
12 Rejoice in hope, be patient in tribulation, be constant in prayer. 13
Contribute to the needs of the saints and seek to show hospitality.

14 Bless those who persecute you; bless and do not curse them. 15 Rejoice
with those who rejoice, weep with those who weep. 16 Live in harmony
with one another. Do not be haughty, but associate with the lowly.
[b] Never be wise in your own sight. 17 Repay no one evil for evil, but
give thought to do what is honorable in the sight of all. 18 If possible,
so far as it depends on you, live peaceably with all. 19 Beloved, never
avenge yourselves, but leave it[c] to the wrath of God, for it is written,
"Vengeance is mine, I will repay, says the Lord." 20 To the contrary, "if

your enemy is hungry, feed him; if he is thirsty, give him something to drink; for by so doing you will heap burning coals on his head." [21] Do not be overcome by evil, but overcome evil with good.

Footnotes:

a. Romans 12:11 Or *fervent in the Spirit*
b. Romans 12:16 Or *give yourselves to humble tasks*
c. Romans 12:19 Greek *give place*

Also, keep in mind what the Lord requires of us:

Micah 6:8 English Standard Version (ESV)

[8] He has told you, O man, what is good; and what does the LORD require of you but to do justice, and to love kindness,[a] and to walk humbly with your God?

Footnotes:

a. Micah 6:8 Or *steadfast love*

Now let's address the next concern:

Can I possibly be saved if I still doubt what He and the Bible says?

In my humble opinion, it is possible... Perhaps you got saved and are not growing in His word. Perhaps some spiritual disciplines are lacking and preventing growth... Because you have questions does not mean that you do not believe that Jesus is the Savior.

To be certain that you are saved is the most important thing you can do. There is no harm in making sure that you are truly saved.

Please go to the following URL, read it, and see if you agree. If so, you can join others by clicking the link informing us of your decision:

http://www.gotquestions.org/how-can-I-be-saved.html

Know this, once you have truly accepted Jesus Christ as your Savior nothing can take you out of His grip!

Romans 8:38-39 English Standard Version (ESV)

38 For I am sure that neither death nor life, nor angels nor rulers, nor things present nor things to come, nor powers, 39 nor height nor depth, nor anything else in all creation, will be able to separate us from the love of God in Christ Jesus our Lord.

In conclusion:

You are asking questions that promote growth as a believer. Keep seeking answers. Study to show yourself approved…

2 Timothy 2:15 English Standard Version (ESV)

15 Do your best to present yourself to God as one approved,[a] a worker who has no need to be ashamed, rightly handling the word of truth.

Footnotes:

a. 2 Timothy 2:15 That is, one approved after being tested

When doubt occurs know that the Christian faith is truth. Salvation is in the eternal security of Gods perfect strength. When you accept Jesus as your Savior it is finished and rest in Gods Hands!

Blessings my friend!

Question: 87

Is it okay for a Christian to own a gun?

Profile: Male 61, North America

Answer: Thanks for writing Lord of Hope Ministries. Friend, I see no reason why a Christian shouldn't own a gun for the purpose of protecting one's family. We live in a wicked society where things are starting to go against those believing and following the Lord!

Also, sick minded people sometimes just go out shooting innocent people (ie… Colorado movie theater)….

If you decide to get one, please, for you and your family sake, keep it in a place where no kids can get to it. Have a safety mechanism enabled such as a pin or lock. Keep the Gun's storage location confidential… Only tell your partner and possibly your grown kids if they need to know where it is.

Another thing to consider… If you and your spouse walk into your home where some intruder was still in the home, forget the gun, and leave if possible, and call the cops. The intruder could have an unfair advantage…

It is sad that we all will need to decide how to protect our families. Pray first and see if God gives you the okay for He knows all…

Remember this… our help ultimately comes from the Lord.

Psalm 121:2 English Standard Version (ESV)

2 My help comes from the Lord, who made heaven and earth.

I pray that you never ever have to use it!

Question: 88

Question regarding Homosexuality...

I got this from an article and I'm wondering if it's true? "If any case, whether homosexuality results from genetics or upbringing, people don't generally choose to be homosexual. Many homosexuals testify how agonizing it is to find yourself with these desires and to fight against them, and they'll tell you they would never choose to be that way. And the Bible doesn't condemn a person because he has a homosexual orientation. What it condemns is homosexual acts. It is perfectly possible to be a homosexual and be a born-again, Spirit-filled Christian. Just as an alcoholic who is dry will still stand up at an AA meeting and say, 'I am an alcoholic," so a homosexual who is living straight and keeping himself pure ought to be able to stand up in a prayer meeting and say, 'I am a homosexual. But by God's grace and the power of the Holy Spirit, I'm living chastely for Christ." And I hope we'd have the courage and love to welcome him or her as a brother or sister in Christ."

Answer: Thanks for writing Gotquestions.org.

Let me first address this issue by mentioning that homosexuality is a choice just like other sins... If the article says what you mentioned above regarding people don't generally choose to be gay, than I would say that information is false. Contrary to what the Gay movement has successfully convinced many people in the current government, homosexuality is not a civil rights issue. It is a choice to act out in a way that is displeasing to the Lord.

God cannot bless sin, and no true Christian would confirm others in a sinful lifestyle – one that merits eternal judgment (1 Corinthians 6). The good news is that many men and women once trapped in homosexuality have found freedom through the same Christ whose words the world distorts.

Is it possible to be a gay Christian? If the phrase “gay Christian” refers to a person who struggles against homosexual desires and temptations – yes, a “gay Christian” is possible. However, the description “gay Christian” is not accurate for such a person, since he/she does not desire to be gay, and is struggling against the temptations. Such a person is not a “gay Christian,” but rather is simply a struggling Christian, just as there are Christians who struggle with fornication, lying, and stealing. If the phrase “gay Christian” refers to a person who actively, perpetually, and unrepentantly lives a homosexual lifestyle – no, it is not possible for such a person to truly be a Christian.

Please read the following articles at GotQuestions.org to help you get a better understanding from a biblical perspective on this subject:

Is it possible to be a gay Christian?

http://www.gotquestions.org/gay-Christian.html

Can a person be born gay?

http://www.gotquestions.org/born-gay.html

What does the Bible say about homosexuality? Is homosexuality a sin?

http://www.gotquestions.org/homosexuality-Bible.html

What does the Bible say about being a lesbian? Does the Bible mention lesbianism?

http://www.gotquestions.org/Bible-lesbian.html

There are former Homosexuals who can give testimony to how the power of God can help a person struggling with this issue. Sadly, many don't get to hear the truth about this awful lifestyle.

Testimonies can be found at:

Testimony of Former Homosexual and Prisoner

http://lightingtheway.blogspot.com/2009/10/testimony-of-former-homosexual-and.html

Former Gay Hairdresser to the Stars gets SAVED!

http://www.youtube.com/watch?v=Ty1QYul0cx8

The statement where the person stands up and announced that they are a homosexual is not something a Christian would need to continue doing if attending such meeting because God has made them a new creation. The power of God can change their life. As they grow in Christ former behaviors and thinking will change.

2 Corinthians 5:17 English Standard Version (ESV)

17 Therefore, if anyone is in Christ, he is a new creation. The old has passed away; behold, the new has come.

Again a person can change from this life style. They will have to leave the people who are enabling them to continue in the homosexual lifestyle.

Prayer can change things. With prayer all things are possible for our great God is listening and answering.

Question: 89

Do we have to honor a parent that is severely immoral and brings out the worst in people? If so, how is it possible?

Profile: Male 31-45 North America

Answer: Thanks for writing us! Yes. Scripture expresses it this way:

Exodus 20:12 English Standard Version (ESV)

12 "Honor your father and your mother, that your days may be long in the land that the LORD your God is giving you.

Ephesians 6:2-3 English Standard Version (ESV)

2 "Honor your father and mother" (this is the first commandment with a promise), 3 "that it may go well with you and that you may live long in the land."

Note: To honor does not mean accepting bad behavior.

There are scriptures showing how others dealt with a bad parent or in-law.

Check out 1Samuel 18-24

Saul tried to kill his son Jonathan's close friend David... David was also Saul's son-in-law...

Even though Saul's jealousy led to Saul trying to kill David, you will see how David still honored God and Saul's leadership position as King. Jonathan tried to balance following his dad and not getting caught up in Saul's craziness and did the right thing in warning his friend David.

The first thing to remember is that God is our loving Heavenly Father who does not just slap down a rule and sit back waiting for us to obey it, but whose rules are there for one reason only—our ultimate good. If we truly desire to obey Him no matter how impossible it seems, He is willing and eager to help us find the way. First and foremost, of course, we must develop a loving, trusting relationship with our Heavenly Father which may be extremely difficult for those who have never known what it is to love and trust. Those in this position must just take one small step and say to God in their heart "I want to learn to love and trust you—please help me." He will move to answer, because that heart cry from one of His children is all He needs. He is the only one who can change emotions and attitudes and mend damaged relationships and broken hearts (Luke 4:18).

Friend, you asked how is it possible to honor an immoral parent.

Honoring your father and mother is being respectful in word and action and having an inward attitude of esteem for their position. The Greek word for honor means "to revere, prize, and value." Honor is giving respect not only for merit but also for rank. For example, some Americans may disagree with the President's decisions, but they should still respect his position as leader of their country. Similarly, children of all ages should honor their parents, regardless of whether or not their parents "deserve" honor.

While we are required to honor parents, that doesn't include imitating ungodly ones (Ezekiel 20:18-19). If a parent ever instructs a child to do something that clearly contradicts God's commands, that child must obey God rather than his/her parents (Acts 5:29).

Honor begets honor. God will not honor those who will not obey His command to honor their parents. If we desire to please God and be blessed, we should honor our parents. Honoring is not easy, is not always fun, and certainly is not possible in our own strength. But honor is a certain path to our purpose in life—glorifying God. "Children, obey your parents in everything, for this pleases the Lord" (Colossians 3:20).

Read the details in the following articles. They will shed further light on this very important topic…

What does it mean to honor my father and mother?

http://www.gotquestions.org/honor-father-mother.html

How do we honor an abusive parent?

http://www.gotquestions.org/honor-abusive-parent.html

Additional Action Steps:

1. Love the Lord your God with all your heart. Matthew 22:37 (ESV)

[37] And he said to him, "You shall love the Lord your God with all your heart and with all your soul and with all your mind.

2. Love your neighbor as yourself. Mark 12:31 (ESV)

[31] The second is this: 'You shall love your neighbor as yourself.' There is no other commandment greater than these."

3. Apply the golden rule. Luke 6:31(ESV)

[31] And as you wish that others would do to you, do so to them.

4. Speak the truth in love.

Ephesians 4:15 English Standard Version (ESV)

[15] Rather, speaking the truth in love, we are to grow up in every way into him who is the head, into Christ,

You may not be able to change the way a parent behaves, but how you respond to them is your choice. You can allow the parent to get to you, or you can surrender it to God.

What else can we do about reacting to a parent who is severely immoral and brings out the worst in people?

It is our own response to this type of situation that fuels our frustration. Only we can stop wearing ourselves out emotionally by allowing interfering parents actions to be the arbiter of our own peace. A parent's behavior is not our responsibility; our response is.

Parents and in-laws should be treated with respect and love, but we must not allow our emotions to entangle us. Consider the best way to disengage an enemy, a trouble maker is to make him an ally. This is done through God's grace. Christians can always give the grace of forgiveness (Ephesians 4:32). It may not stop a parent from being immoral, interfering, or bringing out the worst in people, but it will be a source of strength and peace to stand in (Ephesians 6:11-17). The only place to find true peace of heart is in a personal relationship with God through Christ. Only then can we respond by resting in His peace.

Galatians 5:22-23 English Standard Version (ESV)

22 But the fruit of the Spirit is love, joy, peace, patience, kindness, goodness, faithfulness, 23 gentleness, self-control; against such things there is no law.

Friend, pray for God to increase the fruits of the Spirit in you.

In closing:

2 Timothy 2:15 English Standard Version (ESV)

15 Do your best to present yourself to God as one approved,[a] a worker who has no need to be ashamed, rightly handling the word of truth.

Footnotes:

a. 2 Timothy 2:15 That is, one approved after being tested.

Question: 90

Why did God place humans on earth with the fallen angels? Why didn't He put us on another planet to avoid sin?

Why would He give Satan and the fallen angels a second chance to live and torment us here on earth? Is earth really hell? Shouldn't the fallen angels be in hell somewhere?

I don't know what to believe anymore. So much has changed and has been hidden from us.

Profile: Female 18-30 North America

Answer: Hello Friend. I am really glad that you decided to contact GotQuestions.org seeking answers to your many excellent questions.

Let me begin by saying don't loose heart! If you are a Christ follower, keep holding on, for you do not believe in vain. If you are not a Christ follower, keep seeking answers for we want you to become a Christ follower. Your eternal life is so important to us!

I will provide answers in brief and some links to articles that will give you most of the details. Please take the time to read all of the references that I include, for it is my goal that you will come through this stronger in your faith.

First, God is good, perfect, sovereign, all knowing, always right and He is love. These are just a few of His attributes...

Based on just these few attributes we must conclude that He knows what he is doing.

Why did God place humans on earth with the fallen angels?

God is purposeful. He has a plan that He enacted with full understanding of all occurrences. If I can offer this opinion: It appears that God is using all of life circumstances to build our faith, build our reliance and trust in Him and to test us.

God not only allowed Satan to roam the earth, Satan went back and forth to heaven at a certain period. See below:

The book of Job tells us that, for a time at least, Satan still had access to heaven and to the throne of God. "One day the angels came to present themselves before the LORD, and Satan also came with them. The LORD said to Satan, 'Where have you come from?' Satan answered the LORD, 'From roaming through the earth and going back and forth in it'" (Job 1:6-7). Apparently at that time, Satan was still moving freely between heaven and earth, speaking to God directly and answering for his activities. At what point God discontinued this access is unknown.

Please read the following article posted at GotQuestions.org:

How, why, and when did Satan fall from heaven?

http://www.gotquestions.org/Satan-fall.html

Friend, God did not put the fallen angels on earth without also providing help for his people. Considered the following scripture:

1 Corinthians 10:13 English Standard Version (ESV)

13 No temptation has overtaken you that is not common to man. God is faithful, and he will not let you be tempted beyond your ability, but with the temptation he will also provide the way of escape, that you may be able to endure it.

Friend, God knows how he made us and desires to test our faith.

Please read the following scriptures:

James 1:3 English Standard Version (ESV)

3 for you know that the testing of your faith produces steadfastness.

1 Peter 1:7 English Standard Version (ESV)

7 so that the tested genuineness of your faith—more precious than gold that perishes though it is tested by fire—may be found to result in praise and glory and honor at the revelation of Jesus Christ.

God also provided a way to save people from sin. God gave mankind a way that leads us from this sin filled world to life everlasting free from sin and death. It is a choice that we will all have to make before it is too late.

John 3:16 English Standard Version (ESV)

For God So Loved the World

16 "For God so loved the world,[a] that he gave his only Son, that whoever believes in him should not perish but have eternal life.

Footnotes:

a. John 3:16 Or *For this is how God loved the world*

Please read more about this at the following URL's:

http://www.gotquestions.org/Christian-doctrine-salvation.html

http://www.gotquestions.org/way-of-salvation.html

http://www.gotquestions.org/steps-to-salvation.html

http://www.gotquestions.org/prayer-of-salvation.html

http://www.gotquestions.org/personal-Savior.html

Why didn't He put us on another planet to avoid sin?

God designed earth for humankind. He gave humans free will. Humans have the choice to obey or disobey God. Think on this my friend; even if the fallen angels were not present, the potential for sin existed. Wherever Mankind dwelled they could have chosen to disobey God. Yes, this would be disobedience, and evil. I only mentioned it because the possibility existed.

Know this, God did not create evil, but He does allow evil. If God had not allowed for the possibility of evil, both mankind and angels would be serving God out of obligation, not choice. He did not want "robots" that simply did what He wanted them to do because of their "programming." God allowed for the possibility of evil so that we could genuinely have a free will and choose whether or not we wanted to serve Him.

As finite human beings, we can never fully understand an infinite God (Romans 11:33-34). Sometimes we think we understand why God is doing something, only to find out later that it was for a different purpose than we originally thought. God looks at things from a holy, eternal perspective. We look at things from a sinful, earthly, and temporal perspective. Why did God put man on earth knowing that Adam and Eve would sin and therefore bring evil, death, and suffering on all mankind? Why didn't He just create us all and leave us in heaven where we would be perfect and without suffering? These questions cannot be adequately answered this side of eternity. What we can know is whatever God does is holy and perfect and ultimately will glorify Him. God allowed for the possibility of evil in order to give us a true choice in regards to whether we worship Him. God did not create evil, but He allowed it. If He had not allowed evil, we would be worshipping Him out of obligation, not by a choice of our own will.

For more information please read the following article:

http://www.gotquestions.org/did-God-create-evil.html

Why would He give Satan and the fallen angels a second chance to live and torment us here on earth?

We do not always know why God does something.

Deuteronomy 29:29 English Standard Version (ESV)

[29] "The secret things belong to the LORD our God, but the things that are revealed belong to us and to our children forever, that we may do all the words of this law.

Know this; God is also present for His people. He is seeking to save the lost as well. God has the big picture in mind. He also wants to be involved in his people's lives.

2 Chronicles 7:14 English Standard Version (ESV)

[14] if my people who are called by my name humble themselves, and pray and seek my face and turn from their wicked ways, then I will hear from heaven and will forgive their sin and heal their land.

Jeremiah 29:11 English Standard Version (ESV)

[11] For I know the plans I have for you, declares the LORD, plans for welfare[a] and not for evil, to give you a future and a hope.

Footnotes:

a. Jeremiah 29:11 Or *peace*

Additionally, the Bible does not specifically address the issue of God's giving the fallen angels an opportunity to repent, but we do know principles and can extrapolate from them an educated guess. First, Satan (Lucifer) was one of the highest angels, perhaps the highest (Ezekiel 28:14). Lucifer—and all the angels—were continually in God's presence and had a complete knowledge of the glory of God, unobstructed by the things that keep mankind from knowing Him fully. Therefore, they had no excuse for rebelling against God and turning away from Him. For Lucifer and the other angels to rebel despite what they knew about God is the utmost of evil, and this most likely results in God not giving Satan and the other fallen angels the opportunity to repent.

The Bible gives us no reason to believe they would repent even if God did give them the chance (1 Peter 5:8). The fallen angels seem completely devoted to opposing God and attacking God's people. The Bible tells us that one of the things God judges on is how much knowledge of Him a person possesses (Luke 12:48). The fallen angels, then, are even much more deserving of God's wrath because of the exceedingly great knowledge they had about God.

http://www.gotquestions.org/angels-repent.html

Is earth really hell?

Scripture does not tell us the geological (or cosmological) location of hell. Hell is a literal place of real torment, but we do not know where it is. Hell may have a physical location in this universe, or it may be in an entirely different "dimension." Whatever the case, the location of hell is far less important than the need to avoid going there.

Put another way, this earth is the best it will get for those who reject Jesus as their Lord and Savior.

For more details regarding where is hell please go to the following article:

http://www.gotquestions.org/where-is-hell.html

Shouldn't the fallen angels be in hell somewhere?

Ultimately they are all doomed! Some are locked up now (Jude 6), all of them and Satan will be cast in the lake of fire (Revelation 20:7-10) at the appointed time that God controls. Also see Matthew 25:41.

Here is one example of where some fallen angels are located: It seems that God put an end to demons mating with humans by placing all the demons who committed such an act in the Abyss. Jude verse 6 tells us, "And the angels who did not keep their positions of authority but abandoned their own home—these he has kept in darkness, bound with everlasting chains for judgment on the great Day." Obviously, not all of the demons are in "prison" today, so there must have been a group of demons who committed further grievous sin beyond the original fall. Presumably, the demons who mated with human females are the ones who are "bound with everlasting chains." This would prevent any more demons from attempting such an act.

The future forecast for what will happen to Satan is in the book of Revelation chapter 20.

You mentioned "I don't know what to believe anymore. So much has changed and has been hidden from us".

God has made much known in His word the bible so that you will know what to believe. All that you really need to know from a spiritual standpoint was provided. God provided the information in His book the bible. Spend more time reading the bible over and over again as you do life. The renewing of your mind will occur as you fall in love with the eternal, awesome God of the bible. Ask God for wisdom. Ask God to build your faith.

Romans 1:20 English Standard Version (ESV)

20 For his invisible attributes, namely, his eternal power and divine nature, have been clearly perceived, ever since the creation of the world,[a] in the things that have been made. So they are without excuse.

Footnotes:

a. Romans 1:20 Or *clearly perceived from the creation of the world*

Matthew 7:7 English Standard Version (ESV)

7 "Ask, and it will be given to you; seek, and you will find; knock, and it will be opened to you.

James 1:5 English Standard Version (ESV)

5 If any of you lacks wisdom, let him ask God, who gives generously to all without reproach, and it will be given him.

Please read Job 38 for in this God answers Job who experienced big time troubles and needed answers… Mankind is not going to know all the answers for life troubles. It shows God having it all under control.

Additional study:

Why does God allow evil?

http://www.gotquestions.org/God-allow-evil.html

Keep asking questions. Look for answers because God will provide what's needed to build your faith and trust in Him. This world does not have it right. The systems are going more and more against the word of God. Stay in God's word the bible, to keep your spiritual and moral compass calibrated to God's standards.

Continue looking through the many excellent articles posted at http://gotquestions.org

Know that by doing these things you will know what to believe.

May God Bless your efforts in seeking truth!

Question: 91

Can you baptize yourself?

Answer: Thanks for writing Gotquestions.org.

The meanings of the word 'baptize' is to immerse and change the color of, like to 'dye'. So, literally, a cloth cannot dye itself. It must be done by someone else.

When you are baptized, spiritually you are being changed from 'the old man' to a 'new man', receiving the new spirit of God. You are also showing Jesus' death and resurrection and someone is needed to lead you into this, to proclaim it, and to vouch for your willingness and readiness to do this. Most churches give classes to ensure the person knows some of the bible, the important parts in order to really know what they are doing.

The standard in scripture is the person seeking baptism went to another spiritual leader. Jesus went to John the Baptist and the Ethiopian eunuch went to Philip (Acts 8:26-40).

In my humble opinion, Baptisms need to be performed by a spiritual leader, or other Christ follower who, by doing so, is vouching for the sincerity of the one being baptized.

Jesus said that we must confess his name before men/people and confession is necessary before baptism.

A person acting alone misses the mark here...

Also, we should follow what our leader did, and our leader "Jesus" went to a spiritual leader (e.g. John the Baptist) to get baptized.

What is important is that one be baptized for the right reason that is for the remission of sins. Note: Baptism without a witness or witnesses could become very questionable as no one could prove it. Such would open the door for persons to become members of a congregation without having been baptized if the individuals were dishonest.

The person doing the baptizing in scripture was always a person in authority and a Christ follower. There are no examples in scripture of someone baptizing themselves.

Another thing to consider, Jesus told the disciples to perform the baptisms and did not influence individuals to do there own baptism.

The authority behind baptism in Jesus' Name (name of Father, Son and Holy Spirit) resides in the New Testament, written Word of God. To recognize the authority of Jesus means that we believe in His death, burial, resurrection and ascension into Heaven where He is now Lord of all. We also recognize that He does not act alone but He in concert with the Father and the Holy Spirit who are also God. It was this Divine authority the apostles were commissioned by and commanded to baptize all according to this authority.

Matthew 28:18: And Jesus came up and spoke to them, saying, "All authority has been given to Me in heaven and on earth. Matthew 28:19: "Go therefore and make disciples of all the nations, baptizing them in the name of the Father and the Son and the Holy Spirit, Matthew 28:20 teaching them to observe all that I commanded you; and lo, I am with you always, even to the end of the age."

There is perhaps one exception to this and that is for those in situations where no one is available who is willing to baptize a person. I cannot be dogmatic about it since scripture is silent here but I do not think God will hold this against the person, but will count his or her desire for baptism in place of the baptism itself and give them the grace anyway. This is because God loves us and wants us to have his grace, even when the normal method of communicating is unavailable.

Friend, again, there are no examples in scripture that people baptized themselves without any human assistance. Also, regarding who is authorized to baptize people, as mentioned in Matthew 28:18-20, we understand that disciples of Jesus were commanded to teach about Him and baptize all for the remission of sins in His name.

According to Matthew 28:20, we must learn and follow the apostles teaching, not the traditions of men so we can remain faithful to Him.

Matthew 28:20 teaching them to observe all that I commanded you; and lo, I am with you always, even to the end of the age.

Act 2:42 They were continually devoting themselves to the apostles' teaching and to fellowship, to the breaking of bread and to prayer.

In conclusion, nowhere in scripture does it say a person can baptize themselves. Baptizing a person is not limited to only Pastors. Fellow believers can baptize a person as long as they understand the process…

For more study regarding baptisms please read the following article at GotQuestions.org:

http://www.gotquestions.org/Christian-baptism.html

Question: 92

Can a person be born a Christian if their parent or grandparent was one?

I have a comment that "heaven is not for us, our home is earth. We are going to heaven because GOD loves us and wants to give a better living than what we have on earth. This is because of our sins and what Satan did. So we will go to heaven in the name of Jesus. Other religion teaching false that we will die and go to heaven or hell according to our life with others. I am Indian and here so many people follow many Gods. My grandfather was Christian so I am also by birth. Mankind doesn't know the truth of the world, God, and themselves. Thank you for your great service.

Profile: Male 18-30 Asia

Answer: Thanks for sharing your thoughts with us. You matter to us! I am glad that you sent this with a sincere and open heart seeking answers. My response to your comments needs to address the critical information first and then clarify from a biblical standpoint the matter of heaven and earth.

You have mentioned the following: "my grandfather was Christian so I am also by birth". Please know that this does not make you a Christian especially once you reach a certain age. Please know that a person who has reached the age of accountability needs to make a decision on which belief they will follow. Will they choose the Lord or the false gods?

You are right when you said "So we will go to heaven in the name of Jesus". Friend, a person who has reached the age where they can make their own decision is held responsible for whether they choose to accept Jesus as their savior or not. This person cannot be saved based on what their parents or grandparents decided. So you need to ask yourself "have

I made the decision to follow Christ?" Can you remember a time when you prayed to accept Jesus as your Lord and savior? Below are a couple of Gotquestions.org links. Please spend some time reading them. Then ask yourself "Am I saved? If you have any doubt, please in Jesus name, pray to receive Jesus Christ as your savior. Your eternity with God depends on this critical step. Choose life my friend. Choose Jesus… If you decide to pray to receive Jesus as your Lord, please let us know so we can celebrate this!

Where do I find the age of accountability in the Bible?

http://www.gotquestions.org/age-of-accountability.html

How can I become a Christian?

http://www.gotquestions.org/become-a-Christian.html

You are correct that other religions are teaching falsely that we will die and go to heaven or hell according to our life with others. It is good that you have a good understanding of this.

Regarding heaven, it is a place where those who accepted Jesus as their savior will be with God. Jesus made it clear that there's another home for believers.

John 14:2 King James Version (KJV)

2 In my Father's house are many mansions: if it were not so, I would have told you. I go to prepare a place for you.

So because of what God has done believers will have a home in heaven.

Will we have physical bodies in Heaven? See the following article for additional study:

http://www.gotquestions.org/physical-bodies-heaven.html

Our ultimate home is earth. God will recreate the heaven and earth and establish his New Jerusalem on the new earth.

Revelation chapters 21-22 give us a detailed picture of the new heavens and the new earth. After the events of the end times, the current heavens and earth will be done away with and replaced by the new heavens and new earth. The eternal dwelling place of believers will be the new earth. The new earth is the "heaven" on which we will spend eternity. It is the new earth where the New Jerusalem, the heavenly city, will be located. It is on the new earth that the pearly gates and streets of gold will be.

For a deeper understanding of this please read the following article:

What are the New Heavens and the New Earth?

http://www.gotquestions.org/new-heavens-earth.html

May God bless your study and hunger for the truth. You are loved!

Question: 93

Should a lay person perform a marriage ceremony?

Profile: Male 31-45 North America

Answer: Thanks for writing us! Let's look at the definition of Marriage.

Definition of Marriage

1. The state of being united to a person of the opposite sex as husband or wife in a consensual and contractual relationship recognized by law.
2. The institution whereby individuals are joined in a marriage.

What does the bible say about marriage ceremonies?

The Bible does not give specific details or directions about a marriage ceremony. It does mention weddings in several places. Jesus attended a wedding in John 2. Wedding ceremonies were a well-established tradition in Jewish history and in Bible times. Scripture is very clear about marriage being a holy and divinely established covenant. It is equally clear about our obligation to honor and obey the laws of our earthly governments, which are also divinely established authorities, as long as the government conforms to God's word.

In Malachi 2:14 we see that marriage is a holy *covenant* before God. In the Jewish custom, God's people signed a written agreement at the time of the marriage to seal the covenant. The marriage ceremony, therefore, is meant to be a public demonstration of a couple's commitment to a covenant relationship. It's not the "ceremony" that's important in a marriage; it's the couple's covenant commitment before God and men.

What are the requirements in government? To keep this answer short I will just mentions one USA state.

In the state of Illinois, those who perform marriage ceremonies must be an ordained minister or a Justice of the Peace. These qualifications permit them to perform marriages throughout the state. Various ministries ordain laypeople who have a desire to administer marriage rites to their community, giving many people the opportunity to share in the celebration of marriage in this way.

So after researching this subject, the answer to your question can vary depending on where the person lives. A Lay person can perform the wedding ceremony if they meet certain qualifications. They should be considered Ordained Personnel.

States in America have Government personnel that can do this as well. Justice of the peace, Clerk of Court, Notary…. The state or country you live in may have a variation to these I listed so it depends on where you live.

In a church environment ordained Ministers traditionally performs the weddings.

I hope this helps you as you seek answers… May God bless you!

Question: 94

Should we pity and feel bad for evil men both in history, and nowadays, or hate them? As a child I felt pity for Judas and other evil men/women in the Bible. Is that bad? I obviously do not condone the evil and terrible things Judas or Cain did, but God has created much good from evil. So, I am confused about how I am supposed to feel about these men.

Profile: Male 18-30 North America

Answer: Greetings from GotQuestions.org! Your question tells me something wonderful about you. You have compassion for your fellow man whether they are considered good people or bad. There is absolutely nothing wrong with how you feel. You are wired up in such a way that I can see you being used by God.

You feeling pity for Judas and other evil men and women in the bible suggest that you have a good understanding of the mess that they made of their lives. It did not have to turn out the way it did if they all made better God honoring choices. Friend, you are exhibiting a trait our Lord had when he looked at the crowds he spoke to.

Matthew 9:36 English Standard Version (©2001)

When he saw the crowds, he had compassion for them, because they were harassed and helpless, like sheep without a shepherd.

When God saw how wicked mankind had become he became grieved…

Genesis 6:6 English Standard Version (©2001)

And the LORD was sorry that he had made man on the earth, and it grieved him to his heart.

You asked “should we pity and feel bad for evil men both in history and nowadays or hate them?

Feeling bad for sinners is not a bad thing. God has done this as well!

The bible says we need to be merciful, tender and compassionate.

Please read the following:

Luke 6:36 English Standard Version (ESV)

36 Be merciful, even as your Father is merciful.

Luke 6:36 Amplified Bible (AMP)

36 So be merciful (sympathetic, tender, responsive, and compassionate) even as your Father is [all these].

So scripture says we need to be merciful like our heavenly Father….

Colossians 3:12 English Standard Version (ESV)

12 Put on then, as God’s chosen ones, holy and beloved, compassionate hearts, kindness, humility, meekness, and patience,

This is not just to be used for the people living right but also towards the wicked.

Let’s look at the of Definition of Pitiful - Ευσπλαγχνοι· Tender-hearted; let your bowels yearn over the distressed and afflicted.

The following scripture in various bible versions expresses the meaning with clarity:

1 Peter 3:8 King James Version (KJV)

8 Finally, be ye all of one mind, having compassion one of another, love as brethren, be pitiful, be courteous:

1 Peter 3:8 New King James Version (NKJV)

8 Finally, all *of you be* of one mind, having compassion for one another;
love as brothers, *be* tenderhearted, *be* courteous;

Scripture also tells us to love our enemies instead of hating them.

Luke 6:27-36 English Standard Version (ESV)

Love Your Enemies

27 "But I say to you who hear, Love your enemies, do good to those who
hate you, 28 bless those who curse you, pray for those who abuse you.
29 To one who strikes you on the cheek, offer the other also, and from
one who takes away your cloak do not withhold your tunic either. 30 Give
to everyone who begs from you, and from one who takes away your
goods do not demand them back. 31 And as you wish that others would
do to you, do so to them.

32 "If you love those who love you, what benefit is that to you? For even
sinners love those who love them. 33 And if you do good to those who do
good to you, what benefit is that to you? For even sinners do the same.
34 And if you lend to those from whom you expect to receive, what credit
is that to you? Even sinners lend to sinners, to get back the same amount.
35 But love your enemies, and do good, and lend, expecting nothing in
return, and your reward will be great, and you will be sons of the Most
High, for he is kind to the ungrateful and the evil. 36 Be merciful, even
as your Father is merciful.

Friend, you said that you obviously do not condone the evil and terrible things done. This says a lot! In my humble opinion you are not confused. You have a tender heart for people. That's a good thing!

You are just learning more about yourself as you mature in the faith.

For further study consider reading the following articles:

What does the Bible say about empathy?

http://www.gotquestions.org/Bible-empathy.html

What does the Bible say about compassion?

http://www.gotquestions.org/Bible-compassion.html

Stay in God's word the bible and keep asking questions.

Blessings to you!

Question: 95

What does the Bible say about a ban or shunning? The Amish use the ban. Where do they get this from scripture? And what's the right way to use it?

Profile: Male 18-30 North America

Answer: I am glad that you are seeking answers from the word of God. This is our best resource, a guide almighty God provided for mankind.

Let's start with the definitions and the Amish practice:

Shunning can be the act of social rejection, or mental rejection. Social rejection is when a person or group deliberately avoids association with, and habitually keeps away from an individual or group. This can be a formal decision by a group, or a less formal group action which will spread to all members of the group as a form of solidarity. It is a sanction against association, often associated with religious groups and other tightly knit organizations and communities. Targets of shunning can include persons who have been labeled as, apostates, whistleblowers, dissidents, strikebreakers, or anyone the group perceives as a threat or source of conflict. Social rejection has been established to cause psychological damage and has been categorized as torture. Mental rejection is a more individual action, where a person subconsciously or willfully ignores an idea, or a set of information related to particular viewpoint. Some groups are made up of people who shun the same ideas.

Amish

Shunning occurs in Old Order Amish and some Mennonite churches. Shunning can be particularly painful for the shunned individuals in these denominations, which are generally very close-knit, as the shunned person may have no significant social contact with anyone other than those in their denomination.

Upon taking instruction classes, each applicant must make a confession to uphold shunning of all excommunicated adult members, and also submit to being shunned if they are excommunicated. The stated intention is not to punish, but to be used in love to win the member back by showing them their error. The Amish call shunning *Meidung*, the German word for *avoidance*. Shunning was a key issue of disagreement in the Amish-Mennonite split. Former Amish Ruth Irene Garrett provides an account of Amish shunning in her community from perspective of shunned individuals in *Crossing Over: One Woman's Escape from Amish Life*. Amish shunning is also the subject of popular fiction novels about shunning. Different Amish communities vary in the severity and strictness of shunning employed.

Why do the Amish practice shunning?

Shunning is a practice fundamental to Amish identity. Shunning, or *Meidung*, was one of the reasons Amish Christianity came about, and has been seen as critical to maintaining the integrity of the Amish church. Shunning is often considered harsh by outsiders, and often misunderstood by non-Amish as well as some Amish themselves.

Social shunning occurs when an individual has violated the Ordnung (guidelines for daily living) and has been excommunicated from the Amish church (**also known as being in the *Bann***). Shunning is a form of social avoidance. It is an alteration of behavior towards an individual who has willfully violated rules of the church.

Shunning may take the form of eating separately, not doing business with a person, not accepting gifts or rides from a shunned individual, and generally excluding a person from community activities. Amish will still converse with an individual in the *Bann*, and will offer assistance if needed. But for all intents and purposes, that individual, through his own choice, is considered outside the flock.

Why do Amish practice shunning? Where do they get this from scripture?

Amish practice shunning as a means of enforcing an individual's commitment to God, made along with the Amish congregation. Amish see a Biblical basis for shunning.

Amish base the practice of shunning on numerous Biblical passages:

Passages often cited in support of shunning include Matthew 18; 2 Thessalonians 3:14 ("And if any man obey not our word by this epistle, note that man, and have no company with him, that he may be ashamed"); 1 Timothy 5 (..."Lay hands suddenly on no man, neither be partaker of other men's sins: keep thyself pure"...); 2 Corinthians 13:10 ("Therefore I write these things being absent, lest being present I should use sharpness, according to the power which the Lord hath given me to edification, and not to destruction"); and numerous others.

Amish practice shunning out of "tough love" in order to get a deviant person to see the error in his ways, change behavior, and re-affirm his commitment to the church. Without rules and shunning, the integrity of the Amish church would rapidly disintegrate.

One Amish man explains the purpose of shunning:

"Shunning" as practiced today could perhaps be best described as a ritualistic reminder of having gone astray and having broken your commitment to the Lord Jesus and the body of believers you made your commitment and baptismal promise with. It is also a statement that the rest of the flock has no intention of leaving the fold and that it takes its commitment to the Lord and each other seriously. But most of all it is done so the soul of the deviant may be saved on the Day of Judgment.

As this Amish man explains, shunning is done out of concern for the deviant member. Shunning is also done to protect the body of the church. Shunning in some ways is a fence that keeps the wolves away from the flock. Amish often point out that an individual can't sit on the fence. Were Amish to accept any practice or belief that came along, the body of the church would be in danger of being corrupted and members led astray spiritually. Membership in the Amish church would be meaningless.

When do Amish employ shunning?

Amish place an individual in the *Bann* and employ *shunning* as a last resort. Typically, church leadership will first visit an individual to discuss the issue at hand, often a violation of the *Ordnung*, such as use or ownership of a forbidden technology, or otherwise universally recognized sinful behavior.

Use of unsanctioned technology can bring about discipline from the church.

The aim is to bring about a change of heart and get the individual to cease his errant behavior. In some cases, such efforts are effective. The individual will either make a confession to the bishop, or in front of the church itself, and be placed in a temporary (usually lasting a few weeks, can be as many as 6 weeks) period of excommunication. After this period, all is restored, and the deviant behavior forgiven and forgotten.

But if an individual deliberately flaunts church rules, refuses to change behavior, to "put away" a forbidden technology, or otherwise continues down a sinful path without regret and attempt to change, the bishop will move to excommunicate him or her (also known as being in the *Bann*).

Amish researchers Hurst and McConnell note that in the Holmes County community, even those who refuse to confess will receive a "grace period" of six to twelve months during which members attempt to persuade the disobedient member to change behavior. Later, there is a vote by the members on excommunication, which must be unanimous (*An Amish Paradox*, Hurst and McConnell).

As alluded to above, excommunication is done as a last resort and with much remorse on the part of the church body. As the Amish man, himself twice placed in the *Bann*, explains, "shunning is usually done with great reluctance and only once there is nothing else left to do".

How long does shunning last?

As described above, Amish may be placed in the *Bann* temporarily for minor transgressions for which they show remorse and ask forgiveness. Otherwise, excommunication is for life.

At the same time, the Amish always allow the possibility of return, confession, and reinstatement into the church. Though this is not too common once an individual leaves, when it does happen, it is cause for much joy in a church. "Upon repentance the relationship is restored and what is in the past stays in the past," notes the Amish man.

Different approaches to shunning

Different Amish groups take different approaches to shunning. There remains disagreement among Amish today as to how shunning should be applied, echoing the original issue which led Jakob Amman to break away from the Mennonites and form the Amish branch in the late 17th century.

More conservative Amish are among those who follow strict shunning.

Some Amish, such as those in Lancaster County, and in more conservative affiliations, follow what is called strong shunning, or *streng Meidung*. In this form of shunning, an individual will be subject to *Meidung* for life, unless he or she returns to an Amish church (in some cases, his original church) and makes a confession.

In the milder form of shunning, practiced by numerous Amish communities in the Midwest, the *Bann* will be lifted if the individual joins a related Anabaptist-umbrella church, such as a Beachy Amish or more progressive Mennonite church (as often happens with individuals who leave the Amish).

Individual Amish may vary in their approach to shunning as well. Amish-born scholar John A. Hostetler notes that some Amish dislike the practice of shunning and may only perform it symbolically.

Hostetler cites an anecdote illustrating such behavior:" One mother prepared two separate tables, placed them within several inches of each other, and covered both with one large tablecloth. Each table had separate benches. The children and the excommunicated ate at one table and the members at the other. Only the adults knew what had transpired." (*Amish Society*, Hostetler)

What does the bible say regarding this practice? What is the right way to use it?

At least 2 Passages in the New Testament such as 1Corinthians 5:11-13, and Matthew 18:15–17, suggest shunning as a practice of early Christians, and are cited as such by its modern-day practitioners within Christianity. However, not all Christian scholars or denominations agree on this interpretation of these verses.

Policies governing the use of shunning vary from one organization to another.

The best answer I can give you is in an article regarding church discipline/ excommunication found at GotQuestions.org. I included it here for your convenience:

"What does the Bible say about church discipline / excommunication?"

Answer: Excommunication is the formal removal of an individual from church membership and the informal separation from that individual. Matthew 18:15-20 gives the procedure and authority for a church to do this. It instructs us that one individual (usually the offended party) is to go to the offending individual. If he/she does not repent, then two or three go to confirm the situation and the refusal to repent. If there is still no repentance, it is taken before the church. This process is never "desirable," just as a father never delights in having to discipline his children. Often, though, it is necessary. The purpose is not to be mean-spirited or to display a "holier than thou" attitude. Rather, the goal is the restoration of the individual to full fellowship with both God and other believers. It is to be done in love toward the individual, in obedience and honor to God, and in godly fear for the sake of others in the church.

The Bible gives an example of the necessity of excommunication in a local church—the church at the city of Corinth (1 Corinthians 5:1-13). In this passage, the apostle Paul also gives some purposes behind the biblical use of excommunication. One reason (not directly found in the passage) is for the sake of the testimony of Christ Jesus (and His church) before unbelievers. When David sinned with Bathsheba, one of the consequences of his sin was that the name of the one true God was blasphemed by God's enemies (2 Samuel 12:14). A second reason is that sin is like a cancer; if allowed to exist, it spreads to those nearby in the same way that "a little yeast works through the whole batch of dough" (1 Corinthians 5:6-7). Also, Paul explains that Jesus saved us so that we might be set apart from sin, that we might be "unleavened" or free from that which causes spiritual decay (1 Corinthians 5:7-8). Christ's desire for His bride, the church, is that she might be pure and undefiled (Ephesians 5:25-27).

Excommunication is also for the long-term welfare of the one being disciplined by the church. Paul, in 1 Corinthians 5:5, states that excommunication is a way of delivering the unrepentant sinner "over to Satan, so that the sinful nature may be destroyed and his spirit saved on the day of the Lord." This means that excommunication can somehow involve God's using Satan (or one of his demons) as a disciplinary tool to work in the sinner's life physically to bring about true repentance in his/her heart.

Hopefully the disciplinary action of the church is successful in bringing about godly sorrow and true repentance. When this occurs, the individual can be restored to fellowship. The man involved in the 1 Corinthians 5 passage repented, and Paul encouraged the church to restore him to fellowship with the church (2 Corinthians 2:5-8). Unfortunately, disciplinary action, even when done in love and in the correct manner, is not always successful in bringing about such restoration. But even when church discipline fails to achieve its goal of bringing repentance, it is still needed to accomplish the other good purposes mentioned above.

We have all likely witnessed the behavior of a young boy who has been allowed to do as he pleases with no consistent discipline. It is not a pretty sight. Nor is such parenting loving, for it dooms the child to a dismal future. Such behavior will keep the child from forming meaningful relationships and performing well in any kind of setting. Similarly, discipline in the church, while never enjoyable or easy, is not only necessary, but loving as well. Moreover, it is commanded by God.

Friend, I pray that my answer helps you!

2 Timothy 3:16 English Standard Version (ESV)

16 All Scripture is breathed out by God and profitable for teaching, for reproof, for correction, and for training in righteousness.

Question: 96

1 Thessalonians 4:16 says the Lord will come with a loud command, with the voice of an archangel. Jehovah witnesses say that this is proof that Jesus is Michael. Can you explain this verse for me please? Thank you & God bless!

Profile: Male 31-45 North America

Answer: Thanks for submitting your question.

The Jehovah's Witnesses do not have a good understanding of the true deity of Christ.

They are using a bible (New World Translation) that is corrupt with blatant changes the Watch Tower society made to support their doctrine. They are not the final authority as they try to make themselves out to be. The Jehovah Witness bible has many errors!

This religion is to be avoided and not used to answer biblical questions.

Please read the articles posted via Gotquestions.org to learn more details about this false religious Cult.

http://www.gotquestions.org/New-World-Translation.html

http://www.compellingtruth.org/Jehovahs-Witnesses.html

http://www.gotquestions.org/witnessing-Jehovahs-Witnesses.html

As for the scripture being used (1 Thess. 4:16) to support the Jehovah Witness case, lets look at what the bible is actually saying:

1 Thess. 4:16 KJV

4:16 For the Lord himself shall descend from heaven with a shout, with the voice of the archangel, and with the trump of God: and the dead in Christ shall rise first:

First, I want to make sure I do not speak where scripture is silent. Consider this my friend, no where in this verse does it say the Lord exclusively was the one doing the shouting, or speaking as an archangel or blowing the trumpet…

The shout could be coming from the angels in heaven; the voice could be the archangel speaking while the Lord descends perhaps announcing it, and the trumpet could be being played by an angel or God himself. It does not say that the Lord is an Archangel.

Please read the article “Is Jesus Michael the Archangel” from GotQuestions.org. It is included below for your convenience. It will provide the rest of the answers that you seek.

“Is Jesus Michael the Archangel?”

Answer: Jesus is not Michael the archangel. The Bible nowhere identifies Jesus as Michael (or any other angel, for that matter). Hebrews 1:5-8 draws a clear distinction between Jesus and the angels, “For to which of the angels did God ever say, ‘You are my Son; today I have become your Father’? Or again, ‘I will be His Father, and He will be my Son’? And again, when God brings His firstborn into the world, He says, ‘Let all God’s angels worship Him.’ In speaking of the angels He says, ‘He makes his angels winds, his servants flames of fire.’ But about the Son He says, ‘Your throne, O God, will last forever and ever, and righteousness will be the scepter of your kingdom.’” The hierarchy of heavenly beings is made clear in this passage—angels worship Jesus who, as God, is alone worthy of worship. No angel is ever worshipped in Scripture; therefore, Jesus (worthy of worship) cannot be Michael or any other angel (not worthy of worship). The angels are called sons of God (Genesis 6:2-4; Job 1:6; 2:1; 38:7), but Jesus is THE Son of God (Hebrews 1:8; Matthew 4:3-6).

Michael the archangel is perhaps the highest of all the angels. Michael is the only angel in the Bible who is designated "the archangel" (Jude verse 9). Michael the archangel, though, is only an angel. He is not God. The clear distinction in the power and authority of Michael and Jesus can be seen in comparing Matthew 4:10 where Jesus rebukes Satan, and Jude verse 9, where Michael the archangel "dared not bring a judgment of blasphemy" against Satan and calls on the Lord to rebuke him. Jesus is God incarnate (John 1:1, 14). Michael the archangel is a powerful angel, but still only an angel.

http://www.gotquestions.org/Jesus-Michael-Archangel.html

Thanks you for taking the time to write us. May God lead you on the path He wants you on!

Question: 97

I've often heard we are not to believe in anything that isn't in the scriptures...Is this scriptural even if an experience makes you love or long for God more? Isn't this what the Pharisees did with Jesus? Additionally, I know that the Pharisees said a few things to Jesus in regards to going against scripture...Did he actually go against the scriptures? Thanks.

Profile: Male 18-30 North America

Answer: The comment you heard "we are not to believe in anything that isn't in the scriptures." depends on the context of how it is being used.

Let's look at the definition of the word believe.

Definition of Believe:

intransitive verb

1a : to have a firm religious faith b : to accept something as true, genuine, or real <ideals we believe in>

2: to have a firm conviction as to the goodness, efficacy, or ability of something <believe in exercise>

3: to hold an opinion : think <I believe so>

transitive verb

1a : to consider to be true or honest <believe the reports> <you wouldn't believe how long it took> b : to accept the word or evidence of <I believe you> <couldn't believe my ears>

2: to hold as an opinion : suppose <I believe it will rain soon>

— be·liev·er noun

— not believe

: to be astounded at <I couldn't believe my luck>

The scientists believed the reports.

Many people seem to believe that theory, but I find it hard to believe.

So you can see the various uses of the word believed. You can hold an opinion and it not be in the bible and does not go against the scriptures.

Consider the following use of the word "believe".

A person can certainly believe that in the winter time in the Midwest and Canada that there is a good chance that it can snow. Scripture does not tell us the seasonal weather conditions for these areas.

Another example, a person can believe in their ability to play a sport.

Friend, if you are referring to spiritual matters this is more serious. Although there are no specific scripture verses that put it the way you mentioned, it is a good idea for example to make sure the experience is not misleading you into thinking that you are feeling close to God but in fact it is pulling you away from Him. It may also cause others to stumble who look up to you. One way to avoid this is that we must make sure that the experience is not learned from the many false religious teachings and actions. These include and are not limited to the following: Buddhism, Islam, New Age, and Hinduism, etc… If the experience is rooted in the false religious practices we are not to follow them per the scriptures.

Scripture Support: 2 Peter 2:1-3 English Standard Version (ESV)

False Prophets and Teachers

2 But false prophets also arose among the people, just as there will be false teachers among you, who will secretly bring in destructive heresies, even denying the Master who bought them, bringing upon themselves swift destruction. [2] And many will follow their sensuality, and because of them the way of truth will be blasphemed. [3] And in their greed they will exploit you with false words. Their condemnation from long ago is not idle, and their destruction is not asleep.

We need to use discernment in how we proceed in experiencing God.

See our article: **How can I increase my spiritual discernment?**

http://www.gotquestions.org/spiritual-discernment.html

Did Jesus actually go against the scriptures?

No. Jesus never went against or contradicted scripture!

Jesus was the master teacher in using Old Testament Scripture. His use of Isaiah 61:1, 2 in the synagogue at Nazareth is a good illustration of this. He read the verses before the Rabbis and others in the synagogue service and made application of them to Himself. He told them, "This day is this scripture fulfilled in your ears" (Luke 4:16-21). The people "bear him witness" and wondered at the gracious words He had spoken.

Jesus told His disciples "that all things must be fulfilled, which were written in the law of Moses, and in the prophets, and in the psalms, concerning me" (Luke 24:44). Jesus not only said "all things must be fulfilled," He meant all things. All things in the law, the prophets, the psalms!

Jesus' testimony to the absoluteness of scripture is found in His declaration, "the scriptures must be fulfilled" (Mark 14:49; Matthew 26:54).

Jesus believed the Scripture could be understood and properly applied. Jesus did for His disciples what the evangelist Philip did for the eunuch through a proper use of Old Testament writings. Philip preached Jesus to the eunuch (Acts 8:35) from Isaiah 53:7, 8.

When tempted of the devil in the wilderness, Jesus repeatedly responded, "It is written" (Matthew 4:4, 7, 10).

Jesus' attitude toward the Scriptures is manifested in manifold ways. The Scriptures affected every aspect of Jesus the Christ: His co-existence with the Father, the testimony of the prophets foretelling His coming, His birth, His life and ministry, trial, death, burial, resurrection and ascension.

Nowhere in the bible did the Lord Jesus go against scripture. He supported and fulfilled it.

The Pharisees and the Sadducees earned numerous rebukes from Jesus. Perhaps the best lesson we can learn from the Pharisees and Sadducees is to not be like them. Unlike the Sadducees, we are to believe everything the Bible says, including the miraculous and the afterlife. Unlike the Pharisees, we are not to treat traditions as having equal authority as Scripture, and we are not to allow our relationship with God to be reduced to a legalistic list of rules and rituals.

The Pharisees were wrong in their false accusations about Jesus.

For more study regarding the Pharisees please go to the following article at GotQuestions.org:

http://www.gotquestions.org/Sadducees-Pharisees.html

May God bless you in the study of His word!

Question: 98

Should negative words of knowledge that would hurt someone be announced publicly or conveyed privately to the person concerned?

Profile: Female 46-60 Asia

Answer: Thanks for writing to GotQuestions.org.

The answer to your question depends on the situation. Without knowing the targeted category that is in question please read on as I try to respond.

If your question falls under the following categories then the answer will vary:

1. Dangerous situation
2. Court
3. Work environment
4. Public Figure
5. Church member or visitor
6. Family
7. Heretics

If the negative words put a person in a dangerous situation then it should be avoided.

For example, you don't want to approach privately a person whom you saw murder someone and say I saw what you did and I am going to tell. Guess who will be the next victim?

In a court, a person may have to speak publically expressing negative words about the defendant to help the court convict the criminal.

In a work environment there may be certain protocols to follow in speaking out negativity… A boss certainly should not call an employee names in private or in public.

Public figures are subject to a lot more verbal comments that can be positive or negative.

The President, for example, may receive a lot of negative press for something he may have done wrong or not done. Most people do not have the opportunity to speak to the President of a country privately. It is generally known that once a person becomes a public figure he/she must prepare themselves for comments that will be uttered whether good or bad.

Church and family I will group together. In a church or household that is trying to honor God in how they live daily, they will want to make sure that they follow the rules and examples in scripture. First and foremost one must make sure that they are not getting caught up in gossip. Please read the following bible verses:

Proverbs 11:13, Proverbs 16:28, James 4:11, Philippians 4:8, Ephesians 4:29, Titus 3:2, Proverbs 15:1, 1 Timothy 5:13, Luke 6:31, James 3:5-7

The bible also gives us the best way to handle conflict resolution. You find it in Matthew 18:15-17.

Matthew 18:15-17 English Standard Version (ESV)

If Your Brother Sins Against You

15 "If your brother sins against you, go and tell him his fault, between you
and him alone. If he listens to you, you have gained your brother. 16 But
if he does not listen, take one or two others along with you, that every
charge may be established by the evidence of two or three witnesses.
17 If he refuses to listen to them, tell it to the church. And if he refuses
to listen even to the church, let him be to you as a Gentile and a tax
collector.

For a Christian who refuses to stop a pattern of sin, this is to become public within the church. Read the following:

1 Timothy 5:20 English Standard Version (ESV)

20 As for those who persist in sin, rebuke them in the presence of all, so that the rest may stand in fear.

If a person is a heretic the bible gives us the following instructions:

Titus 3:10 English Standard Version (ESV)

10 As for a person who stirs up division, after warning him once and then twice, have nothing more to do with him,

Conclusion:

Should negative words of knowledge that would hurt someone be announced publicly or conveyed privately to the person concerned?

As mentioned above it depends on the situation.

In my humble opinion, in general one should not go in public and say hurtful things about a person without considering the other person's feelings. We should remember to use the golden rule.

Matthew 7:12 (ESV)

12 "So whatever you wish that others would do to you, do also to them, for this is the Law and the Prophets

http://www.gotquestions.org/Golden-Rule.html

If the negative words of knowledge are calling out a sin in a church environment (Church Discipline), then it needs to be dealt with biblically and can be done publically so all in the congregation can hear it. Know that care should be taken in what words are used. The goal is to try to be open to restore the person to full fellowship with both God and other believers and not to destroy them. It is to be done in love toward the individual, in obedience and honor to God, and in godly fear for the sake of others in the church.

A person who wants to repent will be sorry for their sin.

2 Corinthians 2:7 English Standard Version (ESV)

7 so you should rather turn to forgive and comfort him, or he may be overwhelmed by excessive sorrow.

Negative words are never desirable," just as a father never delights in having to discipline his children. Often, though, it is necessary. The purpose is not to be mean-spirited or to display a "holier than thou" attitude. Rather, the goal is the restoration of the individual to full fellowship with both God and other believers. It is to be done in love toward the individual, in obedience and honor to God, and in godly fear for the sake of others in the church.

A person who do not care and is causing all kinds of trouble behind the scenes should be asked privately to leave.

Hopefully the disciplinary action of the church is successful in bringing about godly sorrow and true repentance. When this occurs, the individual can be restored to fellowship. The man involved in the 1 Corinthians 5 passage repented, and Paul encouraged the church to restore him to fellowship with the church (2 Corinthians 2:5-8). Unfortunately, disciplinary action, even when done in love and in the correct manner, is not always successful in bringing about such restoration. But even when church discipline fails to achieve its goal of bringing repentance, it is still needed to accomplish the other good purposes mentioned above.

Additional articles you may want to read:

http://www.gotquestions.org/church-discipline.html

http://www.compellingtruth.org/church-discipline-excommunication.html

http://www.gotquestions.org/gossip-Bible.html

I hope this helps you in your quest for answers. May God bless you!

Question: 99

What to do when you have abusive parents? I wanted to know what to do in this situation. I am 20 years old and live at home. I have been recently trying to do better in honoring my parents, even though they were abusive to me as a child. When I turned 18 it stopped. Recently I began going to church events more and went to a retreat. When I came home my mom was angry with me and ignored me. My sister says she kept talking about me and calling me horrible names that I don't feel comfortable saying. This morning I saw my mom get out a belt and beat my 8 year old brother and when I was about to step in she stopped and said "What are you looking at me for" and walked away angrily. I knew she was abusive but haven't witnessed it yet, my sister (she is 14 by the way) says my mom always abuses her and beats her when I'm not around and does the same with my younger siblings who are 8 and 3 years old. She is also very verbal and neglectful. How can I honor her when she does this? My sister says one day she's leaving and never coming back. I feel that is not honoring but she says she can't be around someone who is rude to her. She says I should leave too. I feel at times it is my will to stay here and be a good Christian example, but it is so hard. My mom claims its not abuse unless you leave a mark, and she is very careful in making sure to not leave bruises or such, but the abuse still hurts and often leaves a red mark that soon goes away. My questions are: How do I honor her in this? Should I tell someone close about this? Who is right, me, my mom, or my sister?

Profile: Female 18-30 North America

Answer: Thanks for writing to us! I am so sorry that you have to sort this issue out. Know that with God all is possible even changing your Mom's heart and this situation.

Discipline over the years has changed. When I was a child I knew of people who received discipline with the belt, being pinched etc… It was done to correct occasional bad behavior. In the end it worked and all of the people I am referring to are grown and are fine people.

To issue discipline is not always one punishment fits all situations and each individual. Some people are more sensitive then others thus requiring less of an iron hand than those more stubborn and hard headed.

Discipline should not be done while the parent is tilting with anger. The parent can ask the child to stand facing the corner of the wall until they say to come away. During this time the parent can calm down and then either make this the punishment or increase the punishment to really get the attention of the child.

There is a lot to consider here.

Your mom may not know that she is disciplining too harshly especially if this was considered normal in her development.

The spiritual approach:

Is she a Christian? Will she listen to what the bible says?

Is she open to the gospel? I ask this because if she is open, then my answer shifts towards directing her to the cross…

More questions:

What was the reason discipline was performed? Did she try other means and none worked to steer the children on the correct path? Was she brought up in this way by her parents? Is she open to obtaining parenting training by a Christian organization?

Does your mom do other things to punish the children that do not involve hitting with a belt?

Examples:

1. Have child write 25-500 times (depending on their age) "I will not do ____________________".
2. Take fun activities away for an extended period of time…
3. Have the child stand facing the corner of a room until an appointed time…

Is she angry all the time? Where is your dad? Is he silent through all of this? Is he the source of your mom's frustrations? Is he also abusive?

Please read all of the articles that I include in my answer. I pray that afterwards you will gain wisdom to know how to handle the situation.

What does it mean to "spare the rod, spoil the child"?

http://www.gotquestions.org/spare-rod-spoil-child.html

Should a Christian continue spanking his/her children if it is illegal?

http://www.gotquestions.org/Christian-spanking.html

How should Christians discipline their children? What does the Bible say?

http://www.gotquestions.org/disciplining-children.html

What does it mean to train up a child in the way he should go?

http://www.gotquestions.org/train-up-a-child.html

What does the bible say about abuse?

http://www.gotquestions.org/Bible-abuse.html

Friend, we are to hold our parents in high priority. There are a few specific ways in which this applies to abusive parents.

You asked: "How do I honor her in this?"

The following website has an article that gives details on how to handle abuse:

http://www.compellingtruth.org/honor-abusive-parent.html

There are many hurt and damaged people who find this command:

12 "Honor your father and your mother, that your days may be long in the land that the LORD your God is giving you." Exodus 20:12. This may be difficult to obey. Should we honor and obey an abusive parent? Where do we draw the line? Please read the article at Gotquestions.org for a good perspective on this subject:

http://www.gotquestions.org/honor-abusive-parent.html

Conclusion:

Just as Jesus loved us in our sinful state, we can honor an abusive parent. It means showing grace and compassion to those who don't deserve it, so that God is glorified and the obedient are blessed and rewarded (Matthew 5:44-48; 1 John 4:18-21). Remember, "Make every effort to live in peace with all men and to be holy; without holiness no one will see the Lord" (Hebrews 12:14).

Suggestion:

After reading all that is contained in my response and the articles, please pray and re-evaluate what your Mom is actually doing. Does she show any love? Is it always negative? Is there bad name calling and beatings all the time? Is it really child abuse? Is she really punishing in compliance of scripture? If not, you may have to kindly sit her down and have a heart to heart talk with her. This will be very difficult because she may not want to sit and talk. Pray for God to guide you through this…

If she won't listen pray again for discernment and wisdom on what to say to her.

You may have to inform her that she is frustrating your siblings to the point of them not wanting to be there. Encourage her that it does not have to be this way. Ask her to please consider changing the way she disciplines the children. Tell her that the children could be taken away if this abuse gets noticed by outsiders. Sadly the children may end up scattered and not together... Ask her if she wants this to occur and respond kindly regardless of her response.

You asked "Should I tell someone close about this?"

If the discipline is violent and can cause a loss of life or injuries, sadly, you will have to report your mom to someone close who can do something about it and this may require calling "The Department of Child and Family Services. I sincerely hope that this will not occur. It can damage your bond with your mom for a very long time.

You also asked "Who is right me, my mom, or my sister?"

Your sister says "one day she's leaving and never coming back..." She is voicing how she is really feeling deep inside. She is emotionally hurt. There is nothing wrong with her thinking of trying to seek future refuge. Perhaps family counseling can bring the needed healing for everyone involved and then she won't have to leave the family forever...

Your Mom may be right in some regards, but without me seeing the day to day happenings I can only base it on your comments. Based on your comments (that I believe are true), there seems to be a need for counseling, and guidance in performing discipline in the family setting.

I think Conflict resolution training maybe the way to go for your family. I also want to suggest that you may want to call New Life: http://newlife.com/ and asked them to help you find a counselor in your area. Check the website for more information: http://newlife.com/counselors

Perhaps going on this path can prevent calling DCFS. Note: If violence is involved in the discipline as I mentioned before then call for help…

If your parents need help and won't go for help give it to the Lord. Act accordingly.

This may mean that you and eventually your siblings may want to get counseling if needed. Only if you feel it is necessary…

Try to look at the whole situation and pray before acting. Everything is not always as it appears to be. We will keep you in prayer that God shows you the truth and how to respond accordingly.

You have a good heart for your family! You are willing to reach out on their behalf and ask the tough questions. You are right in doing so. May our Great and Powerful God guide you through this to the path of peace in your family!

I leave you with this verse:

Colossians 3:17 ESV

And whatever you do, in word or deed, do everything in the name of the Lord Jesus, giving thanks to God the Father through him.

Question: 100

Why did God Kill Uzzah? It seems he was only trying to keep the Ark from falling.

Profile: Male 50-60 North America

Answer: You are referring to the bible passages references at 2 Samuel 6:1-7 and 1 Chronicles 13:7-14.

This is a question that is quite puzzling on the surface. Let us remember that God is good and there must be a good reason for this.

A closer look at the situation reveals that David was so fascinated with bringing the Ark of the Covenant to Jerusalem that he omitted some of God's instructions (rules) on how to transport the Ark and who was to carry it.

Read what is mentioned below at 1 Chronicles 13:7-14 and 1 Chronicles 15:12-15 to get the full details.

1 Chronicles 13:7-14

English Standard Version (ESV)

7 And they carried the ark of God on a new cart, from the house of
Abinadab, and Uzzah and Ahio were driving the cart. 8 And David and
all Israel were celebrating before God with all their might, with song
and lyres and harps and tambourines and cymbals and trumpets.

9 And when they came to the threshing floor of Chidon, Uzzah put
out his hand to take hold of the ark, for the oxen stumbled. 10 And the
anger of the Lord was kindled against Uzzah, and he struck him down
because he put out his hand to the ark, and he died there before God.
11 And David was angry because the Lord had broken out against Uzzah.

And that place is called Perez-uzza to this day. [12] And David was afraid of God that day, and he said, "How can I bring the ark of God home to me?" [13] So David did not take the ark home into the city of David, but took it aside to the house of Obed-edom the Gittite. [14] And the ark of God remained with the household of Obed-edom in his house three months. And the LORD blessed the household of Obed-edom and all that he had.

1 Chronicles 15: 11-15

English Standard Version (ESV)

[11] Then David summoned the priests Zadok and Abiathar, and the Levites Uriel, Asaiah, Joel, Shemaiah, Eliel, and Amminadab, [12] and said to them, "You are the heads of the fathers' houses of the Levites. Consecrate yourselves, you and your brothers, so that you may bring up the ark of the LORD, the God of Israel, to the place that I have prepared for it. [13] Because you did not carry it the first time, the LORD our God broke out against us, because we did not seek him according to the rule." [14] So the priests and the Levites consecrated themselves to bring up the ark of the LORD, the God of Israel. [15] And the Levites carried the ark of God on their shoulders with the poles, as Moses had commanded according to the word of the LORD.

This important piece of history serves as a constant reminder that there are some instructions that God requires us to follow without deviation. Failure to comply can lead to death.

Bonus Questions

1. If diamonds are millions of years old and we have them in our rings how can people teach that the earth is young?

Male over 50 USA

Answer: The study of the bible from Genesis to Revelation points to a young earth.

First step in answering this question scientifically is to find out if diamonds can be made in less time… It does not take that long to make a diamond. Pressure is important in making diamonds…

Synthetic diamonds

Advances in technology mean that we can now create synthetic diamonds and these have increased our understanding of diamonds.

There are industrial diamonds being manufactured that do not take millions of years to create.

Measuring age

It isn't always possible to find out the age of a diamond by examining it directly. A better method is to look at tiny inclusions, which are crystals made from other minerals that are often found within diamonds. These give out a slight radioactive signal that scientists can measure to find out how old they are.

This means flawless diamonds, that don't have any inclusions, are very difficult to date.

The following speaks of some scientific experiments that point to a relatively young age of the earth:

Steven Boyd refers to one group of scientists called the RATE group who found that a previously unknown phenomenon, accelerated decay of radioactive isotopes, occurred in the past. This means that the age of a rock cannot be derived from radioisotope dating methods. Moreover the presence of helium in zircon crystals, radiohalos from short half lived polonium in biotite, and carbon-14 in diamonds prove that the earth is thousands, not billions of years old.' [Coming to Grips with Genesis, p. 169]

Check out the following ministries website for further study:

http://www.icr.org/

http://www.icr.org/article/icr-radio-news-release/

Check out the RATE group's research…

The evolution belief system (Religion) is responsible for spreading the age of the earth "millions of years" lie in schools, books, in the media (films, news etc…).

This is a deep subject requiring a lot of information. Perhaps looking into industrial diamond websites will give you additional information on how long it takes to make a diamond.

I hope my summarized answer helps!

2. Did Jephthah really offer his daughter up for a burnt offering?

Answer: Whenever I read Judges 11 it brings this sad an unnecessary vow to front and center stage.

Friend, I am not sure. We do have 2 possibilities to consider.

Jephthah believed in the Lord but acted foolishly in that he should have known how God felt regarding human sacrifices. He should have reasoned this through…

Got Questions.org article gives us the best answer:

Did Jephthah sacrifice his daughter to the Lord?

http://www.gotquestions.org/Jephthahs-daughter.html

A judge of Israel, Jephthah, had made a foolish vow to the Lord that if God gave him victory in battle, he would sacrifice whatever first came out of his door when he came home (Judges 11:30-31). Jephthah's daughter was the first thing to come of out his door when he came home (Judges 11:34). The Bible never specifically tells us whether Jephthah actually sacrificed his daughter as a burnt offering. Judges 11:39 seems to indicate that he did: "He did to her as he had vowed." However, since his daughter was mourning the fact that she would never marry instead of mourning that she was about to die (Judges 11:36-37), this possibly indicates that Jephthah gave her to the tabernacle as a servant instead of sacrificing her.

Whatever the case, God had specifically forbidden offering human sacrifices, so God never would have wanted Jephthah to sacrifice his daughter (Leviticus 20:1-5). Jeremiah 7:31; 19:5; and 32:35 clearly indicate that the idea of human sacrifice has "never even entered God's mind." Jephthah serves as an example for us not to make foolish vows or oaths.

3. Is the Word of Faith movement biblical?

Answer: Word of Faith teaching is decidedly unbiblical. Avoid it like the plague… It is a movement that is heavily influenced by a number of high-profile pastors and teachers such as Kenneth Hagin, Benny Hinn, Kenneth Copeland, the late Paul and Jan Crouch, Joyce Meyers, Joel Osteen, Fred Price and many others.

At the heart of the Word of Faith movement is the belief in the "force of faith." It is believed words can be used to manipulate the faith-force, and thus actually create what they believe Scripture promises (health and wealth). Laws supposedly governing the faith-force are said to operate independently of God's sovereign will and that God Himself is subject to these laws. This is nothing short of idolatry, turning our faith—and by extension ourselves—into god.

They teach that man is a little god.

The Word of Faith movement is deceiving countless people, causing them to grasp after a way of life and faith that is not biblical. At its core is the same lie Satan has been telling since the Garden: "You shall be as God" (Genesis 3:5). Sadly, those who buy into the Word of Faith movement are still listening to him. Our hope is in the Lord, not in our own words, not even in our own faith (Psalm 33:20-22). Our faith comes from God in the first place (Ephesians 2:8; Hebrews 12:2) and is not something we create for ourselves. So, be wary of the Word of Faith movement and any church that aligns itself with Word of Faith teachings.

For more excellent details regarding this false teaching please go to the following website:

http://www.gotquestions.org/Word-Faith.html

Friends, if you are following the word of faith teachings please stop. Change course, for your future depends on you breaking free from this and following the one and only true God.

4. Is the rapture biblical?

Answer: Yes. Although the word rapture is not mentioned in many of the popular bible versions the concept of the rapture is clearly mentioned in all of them.

The word rapture is in the latin valgate bible version expressed as "rapiemur". It is also in the greek translation as HarpageeSo'metha/ *harpazō*.

Some scriptural examples:

Thessalonians 4:17 in the Latin Vulgate:

4:17 deinde nos qui vivimus qui relinquimur simul rapiemur cum illis in nubibus obviam Domino in aera et sic semper cum Domino erimus

Thessalonians 4:17 in the Koine Greek

The Koine Greek of 1 Thessalonians 4:17 uses the verb form ἁρπαγησόμεθα (*harpagisometha*), which means "we shall be caught up" or "taken away", with the connotation that this is a sudden event. The dictionary form of this Greek verb is *harpazō* (ἁρπάζω).[15] This use is also seen in such texts as Acts 8:39, 2 Corinthians 12:2-4 and Revelation 12:5

The rapture of the church is the event in which God removes all believers from the earth in order to make way for His righteous judgment to be poured out on the earth during the tribulation period.

The rapture is described primarily in 1 Thessalonians 4:13-18 and 1 Corinthians 15:50-54. Please read these scriptures to see what it says.

Know that God will resurrect all believers who have died, give them glorified bodies, and take them from the earth, along with those believers who are still alive and who will at that time also be given glorified bodies.

1 Thessalonians 4:16-17 English Standard Version (ESV)

16 For the Lord himself will descend from heaven with a cry of command, with the voice of an archangel, and with the sound of the trumpet of God. And the dead in Christ will rise first. 17 Then we who are alive, who are left, will be caught up together with them in the clouds to meet the Lord in the air, and so we will always be with the Lord.

This is simply awesome! For more information please go to the following urls:

What is the Rapture of the church?

http://www.gotquestions.org/rapture.html

What is the Rapture and when will it occur?

http://www.compellingtruth.org/what-is-the-rapture.html

5. How old was Adam and Eve when they were created?

Answer: Scripture does not come out and say how old they were on the first day. They were created as full grown adults.

So based on this let me suggest that Adam and Eve was one day old when they were created. They were not in the womb for 9 months… They were made on a particular day. Adam and Eve were not going to age according to what we know of aging. It was not until sin entered where we see the aging process as we know it. Adam was a grown man at day one when he was created, and Eve was one day old but a grown woman when God made her from Adams rib.

Scripture references:

Adam was created out of the dust of the earth.

Genesis 1:26-27 "Then God said, "Let Us make man in Our image, according to Our likeness; let them have dominion over the fish of the sea, over the birds of the air, and over the cattle, over all the earth and over every creeping thing that creeps on the earth." " 27- So God created man in His own image; in the image of God He created him; male and female He created them."

Genesis 2:7 English Standard Version (ESV)

[7] then the LORD God formed the man of dust from the ground and breathed into his nostrils the breath of life, and the man became a living creature.

Eve's origin: While Adam was made by God out of the dust of the earth, Eve was made from part of the flesh of Adam.

Genesis 2:21-22 English Standard Version (ESV)

[21] So the LORD God caused a deep sleep to fall upon the man, and while he slept took one of his ribs and closed up its place with flesh. [22] And the rib that the LORD God had taken from the man he made into a woman and brought her to the man.

She was created for a specific purpose, as a companion for Adam - "And the LORD God said, "It is not good that man should be alone; I will make him a helper comparable to him" (Genesis 2:18).

Note: The bible does not say that man's creation took a year or 21 years to complete.

We simply cannot be dogmatic about this topic but let me conclude with the following:

It is therefore estimated that Adam and Eve were 1 day old adults…

6. How old were Adam and Eve When they died?

Answer: According to Geneses 5:5, Adam lived 930 years. Eve's age is not mentioned anywhere.

7. Did Adam and Eve have belly buttons?

Answer: We cannot be dogmatic about this, but my logic says, "No". There was no need for it. Note: This feature was in their DNA.

Consider this and draw your conclusion: The absence of navels on this first human couple would be a powerful, long-lasting witness to the creation itself, and to the power of our Creator God. Dr. Gary Parker, quoting from a study by Ken Ham, phrased it this way, and I would completely agree with this analysis: "Lack of a belly-button on Adam and Eve would be one of the biggest tourist attractions in the pre-Flood world, as the grandchildren and the great-grandchildren would come up and say, 'Why don't you have a belly-button?' And they could then recount again and again, to generation after generation, how God had created them special by completed supernatural acts" (Creation Magazine, June, 1996). The absence of a navel would testify to Truth, and our God would be glorified; the presence of a navel could bring about doubt and could testify to a Lie, and our God's glory would thereby be diminished.

8. How old is the earth?

Answer: The genealogies listed in Genesis chapters 5 and 11 provide the age at which Adam and his descendants each fathered the next generation in a successive ancestral line from Adam to Abraham. By determining where Abraham fits into history chronologically and adding up the ages provided in Genesis 5 and 11, it becomes apparent that the Bible teaches the earth to be about 6000 years old, give or take a few hundred years.

For more study on this read the following articles:

What is the age of the earth? How old is the earth?

http://www.gotquestions.org/earth-age.html

Is there any evidence for the Bible's view of a young earth?

http://www.gotquestions.org/young-earth-evidence.html

9. Who are the two witnesses in Revelation?

Answer: We simply do not know and cannot be dogmatic about it.

There are three primary viewpoints on the identity of the two witnesses in Revelation 11:3-12: (1) Moses and Elijah, (2) Enoch and Elijah, (3) two unknown believers whom God calls to be His witnesses in the end times.

Which view is correct? The possible weakness of (1) is that Moses has already died once, and therefore could not be one of the two witnesses, who die, which would make Moses a contradiction of Hebrews 9:27. Proponents of (1) will argue that all of the people who were miraculously resurrected in the Bible (e.g., Lazarus) later died again. Hebrews 9:27 is viewed, then, as a "general rule," not a universal principle. There are no clear weaknesses to view (2), as it solves the "die once" problem, and it makes sense that if God took two people to heaven without dying, Enoch and Elijah, it was to prepare them for a special purpose. There are also no clear weaknesses to view (3). All three views are valid and plausible interpretations that Christians can have.

For the full details regarding this please go to the following article:

Who are the two witnesses in the book of Revelation?

http://www.gotquestions.org/two-witnesses.html

10. Do Jehovah's Witnesses cast out spirits in the Lords name? Do they prophesy? I'm just trying to figure out Matthew 7:21. It makes sense for people who believe in Jesus but don't believe he was physically raised from the dead. That would make the verse make sense. Why would a person who believes correctly and has relationship with Jesus Christ go to hell? Thanks for helping me understand.

I have answered your questions separately below:

Question A: Do Jehovah's witnesses cast out spirits in the Lords name?

Answer: In its history it is possible someone may have tried to do this. I never heard a first hand account of any person doing this in the Jehovah's Witness organization. I have not seen any guidance or provisions in the Watch Tower Bible and Tract Society literature that I was exposed to. A Jehovah's Witness will pray asking Jehovah for protection from the demonic forces if they personally felt attacked.

Question B: Do they prophesy?

Answer: They have made many attempts in the past 100 years of recording prophesies in their magazines and books regarding when the end of the world will occur. All of which were false predictions. Many times after the date completed they changed the end times to a different date… Here is a listing of some of their false predictions:

- **1897** "Our Lord, the appointed King, is now present, since October 1874," (*Studies in the Scriptures*, vol. 4, p. 621).
- **1899** "...the 'battle of the great day of God Almighty' (Revelation 16:14), which will end in A.D. 1914 with the complete overthrow of earth's present rulership, is already commenced," (*The Time Is at Hand*, 1908 edition, p. 101).
- **1916** "The Bible chronology herein presented shows that the six great 1000 year days beginning with Adam are ended, and that the great 7th Day, the 1000 years of Christ's Reign, began in 1873," (*The Time Is at Hand*, forward, p. ii).
- **1918** "Therefore we may confidently expect that 1925 will mark the return of Abraham, Isaac, Jacob and the faithful prophets of old, particularly those named by the Apostle in Hebrews 11, to the condition of human perfection," (*Millions Now Living Will Never Die*, p. 89).
- **1922** "The date 1925 is even more distinctly indicated by the Scriptures than 1914," (*Watchtower*, Sept. 1, 1922, p. 262).
- **1923** "Our thought is, that 1925 is definitely settled by the Scriptures. As to Noah, the Christian now has much more upon which to base his faith than Noah had upon which to base his faith in a coming deluge," (*Watchtower*, Apr. 1, 1923, p. 106).

- **1925** "The year 1925 is here. With great expectation Christians have looked forward to this year. Many have confidently expected that all members of the body of Christ will be changed to heavenly glory during this year. This may be accomplished. It may not be. In his own due time God will accomplish his purposes concerning his people. Christians should not be so deeply concerned about what may transpire this year," (*Watchtower*, Jan. 1, 1925, p. 3).
- **1925** "It is to be expected that Satan will try to inject into the minds of the consecrated, the thought that 1925 should see an end to the work," (*Watchtower*, Sept., 1925, p. 262).
- **1926** "Some anticipated that the work would end in 1925, but the Lord did not state so. The difficulty was that the friends inflated their imaginations beyond reason; and that when their imaginations burst asunder, they were inclined to throw away everything," (*Watchtower*, p. 232).
- **1931** "There was a measure of disappointment on the part of Jehovah's faithful ones on earth concerning the years 1917, 1918, and 1925, which disappointment lasted for a time...and they also learned to quit fixing dates," (*Vindication*, p. 338).
- **1941** "Receiving the gift, the marching children clasped it to them, not a toy or plaything for idle pleasure, but the Lord's provided instrument for most effective work in the remaining months before Armageddon," (*Watchtower*, Sept. 15, 1941, p. 288).
- **1968** "True, there have been those in times past who predicted an 'end to the world', even announcing a specific date. Yet nothing happened. The 'end' did not come. They were guilty of false prophesying. Why? What was missing?.. Missing from such people were God's truths and evidence that he was using and guiding them," (*Awake*, Oct. 8, 1968).
- **1968** "Why are you looking forward to 1975?" (*Watchtower*, Aug. 15, 1968, p. 494).

For more information please go to the following website:

http://carm.org/jehovahs-witnesses-and-their-many-false-prophecies

Question C: Why would a person who believes correctly and has relationship with Jesus Christ go to hell?

Matthew 7:21 English Standard Version (ESV)

I Never Knew You

21 "Not everyone who says to me, 'Lord, Lord,' will enter the kingdom of heaven, but the one who does the will of my Father who is in heaven.

Answer: Jesus goes on to describe those who will be able to call upon His name on the Day of Judgment. It will be those who hear His words and put them into practice, the same ones referred to in verse 21 as those who obediently do the will of the Father in heaven. True believers are the good trees that produce good fruit (Galatians 5:22-23), the true sheep who look to Christ, depend on Him, commit themselves to Him, trust in Him, and believe on Him for righteousness, salvation, and eternal life. These are the ones who will enter into the kingdom of heaven.

Please read the following article for more details:

http://www.gotquestions.org/Matthew-7-21-23.html

or listen to this article at the following url:

http://www.gotquestions.org/audio/Matthew-7-21-23.mp3

Additionally, true belief in Jesus Christ as your Lord and Savior saves the person with a path to heaven not hell. If a person who attends church all their life but never made the decision to accept Jesus as savior they would be doomed to hell. Also, some people are following a different Lord, not the Lord of the bible. If a person is following a false teacher or a cult religion they are not in relationship with the true God.

Friend, since you have asked questions about the Jehovah's Witness organization, I really want to make sure I caution you to avoid the Jehovah's Witness teachings. This is a cult religion that uses a corrupted bible that they designed to suit their beliefs.

Please consider reading the following articles for I really want your eyes to be open to the real truth:

Who are the Jehovah's Witnesses and what are their beliefs?

http://www.gotquestions.org/Jehovahs-Witnesses.html

Is the New World Translation a valid version of the Bible?

http://www.gotquestions.org/New-World-Translation.html

What is the Watchtower Bible and Tract Society?

http://www.gotquestions.org/Watchtower-Bible-Tract-Society.html

What do the Jehovah's Witnesses believe? Who are the Jehovah's Witnesses?

http://www.compellingtruth.org/Jehovahs-Witnesses.html

Should we allow false teachers into our home?

http://www.gotquestions.org/allow-false-teachers-home.html

May God bless your search for answers…

11. Did Enoch and Elijah die before entering heaven?

Answer: Scripture does not specifically say whether they died during the transition from earth to heaven.

So without speaking where the bible does not I conclude that they did not experience death as we know it.

According to the Bible, Enoch and Elijah are the only two people God took to heaven without them dying. Genesis 5:24 tells us,

"Enoch walked with God; then he was no more, because God took him away." Second Kings 2:11 tells us, "...suddenly a chariot of fire and horses of fire appeared and separated the two of them, and Elijah went up to heaven in a whirlwind." Enoch is described as a man who "walked with God for 300 years" (Genesis 5:23). Elijah was perhaps the most powerful of God's prophets in the Old Testament. There are also prophecies of Elijah's return (Malachi 4:5-6).

For more information please visit the following website url:

http://www.gotquestions.org/Enoch-Elijah.html

12. If God took Adams rib why don't males have one less rib than women?

Answer: Consider this... If something happens to someone after they are already here (an acquired trait) that does not affect your genetic code for the next generation. If you cut your hand off it does not mean your next offspring will be missing a hand. So God taking the rib from Adam affected just Adam.

13. Was it a whale or a fish that swallowed Jonah?

Answer: Not sure. If it was a whale or a shark they are considered fish in biblical classification. Our modern classification system has changed thus adding to the confusion...

As for the whale, the Bible doesn't actually specify what sort of marine animal swallowed Jonah. Most people assume that it was a cachalot (also known as the sperm whale). It may very well have been a white shark. The Hebrew phrase used in the Old Testament, *gadowl dag*, literally means "great fish." The Greek used in the New Testament is *këtos* which simply means "sea creature." There are at least two species of Mediterranean marine life that are known to be able to swallow a man whole. These are the cachalot and the white shark. Both creatures are known to prowl the Mediterranean and have been known to Mediterranean sailors since antiquity. Aristotle described both species in his 4th-century B.C. *Historia Animalium*.

If you are not familiar with Jonah, this is a true biblical account. Please read the book of Jonah in the bible and also the following article for more information:

http://www.gotquestions.org/Jonah-whale.html

14. Will we remember our earthy life when we are in heaven?

Answer: Yes. After death the Martyrs depicted in Revelation 6:9-11 clearly remember at least some of what happened on earth, including that they underwent great suffering.

Revelation 6:9-11 English Standard Version (ESV)

9 When he opened the fifth seal, I saw under the altar the souls of those who had been slain for the word of God and for the witness they had borne. 10 They cried out with a loud voice, "O Sovereign Lord, holy and true, how long before you will judge and avenge our blood on those who dwell on the earth?" 11 Then they were each given a white robe and told to rest a little longer, until the number of their fellow servants and their brothers should be complete, who were to be killed as they themselves had been.

So, if they remember that, what wouldn't they remember? There's no reason to assume that in heaven we will forget our lives on earth.

15. Can Angels take on human form?

Answer: At a certain time in history there were some demons that mated with woman and the offspring were called the Nephilim. In this context they were in the form of a human. God has stopped this from occurring around the time of the flood. See the following articles at GotQuestions.org:

http://www.gotquestions.org/Nephilim.html

http://www.gotquestions.org/Nephilim-demons.html

http://www.gotquestions.org/sons-of-God.html

http://www.gotquestions.org/Anakim.html

http://www.gotquestions.org/spirits-in-prison.html

So the answer is: Satan and demons cannot take on human form! Satan does not have creation powers. The demons cannot mate with humans to have offspring that take on human form.

Angels can take on human form by God's power only if God permits it… By God's creative prowess (power), He can cause angels to take on human form.

Scripture says we entertain angels in Hebrews 13:2.

In scripture we see examples of this happening.

Angelophanies: Angelophany is the actual appearance of an angel to man.

1. Isaac's birth promised Genesis 18.
2. The two angels who visited Lot in Sodom and Gomorrah Genesis 19:1-5.

Note: the people of Sodom and Gomorrah saw the angels in human male form.

The bible also mentions other examples of God changing form via Christophanies and Theophanies… Christophany is the appearance of

Jesus in human form which happens in the Old Testament Genesis 3:9 and referenced in Hebrews 1:1.

Theophanies: An appearance of God. Genesis 17:1, 18:1, Exodus 6:2 -3, 24:9-11, Numbers 12:6-8. These are the pre-incarnate Christ because no one on earth has ever seen the father (John 6:46).

God, Christ, and angels (when God permits it) can take on human form.

16. Should a Christian watch the Twilight series?

Answer: Friends, my answer is no with one exception. Unless it is being viewed with someone to discuss the reasons why they should not watch or read the series...

This book and movie series embraces and exalts the sins of the flesh. This should not be enjoyed by Christians. There are too many moral issues in this movie. The character Jacob had his shirt off for most of the movie. If an attractive girl showed that much flesh throughout the movie, the movie would be labeled offensive. Don't be misled, lust goes both ways.

Informal Internet Poll:

What do you think of Twilight Books/Movies

- **30%** Loved them.
- **12%** They were good.
- **6%** Could take or leave them.
- **4%** Did not enjoy.
- **5%** Hated them.
- **44%** Will not read/see them.

363 people have voted in this poll.

As you can see from the informal poll above there are people who are into watching and reading the Twilight stuff.

The Twilight series is showing young people, especially girls about what qualities to look for in a partner. Bella's love interests are vampires and werewolves. What's up with that? There are many images of lust and want that remain burned in the subconscious of the viewers and especially a young child's mind. Much of the twilight films revolve around 50 mph piggy back rides and tree climbs, Edward protecting Bella from dangers that were brought into her life by him, co-dependent love to the point of being suicidal if it is interrupted, and so on. There are too many moral issues in this movie series. Most young girls have said that Edward's chivalry and gentlemanly behavior is what attracts them, but I do not believe he would be as attractive without his darkness, his powers, and the danger surrounding him. This is teaching young girls the absolute wrong circumstances for a relationship. While many Christians are understandably praising the absence of sex in the Twilight saga, we must not lose sight of the fact that sex is not the only destructive relationship decision one can make.

As a Christian, the will of God is for us to remain in a constant pursuit of holiness. Romans 12:1-2 provides us a clear charge to be transformed by the renewing of the mind – in Christ. As our culture continues to saturate itself in things such as vampires, *Harry Potter*, and *New Moon* – should the Christian embrace such books, literature, games, and movies? Do Christians have liberty and freedom in Christ to enjoy such things? I believe the answer is clearly recorded down in the bible book of Galatians 5. In that chapter, Paul is writing to the Galatians who were being attacked with a false gospel that literally choked the life out of the church in that city. Paul spoke to them in the latter part of the chapter about Christian liberty and freedom in Christ. However, he also warned them to refrain from using their Christian liberty as a license to sin (Galatians 5:13-26)!

In that passage of Scripture, Paul outlines some of the sins of the flesh…

Galatians 5:19-21: Now the works of the flesh are evident: sexual immorality, impurity, sensuality, idolatry, sorcery, enmity, strife, jealousy, fits of anger, rivalries, dissensions, divisions, envy, drunkenness, orgies, and things like these. I warn you, as I warned you before, that those who do such things will not inherit the kingdom of God.

As we read this passage of Scripture, we should pay close attention to what it says about witchcraft (sorcery) in verse 20. Notice that it lumps that sin in with other sins like adultery and murder! Then Paul goes on to say that anyone who practices such things will not inherit the Kingdom of God. That is no little statement by the Apostle Paul. That is a powerful warning that every Christian who is dabbling in things such as *Harry Potter* and the *New Moon* should repent immediately.

It should be noted that God has always opposed witchcraft. This is extremely important to understand. In Deuteronomy 18:9-10, God commands His people to refrain from it! He calls it an abomination! In Isaiah 8:19, God again warns against such practices as communicating with the dead. It should also be pointed out that in Revelation 21:8, the Apostle John warns that all sorcerers will have their part in the lake of fire and brimstone. Therefore, the totality of God's Word stands opposed to witchcraft and the evil that surrounds such practices.

After the description of the life before Christ by Paul in Galatians 5, Paul then describes the life in Christ. He points out that the Christian will manifest the fruit of the Spirit. As we read the list from Galatians 5:22-23, we see that the true Christian will demonstrate a life that reflects Christ – not a sinful corrupt world. Believers, please don't be like the world! Christians are people of light – not darkness. Therefore, we should stand opposed to the darkness of sin – no matter how popular or attractive it may seem in books, movies and amongst your peers. If you have been sucked into the New Moon, Harry potter world view, repent! Destroy the posters and paraphernalia. Purge the content out of your homes etc… Be a bold Christian and stand for Christ – not the world. Never use your freedom in Christ as a license to sin.

There is a danger in how what we are watching can affect our hearts and how it affects others. For ourselves, if the scene we see brings a feeling of lust, anger, or hatred, then we have sinned. See Matthew 5:22, 28.

We must all do what we can to avoid this from occurring again. One other thing to consider is it can be a stumbling block to someone who is struggling with a habit or behavior that is coming between them and God. Ref: 1 Corinthians 10:25-33, Romans 14:13.

Please don't fight me on this. Repent immediately! I care about your future in Christ.

Galatians 5:13 (ESV)– For you were called to freedom, brothers. Only do not use your freedom as an opportunity for the flesh, but through love serve one another.

In conclusion:

In my humble opinion, Christians should avoid reading and watching the twilight series and others like it! Don't let the world desensitize you to the real truth!

Follow the higher calling that scripture prescribes for all of us:

Philippians 4:8 English Standard Version (ESV)

8 Finally, brothers, whatever is true, whatever is honorable, whatever is just, whatever is pure, whatever is lovely, whatever is commendable, if there is any excellence, if there is anything worthy of praise, think about these things.

17. Someone I know asked a questioned that I don't know the answer to... Who is the 144,000?

Profile: Male over 60

Answer:

Thanks for asking "LORD OF Hope Ministries" your bible Question:

Short answer: After the Rapture there will be Jews who accept Jesus as their savor. These are the 144,000 mentioned in the bible.

For more details please read the following articles:

http://www.gotquestions.org/144000.html

http://www.compellingtruth.org/144000.html

Details Summarized:

When taken at face value: "Then I heard the number of those who were sealed: 144,000 from all the tribes of Israel" (Revelation 7:4), nothing in the passage leads to interpreting the 144,000 as anything but a literal number of Jews—12,000 taken from every tribe of the "sons of Israel."

These Jews are "sealed," which means they have the special protection of God from all of the divine judgments and from the Antichrist to perform their mission during the tribulation period (see Revelation 6:17, in which people will wonder who can stand from the wrath to come). The tribulation period is a future seven-year period of time in which God will enact divine judgment against those who reject Him and will complete His plan of salvation for the nation of Israel. All of this is according to God's revelation to the prophet Daniel (Daniel 9:24-27). The 144,000 Jews are a sort of "first fruits" (Revelation 14:4) of a redeemed Israel which has been previously prophesied (Zechariah 12:10; Romans 11:25-27), and their mission is to evangelize the post-rapture world and proclaim the gospel during the tribulation period. As a result of their ministry, millions—"a great multitude that no one could count, from every nation, tribe, people and language" (Revelation 7:9)—will come to faith in Christ.

May God bless your study of His word!

18. "If a man has multiple wives and becomes a Christian, what is he supposed to do?"

Answer: Thanks for asking Lord of Hope Ministries your bible question.

Since polygamy is frowned upon in most societies, this is not a question too many people think about. But there are still numerous places in the world where polygamy is accepted. Many Muslim countries allow polygamy. For a man to have multiple wives is somewhat common in several African nations. Even in the United States, there are some communities which endorse polygamy. However, virtually all Bible scholars agree that polygamy is not for Christians. Please see the GotQuestions.org article:

Why did God allow polygamy / bigamy in the Bible?

http://www.gotquestions.org/polygamy.html

What, then, should a polygamist do if he places his faith in Jesus Christ and becomes a Christian?

Most people immediately give an answer like "He should divorce all of his wives but one." While that seems to be an ethical solution, the situation is usually not quite that simple. For example, which wife does he keep? His first wife? His last wife? His favorite wife? The wife that has borne him the most children? And what about the wives he divorces? How do they provide for themselves? In most cultures that allow polygamy, a previously married woman has very little opportunity to provide for herself and even fewer possibilities of finding a new husband. And what happens to the children of these wives? The situation is often very complicated. There is rarely a simple solution.

We do not believe polygamy is something God approves of in this era. However, the Bible nowhere explicitly gives a "thou shalt not marry multiple wives" command. In the New Testament, a polygamist is ineligible for church leadership (1 Timothy 3:2, 12; Titus 1:6), but polygamy itself is not forbidden. Polygamy was not God's original intent (Genesis 2:24; Ephesians 5:22-33), but it was also something He allowed (see the examples of Jacob, David, and Solomon). The closest the Bible comes to forbidding polygamy is Deuteronomy 17:17, which is properly understood as God's command against a king of Israel taking *many* wives. It cannot be understood as a command that no man can ever take more than one wife.

So, if a man has multiple wives and becomes a Christian, what is he supposed to do? If polygamy is illegal where he lives, he should do whatever is necessary to submit to the law (Romans 13:1-7), while still providing for his wives and children. If polygamy is legal, but he is convicted that it is wrong, he should divorce all but one wife, but, again, he must not neglect providing for all of them and their children. They are his responsibility. If polygamy is legal and he has no conviction against it, he can remain married to each of his wives, treating each one with love, dignity, and respect. A man who makes this decision would be barred from church leadership, but it cannot be said that he is in explicit violation of any command in Scripture.

The above Answer is from article:

http://www.gotquestions.org/multiple-wives.html

19. Since God is the Father, the Son and the Holy Spirit, do I have to pray to God or can I just pray to Jesus, since Jesus is God? When I pray to Jesus, am I praying to God?

When I pray to Jesus and my prayers are answered, is God the one who is answering my prayers?

Answer

Thank you for writing to Lord of Hope Ministries. May God bring you the answer that you seek!

I am also a staff writer for Gotquestions.org. At GotQuestions.org we have an article that addresses this subject. You can read it below or click the link to listen to the mp3 version. You will need an internet connection to hear the mp3.

"To whom are we to pray, the Father, the Son, or the Holy Spirit?"

All prayer should be directed to our triune God—Father, Son, and Holy Spirit. The Bible teaches that we can pray to one or all three, because all three are one. To the Father we pray with the psalmist, "Listen to my cry for help, my King and my God, for to you I pray" (Psalm 5:2). To the Lord Jesus, we pray as to the Father because they are equal. Prayer to one member of the Trinity is prayer to all. Stephen, as he was being martyred, prayed, "Lord Jesus, receive my spirit" (Acts 7:59). We are also to pray in the name of Christ. Paul exhorted the Ephesian believers to always give "thanks to God the Father for everything, in the name of our Lord Jesus Christ" (Ephesians 5:20). Jesus assured His disciples that whatever they asked in His name—meaning in His will—would be granted (John 15:16; 16:23). Similarly, we are told to pray to the Holy Spirit and in His power. The Spirit helps us to pray, even when we do not know how or what to ask for (Romans 8:26; Jude 20). Perhaps the best way to understand the role of the Trinity in prayer is that we pray to the Father, through (or in the name of) the Son, by the power of the Holy Spirit. All three are active participants in the believer's prayer.

Equally important is whom we are not to pray to. Some non-Christian religions encourage their adherents to pray to a pantheon of gods, dead relatives, saints, and spirits. Roman Catholics are taught to pray to Mary and various saints. Such prayers are not scriptural and are, in fact, an insult to our heavenly Father. To understand why, we need to look at the nature of prayer. Prayer has several elements, and if we look at just two of them—praise and thanksgiving—we can see that prayer is, at its very core, worship. When we praise God, we are worshipping Him for His attributes and His work in our lives. When we offer prayers of thanksgiving, we are worshipping His goodness, mercy, and loving-kindness to us. Worship gives glory to God, the only One who deserves to be glorified. The problem with praying to anyone other than God is that He will not share His glory. In fact, praying to anyone or anything other than God is idolatry. "I am the LORD; that is my name! I will not give my glory to another or my praise to idols" (Isaiah 42:8).

Other elements of prayer such as repentance, confession, and petition are also forms of worship. We repent knowing that God is a forgiving and loving God and He has provided a means of forgiveness in the sacrifice of His Son on the cross. We confess our sins because we know "He is faithful and just to forgive us our sins, and to cleanse us from all unrighteousness" (1 John 1:9) and we worship Him for it. We come to Him with our petitions and intercessions because we know He loves us and hears us, and we worship Him for His mercy and kindness in being willing to hear and answer. When we consider all this, it is easy to see that praying to someone other than our triune God is unthinkable because prayer is a form of worship, and worship is reserved for God and God alone. Whom are we to pray to? The answer is God. Praying to God, and God alone, is far more important than to which Person of the Trinity we address our prayers.

You may listen to above article being read at the following url:

http://www.gotquestions.org/audio/pray-Father-Son-Spirit.mp3

Additional reading: http://www.gqkidz.org/who-pray-to.html

How to pray? What is the proper way to pray?

Your may listen to this article being read at the following url:

http://www.gotquestions.org/audio/how-to-pray.mp3

Additional reading: http://www.gqkidz.org/how-pray.html

At Gotquestions.org we have over 495,000+ bible questions answered. If your question is not there you can also submit it through a link at http://www.Gotquestions.org or as you have done through Lord of Hope Ministries.

May God bless your study of His word the Bible!

20. How do I become born again (Saved)?

Answer

Open your heart and mind and read this carefully!

Please read the following because we really want you to understand why you need to be saved.

Salvation:

Why do I need to be saved?

God leaves no doubt about our condition. We set our standards of right and wrong by society's values. God's standard for us is His own holiness. How do we measure up? "All have sinned, and come short of the glory of God" (Romans 3:23). It's only fair that God demands holiness; that's how He first created mankind. We have rebelled against Him as a race and as individuals.

Our pathway away from God has brought its consequences. "The wages of sin is death" (Romans 6:23a). The Bible compares sin to a cruel slave master. There is no mercy in suffering, no freedom from bondage, no lasting joy, and no hope for the future. But most scary is the final consequence of sin. The Bible warns that without Gods salvation, death is the doorway to eternal punishment (Hebrews 9:27).

It is from this that we need to be saved from our own sin, from its bondage, from its consequences. "How shall we escape if we neglect this great salvation?" (Hebrews 2:3).

How does God say I can be saved?

God is holy and God is love. His holiness demands that our sin be punished infinitely. His love provides a way for us to be saved from this punishment. How is this possible? Another was willing to suffer what we deserve. Our substitute had to be a sinless man, able to suffer the infinite anger of God against our sin. The only one able to take our place was God's only Son (Jesus Christ).

The greatest display of God's love unfolded as His Son left heaven to become a man. Born of a virgin 2000 years ago, Jesus Christ lived with His creation. Unable to sin Himself, yet He showed compassion to sinners all around Him. However, men hated Him because His holiness revealed their sinfulness. He willingly allowed them to nail Him to a cross of wood outside Jerusalem. They suspended Him so they could sit and watch Him die. The climax of God's plan of salvation had arrived as God covered the earth with darkness. The Bible tells us that for three hours He laid on His Son the infinite punishment we deserve for our sin. The darkness was broken when Jesus Christ called out with a loud voice "It is finished". He had accomplished the mighty work, God's great plan of salvation.

After three days in death, Christ Jesus rose from the dead. This is evidence to all that saw him afterwards and to all who read God's word that Christ suffering completely satisfied His father. He was victorious over death itself the ultimate consequence of our sin.

God's plan of salvation brings us into the good of Christ suffering, death, and victory. "For when we were yet without strength, in due time, Christ died for the ungodly" (Romans 5:6). "For God so loved the world, that He gave His only begotten Son, that whosoever believeth in Him should not perish, but have everlasting life" (John 3:16).

If after reading this book, or you have been led to making a decision to follow Jesus Christ as your Lord and savior, please pray the following prayer and mean it from your heart:

Salvation Prayer:

Dear Lord Jesus, I know that I am a sinner and need your forgiveness.

I believe that you died for my sins.

I want to turn from my sins. I now invite you to come into my heart and life.

I want to trust and follow you as Lord and Savior. In Jesus name Amen.

If you truly meant this prayer:

You are saved!

You are a Child of God!

You have everlasting life!

If you prayed to have Jesus Christ be Lord of your life and the forgiver of your sins we would love to hear from you. Please send us a letter informing us that you said the salvation pray. We want to celebrate in our hearts for you!

Now go out and get connected to a bible teaching church and get involved by serving the Lord.

Love you!

Pastor Roscoe and Teacher & Counselor Revita De Chalus

Lord of Hope Ministries

P.O Box 160

Streamwood, IL. 60103

e-mail address: info@lordofhopeministries.com

Appendix

STATEMENT OF FAITH

1. We believe in the Trinity, that God is three in one: the Father, the Son and the Holy Spirit.
2. We believe the Son, Jesus Christ, God as flesh was born of a virgin, was crucified (died) for our sins and rose from the dead 3 days later to sit at the right hand of God.
3. We believe that the Bible is the undisputed word of God, inspired by God, was given to mankind to guide them in their daily activities.
4. We believe in heaven and hell, that God is alive and that Satan wants to destroy us.
5. We believe salvation (hope) is available to all who call upon the Lord, repent of their sins, and believe in Jesus Christ.
6. We believe faithfully in One God.

References

ESV Bible
KJV Bible, and New King James Version (NKJV).

Lord of Hope Ministries http://www.lohmin.org

Got Questions Ministries http://gotquestions.org

www.deceptioninthechurch.com
http://cephas-library.com/evangelists_bonnke.html
http://www.letusreason.org/Popteac13.htm
http://bible.org/seriespage/false-teachers-2-peter-21-3

http://bible.org/seriespage/instruction-concerning-false-teachers-church-titus-110-16

www.brethren.org
www.ucg.org
http://www.parsonage.org/p2p/index.cfm

http://www.focusonlinecommunities.com/blogs/Finding_Home/2007/12/03/pastor-to-pastor-hotline

http://www.parsonage.org/info/contactus.cfm
http://www.equip.org/articles/christianity-still-in-crisis-
http://www.youtube.com/watch?v=pKF_QgNezBY
http://today.msnbc.msn.com/id/6894347
http://www.watchman.org/profile/wordpro.htm
http://www.av1611.org/osteen.html
http://www.letusreason.org/JW52.htm

http://www.christianbook.com/are-seventh-day-adventists-false-prophets/wallace-slattery/9780875524450/pd/5524451?event=AFFp=1011693&

http://www.amazon.com/Bones-Contention-Creationist-Assessment-Fossils/dp/0801065232
http://www.whoinventedit.net/who-invented-the-atomic-bomb.html

http://www.letusreason.org/JW52.htm

http://www.letusreason.org/7thAd26.htm

http://www.equip.org/articles/is-jesus-christ-the-spirit-brother-of-satan-

http://news2.onlinenigeria.com/headlines/158961-prophet-temitope-balogun-joshua-banned-from-cameroun.html

http://tbjoshuawatch.wordpress.com/

http://www.deceptioninthechurch.com/buyamiracle.html

http://newlife.com/contact

http://newlife.com/

http://greeknewtestament.com/B52C004.htm

Creation Magazine June 1996 (Dr. Gary Parker, Ken Ham).

http://www.biblegateway.com

http://www.thegracewellnesscenter.com

http://thrivingPastor.com/caregiving-ministries/index.html

http://thrivingPastor.com/category/Pastor-to-Pastor/

http://carm.org/jehovahs-witnesses-and-their-many-false-prophecies

An Amish Paradox, Hurst and McConnell.
Crossing Over: One woman's escape from Amish life.
John A. Hostetler note/reference (Amish Society Hostetler).
Coming to Grips with Genesis, P169

http://www.icr.org
http://www.icr.org/article/icr-radio-news-release/

About The Author

Pastor Roscoe De Chalus M. Min. is the President of Lord of Hope Association, and the President and Senior Pastor for Lord of Hope Ministries. He and his wife Revita are also Radio Bible Teachers and have served as Telephone Ambassadors for the Billy Graham Evangelistic Association.

Pastor Roscoe De Chalus is on the board of the Psalm 119 Association (Woodrow Kroll Ministries). http://www.psalm119association.org or http://wkministries.com/

Graduate of Masters International University of Divinity: Masters of Ministry, Pastoral Ministry Degree.

Lord of Hope Ministries

www.lohmin.org

Roscoe has co-founded this ministry with his lovely wife Revita on August 18, 2002.

Roscoe and his wife Revita's sermons have been broadcasted on LESEA Shortwave, and FM radio, and currently on Spirit Network Radio International that delivers programming throughout the world on satellite and satellite IP services reaching over 4.3 million subscribers.

SNRI's Internet Radio Service can be heard on www.spiritnetworkradio.

com as well as on 67 other platforms around the world. The network's iPhone and iPad apps are available to the over 100-million smart phone users around the world. Also, Spirit Network Radio is carried throughout North and South America on the Global Gospel Network and UnoRed/ One Network.

In addition to the above Spirit Network Radio launched IP Radio streams to the following countries: Brazil, Netherlands, Congo, Democratic People, Republic of United Kingdom, Canada, Kenya, Korea, Republic of, Slovak Republic, Venezuela, Mexico, Finland, India, South Africa, Singapore, Australia, Austria, Germany, Spain, Russia, Bahamas, Greece, Nigeria, Peru, Egypt, Chile, Angola, Argentine, Romania, Madagascar, Philippines, Slovenia, Sweden, Norway, Colombia, Norway, Germany, Switzerland, Netherlands, United Kingdom, Austria, Canada, Brazil, France, Czech Republic, Singapore, Japan, South Africa, Ethiopia, India, Ireland, Poland, Mexico, Romania, Italy, Argentina, Trinidad and Tobago, Republic of Korea, Australia, Philippines, Hungary, China (People's Republic of), Puerto Rico, Paraguay, Guatemala, Venezuela, Portugal, Panama, Belgium, Sweden, Peru, Finland, Uganda, Denmark, Spain and Bulgaria.

We get questions submitted to Lord of Hope Ministries (Ask a Pastor) and from GotQuestions.org.

Pastor Roscoe De Chalus is a volunteer writer for GotQuestions.org.

A lot of the questions in this book were assigned to Pastor Roscoe to answer for GotQuestions.org.

Pastor Roscoe sends many thanks to GotQuestions.org for letting him be part of this magnificent ministry team!

Pastor Roscoe also serves in the music ministry at Harvest Bible Chapel. http://www.harvestbiblechapel.org/

Pastor Roscoe has a passion for Christian apologetics and also getting God's word to you through various methods.

Pastor Roscoe also serves as a Guest Pastor in the USA…

To feed your faith and to learn even more about Pastor Roscoe and His wife Revita feel free to go to our ministry website:

Lord of Hope Ministries

www.lohmin.org

You can follow Pastor Roscoe De Chalus on Twitter:

http://twitter.com/#!/internetpastor

Pastor Roscoe is listed in the Masters International Registry.

Printed in the United States
By Bookmasters